Dark Sides of the Startup Nation

Israeli national neoliberalism has promoted innovation policies leading to an ostensible paradox: At the center is a startup nation with a vibrant and successful high-tech entrepreneurial ecosystem, accumulating resources and enabling constant growth. At the geographical and social periphery, there has emerged a parallel society with often-marginalized groups not able to keep up. In one of the most unequal countries with a high rate of poverty, entrepreneurial heroes are celebrated at the center, promoting a myth that all could be self-made successes. At the periphery, entrepreneurs are struggling to survive, often pushed into precarious working and living conditions.

Applying critical theory discourse, this book illustrates how neoliberalism and entrepreneurship are intertwined and how the startup nation has evolved in Israel. It explores how national neoliberal state policies have targeted technological innovation as a tool to obtain a competitive advantage in the international arena rather than aiming at increasing economic achievements and well-being for all. It will demonstrate that the Israeli entrepreneurship scene exemplifies the existence of parallel entrepreneurial societal spaces, analyze the positionality of entrepreneurs belonging to a variety of groups that characterize Israeli society, and uncover structural disadvantages and related levels of precarity as well as existing links between entrepreneurial advantages and disadvantages, mobility and varying degrees of social marginality.

Dark Sides of the Startup Nation sheds light onto the problematic and sometimes contradictory myth that entrepreneurship is meritocratic and that neoliberal capitalism provides everyone with equal opportunities to succeed. The book will be of interest to researchers, academics, policy makers and students in the fields of entrepreneurship and small business management, responsibility and business ethics, and technology and innovation.

Sibylle Heilbrunn is Full Professor of Organizational Sociology and Dean of the Faculty of Social Sciences and Humanities at Kinneret Academic College on the Sea of Galilee, Israel.

Routledge Studies in Entrepreneurship

This series extends the meaning and scope of entrepreneurship by capturing new research and enquiry on economic, social, cultural and personal value creation. Entrepreneurship as value creation represents the endeavours of innovative people and organisations in creative environments that open up opportunities for developing new products, new services, new firms and new forms of policy making in different environments seeking sustainable economic growth and social development. In setting this objective the series includes books which cover a diverse range of conceptual, empirical and scholarly topics that both inform the field and push the boundaries of entrepreneurship.

Entrepreneurship in Creative Crafts
Edited by Vanessa Ratten

Immigrant Entrepreneurship
Cases from Contemporary Poland
Edited by Beata Glinka and Adam W. Jelonek

Entrepreneurship, Dyslexia, and Education
Research, Principles and Practice
Edited by Barbara Pavey, Neil Alexander-Passe, and Margaret Meehan

Entrepreneurship in Spain
A History
Edited by Juan Manuel Matés-Barco and Leonardo Caruana de las Cagigas

Dark Sides of the Startup Nation
Winners and Losers of Technological Innovation and Entrepreneurship in Israel
Sibylle Heilbrunn

For more information about this series please visit: www.routledge.com/Routledge-Studies-in-Entrepreneurship/book-series/RSE

Dark Sides of the Startup Nation

Winners and Losers of Technological Innovation and Entrepreneurship in Israel

Sibylle Heilbrunn

Routledge
Taylor & Francis Group
NEW YORK AND LONDON

First published 2023
by Routledge
605 Third Avenue, New York, NY 10158

and by Routledge
4 Park Square, Milton Park, Abingdon, Oxon, OX14 4RN

Routledge is an imprint of the Taylor & Francis Group, an informa business

Library of Congress Cataloging-in-Publication Data
Names: Heilbrunn, Sibylle, 1958- author.
Title: Dark sides of the startup nation : winners and losers of technological innovation and entrepreneurship in Israel / Sibylle Heilbrunn.
Description: New York, NY : Routledge, 2022. | Series: Routledge studies in entrepreneurship | Includes bibliographical references and index.
Identifiers: LCCN 2022025840 | ISBN 9780367548902 (hardback) | ISBN 9780367548926 (paperback) | ISBN 9781003091042 (ebook)
Subjects: LCSH: Entrepreneurship—Government policy—Israel. | High technology industries—Government policy—Israel. | New business enterprises—Government policy—Israel. | Neoliberalism—Israel.
Classification: LCC HC415.25.Z9 H5344 2022 | DDC 338/.04095694—dc23/eng/20220906
LC record available at https://lccn.loc.gov/2022025840

ISBN: 978-0-367-54890-2 (hbk)
ISBN: 978-0-367-54892-6 (pbk)
ISBN: 978-1-003-09104-2 (ebk)

DOI: 10.4324/9781003091042

Typeset in Bembo
by Apex CoVantage, LLC

To my family and friends in Israel and in Germany.
Thank you for your support and patience.

Contents

Figures

Tables

Foreword

In recent years, narratives depicting the growth of Israeli high-tech in terms of "economic miracle" have taken an increasingly important part in the public and academic debate. In most cases, the economic press and academic literature present the rise of high-tech as a success story and a source of national pride, and downplay the problematic aspects that result from the rapid enrichment of a very specific and small social group. When critical voices succeed in penetrating the wall of consensus, they make sure to maintain a cautious tone, and condition the spot criticism on a general recognition of the contribution of high-tech to the Israeli economy. Not that we are against the high-high - they make it clear again and again - high-tech is the "engine of growth" of the Israeli economy. In a nutshell we would just feel more comfortable if inequality would be a little less blatant, and that the rich be a little politer.

In this book I propose to discuss entrepreneurship and high-tech not only in "neutral" technological and economic terms that emphasize the transition from a traditional economy to a knowledge economy, but also in a way that emphasizes the connections between the rise of high-tech and the establishment of the neoliberal order and rising inequalities in Israel. In Israel, a communities' geographical location profoundly affects the life of people in terms of socio-economic status, access to high quality high-school education and higher education, chances of labor market participation and quality of social services provided by municipalities. The center periphery divide – which deepened with the rise of the high-tech – configures intersecting geographic, ethnic/religious and national divides.

To my opinion, the overreliance of Israel's national strategy on the startup nexus and the high-tech industry bares considerable risks for two main and overlapping reasons. The first concerns the lack of spillover of the achievements of the high-tech industry to the peripheries and the resulting inequalities and exclusion of entire groups of population. This reason is discussed extensively in the book. The second reason, not discussed in the book[1] - concerns what has been called the recent decline of the Israeli advantage. At the TheMarker *Technovation* 2022 conference the CEO of the Israeli Innovation Authority cautioned that cities such as Paris, Berlin and Singapore are closing gaps versus Israeli high-tech and are increasingly competitive. In addition he related to the ongoing extremely high productivity and skill gap that exists in Israel in comparison to OECD countries.

What if the "engine of growth" will not provide growth anymore? Is the growth model still viable? Maybe, in order to face the existential future challenges, a change of discourse is needed, towards a political strategy targeting sustainability of Israeli society for all its population groups? And maybe not for Israel alone? I hope that this book will provoke such a change in the Israeli high-tech discourse.

1 I started to work on this book during the winter months of 2019 and the gathered most of the data and background information during the year 2020. While writing the final draft I updated the data where possible, however, very recently some trends emerged in the Israeli high-tech industry that are not discussed in this first edition of the book. The Annual Innovation Report on the State of the High-Tech 2022 published by the Israel Innovation Authority presents these trends.

Acknowledgments

Many people have been involved in the process of writing this book, some directly, some indirectly, and I think that everybody I met during the last two years knows about it. The idea of the book definitely has its roots at Kinneret Academic College, where I have been serving as dean for the last years. Observing the development of the high-tech startup nation from the northern periphery, made me think once and again about our students and their chances to be part and to take part. My students and their future in Israeli society motivated me to investigate the startup nation phenomenon from another, a bit more critical perspective.

I want to thank all those who accompanied me during the journey of writing the book. To my husband Alex who has always been standing at my side; to our daughter Jonit and her partner Shahar, who have given us two wonderful grandsons and have accepted and supported my choices; to Yaron who is always there to talk and who has become a wonderful and engaged young man.

To all the interviewees who contributed their knowledge and shared their personal views, I am very grateful for your investing very precious time and sincere attention. I did learn a lot from you all. To Noa Gani, Noa Berger and Yaari Hodara, who were much more than research assistants, without you this would not have happened. To my friends in Israel and Germany, who have been patient and understanding.

To my colleagues and friends at Kinneret College, thank you for your support and encouragement.

Finally, to my grandson Nitai, who asked me to write the next book only for him—and that I will do. To Maria, who was always there to talk, discuss and comment, it is a pleasure to have you in our family and see you grow. And last but not least to my son Ran, who is my academic soul mate and intellectual partner and who's always critical comments definitely improve my work.

Thank you!

Introduction

On the 1st of December 2021, Tel Aviv was declared the most expensive city in the world. According to the latest findings of the Worldwide Cost of Living Survey of the Economist Intelligence Unit (EIU) (Economist Intelligene, 2021), Paris and Singapore were jointly second, followed by Zurich and Hong Kong. New York ranked sixth. Tel Aviv has risen five places since 2020, and in 2021 prices of goods and services are higher than in any other city globally. The cost-of-living survey compares prices of more than 200 products and services in 173 cities around the world, and companies use it frequently for evaluating relocation compensation. The report also reveals that cities everywhere are becoming more expensive, mainly due to rising inflation rates caused primarily by supply-chain disruption stemming from the Covid pandemic. Retailers have to deal with extremely high cargo costs and shortages because of impeded production, and they pass the costs on to consumers. The reasons for Tel Aviv's champion status in cost of living are mainly the strength of the shekel against the dollar and—like everywhere—an increase in prices in general and for transportation and grocery in particular (Shulman & Samet, 2021). During the last years, Tel Aviv has been booming, and therefore, for many experts, the champion rank is not a big surprise. Technological companies located at the center of Tel Aviv have continuously raised capital and gradually moved into office space, either renting or acquiring buildings. The wage level of high-tech employees have increased as a result the cost of living.[1] For some years now, rising costs in transportation, housing and everyday products have led to an affordability crisis and pushed people who are not employed in the high-tech sector out of the city (Squires, 2021). According to data from the Central Bureau of Statistics (CBS), an apartment in Tel Aviv costs about three times more than an equivalent apartment in Haifa and about 20% more than about three years ago (CBS, 2022). Peretz (2022) explains that insufficient supply of new housing projects, foreign investors' interest leading to increasing demand and government failure in releasing land to the market and approving construction plans are the main reasons for the unaffordability crisis. In addition, he maintains that the purchasing power of high-tech employees affects not only housing but also all other services, and the influx of foreign investors in local

DOI: 10.4324/9781003091042-1

investments strengthens the shekel and makes Israel even more expensive. Like Squires (2021) and Tversky (2021), Peretz (2022) predicts that Tel Aviv will become a city for the rich only and cites the city's major Ron Huldai:

> The middle class needs to have access to the heart of the metropolis. In other words, a teacher, nurse or police officer, people an orderly society cannot do without, must be able to live in the city. Some senior cabinet members think that a teacher in a Tel Aviv school should live in Holon.[2]
>
> (Melnitcki, 2021)

Huldai refers to a possible scenario where people working in service professions such as education or healthcare in Tel Aviv will not be able to live in the city but will need to move to the periphery of the metropole. The sustainability of such a scenario is questionable and is one of the concerns of this book.

In 2009, Dan Senior and Saul Singer first published the book *Start-Up Nation: The Story of Israel's Economic Miracle* (Senor & Singer, 2011). Since then, Israel labeled itself and has been labeled as a startup nation. The Israeli startup nation is geographically concentrated in the most expensive city of the world. The major theme of this book concerns those who are not included in the startup scene of Tel Aviv, those who are left behind or often called "all the rest" by Israelis. They are the 80% of the population, some in the geographic periphery, some in the social periphery and some in both. In this book, I will try to highlight that Israel is not only about the startup nation. Israel is not only Tel Aviv, and it is not only high-tech. While the high-tech industry is an important driver of growth, it also drives inequalities. What are the implications of a reality in which a city is for the rich only? What does it mean for the others, those who cannot afford to live there? This book starts out elaborating on the subject of inequality since I believe that inequality is and will be a major challenge for Israel—for the startup nation and for "all the rest."

In the following paragraph, I will briefly discuss inequality and its relevance for the remainder of this book.

Inequality

Reducing inequalities is one of the 17 Sustainable Development Goals of the United Nations. These goals address 17 global challenges (such as poverty, climate change, environmental degradation, peace and justice); one of them is inequality (UN, 2022).

The 2020 World Social Report (UN, 2020) published by the UN Department of Economic and Social Affairs (DESA) shows that in most developed countries and some middle-income countries, income inequality has increased over the years. In the foreword to the report, UN chief António Guterres writes, "Income disparities and a lack of opportunities are creating a vicious cycle of inequality, frustration and discontent across generations." Not surprisingly, the data reveal that the richest 1% of the population are the big winners in the changing global economy, increasing their share of income between 1990 and 2015. Correspondingly, the bottom 40% of that population earned less than a quarter of the average income in the surveyed countries. The report points to a correlation between level of inequality and economic growth. In addition, unequal healthcare and educational services prevent mobility and perpetuate poverty over generations.

In 2019, the Nobel Prize in Economics was awarded to Abhijit Banerjee and Esther Duflo—both MIT professors—for their research aimed at exploring the most effective solutions to alleviate extreme poverty, stating a convincing case for an intelligent interventionism and a society built on compassion and respect. And lately, a number of famous authors have argued that income inequality is a major—if not the major—contemporary concern (Stiglitz, 2012, 2013; Piketty, 2014, 2020; Milanovic, 2016).

There seems to be a consensus that growing inequality is undesirable, with a variety of argumentations as to the why. Above and beyond the intrinsic ethical reasons, some researchers argue that it contributes to populism, protectionism and social stress in general (Alesina & Rodrik, 1994; Persson & Tabellini, 1991; Alesina et al., 2018; Aiyar & Ebeke, 2019). Examples of some Latin American countries in the past and some post-communist countries presently show that a highly unequal society tends to advance toward unstable political situations and often authoritarian regimes (Stiglitz, 2013). Furthermore, following Tridico (2018), inequality can and has led to economic instability and financial crisis, when the financial sector attempts to compensate for the lack of consumption and aggregate demand with credit availability and debt-led growth (Stockhammer, 2015). Moreover, as Inglehart and Norris (2016) explain in their book on "cultural backlash," stagnant middle-class wages and limited job mobility provide convincing objectives for resentment toward "outsiders" whom they perceive as competing for jobs and benefits. This, so the authors argue, is particularly prevalent under conditions of growing social fragmentation and eroded traditional collective structures (Inglehart & Norris, 2016).

Thus, empirical and theoretical literature describes a trend showing that economic insecurity fosters and calls for authoritarian leadership, nativist political parties and an increasing demand for protectionism.

Although it is beyond the scope of this book to provide a detailed review of the reasons why inequality is a major concern, the academic literature and empirical data of the last decades allow us to assume that increasing and persistent inequality is intrinsically undesirable.

Inequality and Growth

An additional issue to be discussed in the framework of this discourse is the relation between inequality and growth. Whether income inequality impedes or fosters growth is widely disputed in the relevant literature (Kharlamova et al., 2018). Some argue that high incomes could increase growth at the same time as inequality, and others point to a decrease of overall productivity due to the fact that entire segments of people are excluded from the labor market (Stiglitz, 2013). Empirical data are inconclusive too. Some studies show a negative effect of inequality on growth (Ostry & Berg, 2011; Ostry et al., 2014; Cingano, 2014; Berg et al., 2018; Seo et al., 2020) while others did not find this effect (Forbes, 2000; Panizza, 2002; Kraay, 2015; Jianu et al., 2021). Furthermore, recent empirical research found that income inequality impacts growth positively in developed EU member states, whereas in developing EU member states, the influence of inequality on growth was found to be negative (Jianu et al., 2021). Inequality had a significant impact on economic growth when interacting with high levels of poverty. This negative impact increases as poverty increases (Breunig & Majeed, 2020). Finally, the type of economy also impacts the relationship between inequality and growth. More specifically, in wage-led economies, an increase in the wage share with a parallel decrease in the profit share increases economic activity and growth, whereas in a profit-led economy, the reverse effect can be found. Onaran and Galanis (2013) explain that in wage-led countries such as Germany, France and Italy, a decrease in wage share leads to lower growth, whereas in profit-led countries such as Canada, Australia, Israel and China, it stimulates growth.

Lastly, it is assumed that the level of equality of opportunity also impacts growth. For example, Aiyar and Ebeke (2019) hypothesize that there is a connection between the level of equality of opportunity and the impact of inequality on growth. More specifically, they maintain that in economies with low equality of opportunity, income inequality affects growth negatively, whereas in economies with higher equality of opportunity, increase in income inequality has a less harmful impact on growth. Generally, most studies maintain that income inequality is detrimental to economic growth, particularly if the population perceives it as unjust and insuperable (OECD, 2018; Mourao & Junqueira, 2021).

Following the UN report mentioned previously, four main global megatrends affect inequalities: technological innovation, climate change, urbanization and international migration. In this book, I will focus on technological innovation since it concerns those winning or losing from it. Most certainly, technological innovation can substantially improve education, communication, healthcare and productivity and thereby support economic growth. However, at the same time, it can also lead to increased wage inequality, harming the more vulnerable groups of workers. Notwithstanding potential negative outcomes, technological change and development is widely considered the "engine of growth." The technological evolution is perceived as a main feature of the 21st century, as are the constant growth of financial capital and the stagnation of classical production (Andersson & Stone, 2017;

Zygmunt, 2017). The following part will discuss the relationship between technological innovation and inequality.

Technological Innovation and Inequality

As early as 1957, Robert Solow (1957) linked the level of skilled labor in production technology to an increase in wage inequality. Since then, studies in a variety of fields dealt with the interconnection of technological innovation and increasing income inequality. The World Social Report of 2020 (UN, 2020) includes a chapter on the winners and losers of the technological revolution. The authors of the report state at the very beginning of the chapter, "For all its promise, technological innovation is already creating winners and losers. Highly skilled workers are benefitting more from new technologies than other workers, resulting in greater income and wage inequality" (UN, 2020, p. 59). Furthermore, they call for strategies and policies to ensure that opportunities to augment equality outperform the risks of technological innovation and change. Thus, there is an overall concern as to the consequences of technological innovation.

Piketty's argumentation points to the skill-based explanation as an important aspect for the account of rising inequality and the role of technological innovation. The "race between the demand and the supply for high skills" in the knowledge-based economy is constantly increasing the income gaps. Salaries of what Piketty calls "super managers" therefore hit unseen levels, and this adds to an ever-growing concentration of wealth. He believes that technological progress will lead to "the triumph of human capital over financial capital and real estate, capable managers over fat cat stockholders, and skill over nepotism" as largely illusory (Piketty, 2014, p. 29). In a similar vein, Brynjolfsson and colleagues (2014) believe that technological innovation is a main driver of increasing inequality, with a growing number of workers left behind. In parallel, he upholds that robots and automation eradicate routine jobs but can also enhance the creation of new and better jobs. Like Piketty, Brynjolfsson believes that the main cause for increasing inequality is not technological innovation in itself. The cause for increasing inequality lies rather in the fact that in technology-driven economies and small groups of successful people who evolve are extremely highly awarded. Therefore, the winners of the knowledge economy are not the owners of conventional capital but the owners of innovative ideas and successful business models. In an article called "New World Order" published in Foreign Affairs, Brynjolfsson, McAfee and Michael Spence (Brynjolfsson et al., 2014), a Nobel laureate and professor at New York University, argued that "superstar-based technical change . . . is upending the global economy." That economy, they conclude, will increasingly be dominated by members of the small elite that "innovate and create" (Brynjolfsson et al., 2014, p. 49). Whereas both Piketty and Brynjolfsson perceive growing inequality as a problem, they disagree about the cause. Piketty worries about inherited wealth leaving people without opportunity for mobility, and Brynjolfsson is concerned with the unequal distribution of the outcomes of the technologically driven and innovative economy. It is beyond the scope of this chapter to further discuss the differences and implications of the approaches of Piketty and Brynjolfsson. In the framework of the argumentation of this book, the point of importance is that rising inequality has potentially negative social and political consequences, and the causes of rising inequality are various. Throughout history, those who innovated and created new ideas progressed more than others. The progress and growth of present technological innovation is much more exponential than in the past, and it is globally scalable; therefore, it seems to perpetuate inequality on national and international levels. Distinguishing between two types of technology can contribute to further clarification—skill-based technology and labor-saving technology. Skill-based technologies increase productivity and the demand for highly skilled workers. More specifically, new technologies lead to higher productivity, but only few workers have the necessary skills to use these technologies. Therefore, employers are prepared to raise the wages of the skilled workforce, who are complements with the new technology (Machin, 2001). Labor-saving technical change in the form of automation is another reason for growing income inequality. Technological progress is displacing unskilled labor in favor of capital and skilled labor and is therefore lowering the share of labor overall and, within that, the share of unskilled labor (Graetz, 2015). Thus, labor-saving technologies reduce the need for labor. Skill-based technologies influence the composition of the labor force as well as the income distribution. Labor-saving technologies are a major driver of the declining income share of workers. In developed countries, technological innovation have also caused a shift from labor to capital in production, thereby reducing the share of workers in national economies (Autor et al., 2017). In parallel, the emergence of a rather small number of dominant firms such as Google, Apple, Amazon and Facebook have increased market concentration and decreased the labor share. Overall and as a result of the previously briefly described trends, highly skilled workers have benefitted most from technological innovations (Mirza et al., 2019).

Silicon Valley

The scenario that often serves to exemplify these developments is Silicon Valley in California. In Silicon Valley, less than a quarter of the inhabitants work in the lucrative high-tech ecosystem where wealth is highly concentrated. As a result, the so-called "spillover effect" is increasing the costs of living (housing, transportation, etc.), with growing demand for employees in retail, hospitality and what was once called blue-collar jobs, a sector in which wages are declining. At the same time, middle class households are being replaced with low- and upper-income households, thus reflecting a polarization of populations along geographic locations overlapping with socioeconomic status. The growth generated in Silicon Valley by the high-tech industry has primarily benefited the wealthiest households. Thus, Silicon Valley illustrates the winner and loser scenario of technological innovation well, and a report funded partly with the support of the Silicon Valley Community Foundation concludes that "the compounded effects of widening inequality, declining mobility, and declining prosperity threaten the economic well-being of individual families, the economic prospects of future generations, and longer-term economic growth" (Reidenbach, 2016, p. 3).

Recently, Ephraim Malkin, Deputy Head of Wages and Labor at the Israeli Finance Ministry, compared Tel Aviv to Silicon Valley (Tversky, 2021), where service workers cannot afford to live anymore. Indeed, as I will show in detail in Chapter 4 of this book, Tel Aviv exemplifies wealth accumulation and social disparities as good as Silicon Valley.

Finally, yet importantly, I would like to point to a number of strategy and policy suggestions aimed to address the potentially problematic consequences of recent technological progress. In developed countries, the discourse about these strategies and policies is based on the assumption that inequality will rise in the absence of government interventions. Moreover, Piketty (2014) predicts that either government intervention or catastrophic events such as world wars or depressions can impede rising inequality.

Suggested strategies and policies to deal with inequality include an inclusive progressive educational system promoting relevant lifelong learning for all. Importantly, research shows that differential levels of achievement are often determined before children enter kindergarten and are closely related to the socioeconomic status of parents. The World Social Report 2020 of the United Nations (UN, 2020) suggests, in addition to education, expanding social protection systems and adapting them to contemporary labor market features such as nonstandard employment modes. At the same time, infrastructures need to be improved in order to enable connectivity, especially for historically marginalized groups. Redistribution by progressive tax, including global wealth tax, has been suggested by Piketty et al. (2018), and creative solutions to share technological innovations more broadly could be achieved via public investment in R & D, state funds to attain stakes in technological innovation and commercialization, tax incentives, and prioritizing of job creating technologies. At least, in the public discourse, there seems to be a consensus that innovative technologies themselves should be accessible to everyone.

Back to Tel Aviv

This book is about the winners and losers of technological advancement in Israel. Following the World Inequality Report, Israel ranks extremely high in inequality, and this trend has been going on for years. Therefore, the gap between the richest and the poorest is constantly growing. In Israel, there are many losers of technological innovation.

The winners personify the startup nation, but they are few. The startup nation has been called an economic miracle and enabled Israel to join the OECD in 2010. Chapter 2 of this book describes and analyzes the process of Israel's path to becoming the startup nation. However, the impressive growth in the high-tech industry has led to a dual economy, with about 10% high-tech employees and a community of high-tech entrepreneurs at the center. There was no spillover to the second Israeli economy, where wages and productivity are stagnating or declining (Breznitz, 2021). In fact, a research project of the researcher Moran Ofir examining the socioeconomic consequences of companies going IPO (initial public offering—entering the stock market) in the USA found that within three kilometers from the area where the headquarters of the issuing companies are located, spillover effects did occur (Heruti-Sover, 2021). There was increasing demand for employees, new businesses and increased use of credit cards—apparently positive spillover effects, within a radius of three kilometers though. In addition, one or two years after the IPO, residential real estate prices increased, as well as the demand for commercial real estate. She maintains that the headquarters of the companies that issue IPOs became so expensive until they caused a population turnover, pushing local populations out. These processes are already taking place in Tel Aviv, reinforcing polarization and the dual economy.

In Israel, the achievements of the high-tech ecosystem are nationally celebrated and internationally acknowledged, with the darker sides seldom in the limelight. In Israel, it was national strategy that led to technological innovation, but there is no national strategy dealing with inequality and its results. The startup nation—a small group of high-tech employees and entrepreneurs—has happily adopted the entrepreneurial imperative and the neoliberal rationality shifting the responsibility for success and failure to the individual, legitimizing emerging inequalities.

Trapped in the myth of meritocracy, the public discourse in Israel has little moral concern for inequalities. In fact, contemporary Israeli society is characterized by lack of social solidarity, worship of personal success and selfish priorities (Tamir, 2019).

Israel is very much "the high-tech and all the rest," and it is this feature I chose to focus on in this book. Generally, the first part of the book deals with the question of how the high-tech industry in Israel has been initiated and developed and finally became so dominant, influential, impactful and successful. In this part of the book, I discuss the knowledge economy and entrepreneurship in Chapter 1, followed by a discourse on national neoliberalism and the Israeli startup nation in Chapter 2. These two chapters set the stage and present the more macropolitical outline. In Chapter 3, the center-periphery divine is discussed theoretically, and data are presented for the Israeli case. Chapter 4 introduces the Israeli startup ecosystem in Tel Aviv. This startup ecosystem includes high-tech employees and entrepreneurs, a very homogenous and small group of people, a rather closed circle, almost inaccessible for "the rest." The second part of the book focuses on "the rest" in an attempt to exemplify the positions of high-tech entrepreneurs from a variety of population groups. Some of these populations are part of the second economy, although they make up a substantial part of the Israeli population.

Chapter 5 presents the theoretical and conceptual framework of social positionality, which I used to describe and analyze technological entrepreneurship in social and geographical peripheries of the country. Chapters 6 through 11 concern technological entrepreneurs of the Ethiopian community (Chapter 6), Kibbutz members (Chapter 7), immigrants from the Former Soviet Union (Chapter 8), women in high tech (Chapter 9), the ultra-Orthodox (Chapter 10) and finally, the Arab-Palestinian Israelis (Chapter 11).

Chapter 12 includes the comparative analysis of the various groups as to their social positionality and attempts to identify level, causes and consequences of exclusion from the high-tech industry. For each group, the interconnectedness of entrepreneurial agency within their respective contexts in terms of cultures and structures of particular communities is analyzed, thereby uncovering structural disadvantages and related levels of precarity as well as existing links between entrepreneurial advantages and disadvantages, mobility and varying degrees of social marginality. Importantly, I attempt to challenge the existing conceptualization of the heroic male entrepreneurship belonging to the dominant elite and highlight the personal experiences of the "other" entrepreneurs. This book attempts to caution the tendency to forget about the losers.

Finally, during the months of writing this book, I interviewed a number of experts from the industry, politics, academia and media. Their insights, opinions and thoughts about the causes for lack of spillover of the achievements of the Israeli high-tech ecosystems to the social and geographic periphery are presented throughout the book and in the concluding chapter, in which I attempt to outline future developments.

I would like to close this introduction with a quote from Piketty's *Capital in the Twenty First Century*: "Every human society must justify its inequalities: unless reasons for them are found, the whole political and social edifice stands in danger of collapse."

Notes

1. For a detailed description of these trends, see chapter 4.
2. A city at the southern outskirts of Tel Aviv

References

Aiyar, S., & Ebeke, C. (2019). Inequality of opportunity, inequality of income and economic growth. *SSRN Electronic Journal*.

Alesina, A., & Rodrik, D. (1994). Distributive politics and economic growth. *The Quarterly Journal of Economics*, *109*(2), 465–490. https://doi.org/10.2307/2118470

Alesina, A., Stantcheva, S., & Teso, E. (2018). Intergenerational mobility and preferences for redistribution. *American Economic Review, 108*(2), 521–554. https://doi.org/10.1257/aer.20162015

Andersson, M., & Stone, T. A. (2017). Global sourcing and technical efficiency—a firm-level study on the ICT industry in Sweden. *Journal of Business Economics and Management, 18*(5), 877–896. https://doi.org/10.3846/16111699.2017.1356367

Autor, D., Dorn, D., Katz, L. F., Patterson, C., & Reenen, J. V. (2017). *Concentrating on the fall of the labor share.* National Bureau of Economic Research.

Berg, A., Ostry, J. D., Tsangarides, C. G., & Yakhshilikov, Y. (2018). Redistribution, inequality, and growth: New evidence. *Journal of Economic Growth, 23*(3), 259–305. https://doi.org/10.1007/s10887-017-9150-2

Breunig, R., & Majeed, O. (2020). Inequality, poverty and economic growth. *International Economics, 161*, 83–99. https://doi.org/10.1016/j.inteco.2019.11.005

Breznitz, D. (2021). *Innovation in real places: Strategies for prosperity in an unforgiving world.* Oxford University Press. https://doi.org/10.1093/oso/9780197508114.001.0001

Brynjolfsson, E., McAfee, A., & Spence, M. (2014). New world order: Labor, capital, and ideas in the power law economy. *Foreign Affairs, 93*(4), 44–53.

CBS. (2022). *Price statistics monthly*. Central Bureau of Statistics.

Cingano, F. (2014). Trends in income inequality and its impact on economic growth. *OECD Social, Employment and Migration Working Papers.* https://doi.org/10.1787/5jxrjncwxv6j-en

Economist Intelligene. (2021). *Worldwide cost of living 2021: Explore the rise and fall of living costs in 173 cities.* The Economist Intelligence Unitk.

Forbes, K. (2000). A reassessment of the relationship between inequality and growth. *American Economic Review, 90*(4), 869–887. https://doi.org/10.1257/aer.90.4.869

Graetz, G. (2015). Rise of the machines: The effects of labor-saving innovations on jobs and wages. *SSRN Electronic Journal.* https://doi.org/10.2139/ssrn.2564969

Heruti-Sover, T. (2021, October 4). Before Herzliya becomes silicon valley: What happens to the region once a company issues? (Hebrew). *The Marker.* Retrieved April 11, 2022, from www.themarker.com/career/.premium-1.10262861

Inglehart, R. F., & Norris, P. (2016). Trump, Brexit, and the rise of populism: Economic have-nots and cultural backlash. *SSRN Electronic Journal.* https://doi.org/10.2139/ssrn.2818659

Jianu, I., Dinu, M., Huru, D., & Bodislav, A. (2021). Examining the relationship between income inequality and growth from the perspective of EU member states' stage of development. *Sustainability, 13*(9). https://doi.org/10.3390/su13095204

Kharlamova, G., Stavytskyy, A., & Zarotiadis, G. (2018). The impact of technological changes on income inequality: The EU states case study. *Journal of International Studies, 11*(2), 76–94. https://doi.org/10.14254/2071-8330.2018/11-2/6

Kraay, A. (2015). *Weak instruments in growth regressions: Implications for recent cross-country evidence on inequality and growth.* World Bank Group. https://doi.org/10.1596/1813-9450-7494

Machin, M. (2001). The changing nature of labour demand in the new economy and skill-biased technology change. *Oxford Bulletin of Economics and Statistics, 63*, 753–776. https://doi.org/10.1111/1468-0084.63.spe1.8

Melnitcki, G. (2021, December 1). 'Tel Aviv is heading toward an explosion,' says the mayor of the world's most expensive city. *Haaretz.* Retrieved April 11, 2022, from www.haaretz.com/israel-news/.premium.HIGHLIGHT.MAGAZINE-tel-aviv-heading-explosion-says-mayor-of-world-most-expensive-city-ron-huldai-1.10430867

Milanovic, B. (2016). *Global inequality*. Harvard University Press. https://doi.org/10.4159/9780674969797

Mirza, M. U., Richter, A., van Nes, E. H., & Scheffer, M. (2019). Technology driven inequality leads to poverty and resource depletion. *Ecological Economics*, *160*, 215–226. https://doi.org/10.1016/j.ecolecon.2019.02.015

Mourao, P., & Junqueira, A. (2021). Through the irregular paths of inequality: An analysis of the evolution of socioeconomic inequality in Brazilian states since 1976. *Sustainability*, *13*(4). https://doi.org/10.3390/su13042356

OECD. (2018). *Opportunities for all: A framework for policy action on inclusive growth*. OECD Publishing. https://doi.org/10.1787/9789264301665-en

Onaran, Ö., & Galanis, G. (2013). Is aggregate demand wage-led or profit-led? A global model. In M. Lavoie & E. Stockhammer (Eds.), *Wage-led growth* (pp. 71–99). Palgrave Macmillan. https://doi.org/10.1057/9781137357939_4

Ostry, J. D., Berg, A., & Tsangarides, C. G. (2014). *Redistribution, inequality, and growth*. International Monetary Fund—Research Department.

Ostry, M. J., & Berg, M. A. (2011). Inequality and unsustainable growth: Two sides of the same coin? *Staff Discussion Notes*, *11*(8). https://doi.org/10.5089/9781463926564.006

Panizza, U. G. (2002). Income inequality and economic growth: Evidence from American data. *Journal of Economic Growt*, 7(1), 25–41. https://doi.org/10.1023/a:1013414509803

Peretz, S. (2022, January 2). Tel Aviv was crowned the world's most expensive city. Can it be dethroned? *Haaretz*. Retrieved April 11, 2022, from www.haaretz.com/israel-news/.premium.MAGAZINE-tel-aviv-was-crowned-the-world-s-most-expensive-city-can-it-be-dethroned-1.10499094

Persson, T., & Tabellini, G. (1991). *Is inequality harmful for growth? Theory and evidence*. National Bureau of Economic Research. https://doi.org/10.3386/w3599

Piketty, T. (2014). *Capital in the 21st century*. The Belknap Press of Harvard University Press.

Piketty, T. (2020). *Capital and ideology*. Harvard University Press. https://doi.org/10.4159/9780674245075

Piketty, T., Saez, E., & Zucman, G. (2018). Distributional national accounts: Methods and estimates for the United States. *The Quarterly Journal of Economics*, *133*(2), 553–609. https://doi.org/10.1093/qje/qjx043

Reidenbach, L. (2016). *Inequality and economic security in silicon valley*. California Budget & Policy Center.

Senor, D., & Singer, S. (2011). *Start-up nation: The story of Israel's economic miracle*. Random House Digital, Inc.

Seo, H. J., Kim, H., & Lee, Y. S. (2020). The dynamic relationship between inequality and sustainable economic growth. *Sustainability*, *12*(14), 5740. https://doi.org/10.3390/su12145740

Shulman, S., & Samet, L. (2021, December 2). If Tel Aviv is as expensive as San Francisco, which city will be Israel's Texas? *Calcalist*. Retrieved April 11, 2022, from www.calcalistech.com/ctech/articles/0,7340,L-3923937,00.html

Solow, R. M. (1957). Technical change and the aggregate production function. *The Review of Economics and Statistics*, *39*(3), 312–320. https://doi.org/10.2307/1926047

Squires, C. (2021, December 2). How Tel Aviv got to be the world's most expensive city. *Quartz*. Retrieved April 11, 2022, from https://qz.com/2097059/how-tel-aviv-got-to-be-the-worlds-most-expensive-city/

Stiglitz, J. E. (2012). Macroeconomic fluctuations, inequality, and human development. *Journal of Human Development and Capabilities*, *13*(1), 31–58. https://doi.org/10.1080/19452829.2011.643098

Stiglitz, J. E. (2013). *The price of inequality*. Norton.

Stockhammer, E. (2015). Rising inequality as a cause of the present crisis. *Cambridge Journal of Economics*, *39*(3), 935–958. https://doi.org/10.1093/cje/bet052

Tamir, Y. (2019). Shall the crooked be made straight? The education plateau and the challenge of inequality. In H. Ayalon, N. Nachum Blass, Y. Feniger, & Y. Shavit (Eds.), *Educational inequality in Israel* (pp. 5–11). Taub Center for Social Policy Studies in Israel.

Tridico, P. (2018). The determinants of income inequality in OECD countries. *Cambridge Journal of Economics*, *42*, 1009–1042. https://doi.org/10.1093/cje/bex069

Tversky, D. (2021, December 22). Tel Aviv: The real cost of being the world's most expensive city. *Davar*. Retrieved April 11, 2022, from https://en.davar1.co.il/349835/

UN. (2020). *World social report 2020*. United Nations—Department of Economic and Social Affairs. https://doi.org/10.18356/7f5d0efc-en

UN. (2022, April 11). *Take action for the sustainable development goals*. United Nations. www.un.org/sustainabledevelopment/sustainable-development-goals/

Zygmunt, A. (2017). Innovation activities of Polish firms. Multivariate analysis of the moderate innovator countries. *Oeconomia Copernicana*, *8*(4), 505–521. https://doi.org/10.24136/oc.v8i4.31

1 Neoliberalism and Entrepreneurship

Introduction

Having parents with money and a technological or science background plays an important role in predicting the likelihood of success in high-tech entrepreneurship. A report of the Israeli Finance Ministry prepared by Hackett and published in January 2021 identified parental education and financial security as key factors for success in high-tech entrepreneurship. The report found that the financial stability of the family impacts the entrepreneurial success of young people more than academic achievements. Academic skills—explained Hackett—do not predict entrance into, or success of, technological entrepreneurship well. Instead, since in the startup process's initial capital investment is needed along with financial security enabling the entrepreneur to live without a regular income, financial security (usually of the family) is an important explanatory variable. Moreover, the relationship between academic success and the probability of becoming an entrepreneur increased in correlation with the parents' income (Hackett, 2021)—so much for meritocracy.

The present and first chapter of this book sets out to explain the interrelationship of neoliberalism and entrepreneurship and the emergence of entrepreneurship as an inherent component of neoliberal ideology. Entrepreneurship has come to symbolize the principles of modern socioeconomic activities globally, where markets synonymously signify societies, which are then called "entrepreneurial societies." This interconnection between neoliberalism and entrepreneurship is a key concern for understanding the Israeli case presented in this book.

Neoliberalism and Entrepreneurship

The collapse of Lehman Brothers in September 2008 was believed by some as the beginning of the end of the age of neoliberalism, followed by Brexit and the Trump presidency in 2016. Doubtlessly, with ever-increasing inequalities and reoccurring crises, even the International Monetary Fund admitted that financial deregulation and retreating government interventions

DOI: 10.4324/9781003091042-2

have been overestimated and "the signature project of neoliberalism—globalization—has come under fire" (Schechter, 2018). Nonetheless, it seems too early to pronounce the death of neoliberalism, which lately coexists smoothly with the so-called economic nationalism.

The concept of neoliberalism has become associated with a radical form of market fundamentalism (Boas & Gans-Morse, 2009) encompassing features such as deregulation and preference for small government; privatization of public facilities; low taxes; minimal regulation of markets; a shareholder focus on the exclusion of a wide range of possible stakeholders; a preoccupation with short-term outcomes; high market capitalization; flexible labor markets, including the ability to fire at will and pay low wages; minimal worker-unemployment support; and many others (Bergsteiner & Avery, 2019; Murtola, 2020). Increasing competition is achieved by opening domestic markets for foreign investments and producers and reducing the role of the state in regulating the economy. Indeed, neoliberal policies have deeply affected all spheres of life. Leaning upon Foucault, Wendy Brown terms neoliberalism a "governing rationality" and explains neoliberalism as a governing rationality through which everything is "economized." "Human beings become market actors and nothing but market actors every field of activity is seen as a market, and every entity (whether public or private, whether person, business, or state) is governed as a firm." Neoliberalism also infiltrates non-wealth-generating spheres, such as learning and dating in market terms—according to Brown—and "submits them to market metrics, and governs them with market techniques and practices. Above all, it casts people as human capital who must constantly tend to their own present and future value" (Shenk, 2005).[1]

Neoliberalism Is Producing Winners and Losers

Evidence shows that a purely neoliberal organization of societies will generate winners and losers (McGuigan, 2014; Bal & Dóci, 2018), with a centralization of few organizations and key figures controlling a substantial share of the global resources and markets (Vitali et al., 2011). This happened primarily because deregulation, privatization and governmental withdrawal from social provisions led to a shift in power from governments to mostly multinational corporations (George, 2014). Consequently, competition between players about shareholder value and profit maximization in this so-called "free" market inevitably generates winners and losers (Lazonick, 2014; Porter, 2011). These trends have increased the gap between powerful multinationals and the "others," often national midsize companies, causing a concentration of a considerable portion of national and global markets in the hands of few (Vitali et al., 2011) and thereby ultimately increasing inequality (Bidwell et al., 2013; Adam Cobb, 2016; Galbraith, 2012). The "others," though, are not only companies and small businesses but also workers, employees who have to sell their labor power in the labor market. These "others" are expected and even demanded to be self-reliant and the absence of governmental regulations in healthcare, housing, education, unemployment, etc., in order to buffer the results of inequality, leaves the weaker segments of societies increasingly vulnerable. Stiglitz (2012) explains that as a result of the growing inequality, ideology and the experiences of people are increasingly dissonant (Wisman, 2013; Stiglitz, 2012; Bal & Dóci, 2018).

In the following, I will attempt to highlight the complexity of this dissonance more in detail. Alas, neoliberal ideology postulates that governments should withdraw from markets so that the "invisible hand" can promote a system in which those who work hard will succeed and are rewarded accordingly (Bal & Dóci, 2018). Thus, work is exchanged as a commodity on the market, often individually, rather than within frameworks of unions, which are perceived as troublemaking interventionists, disturbing the "natural" flow of the free market. Subsequently, neoliberal players are perceived as rational agents—also called "homo economicus" (Brown, 2015), strategically promoting their own interests and goals. Therefore, governments' intervention in the so-called free market is counterproductive, and governments should deregulate, privatize the public sector and withdraw as much as possible from social provisions, such as unemployment, healthcare benefits and social housing (Bal & Dóci, 2018; Peck & Shu, 2009). The neoliberal rationality shifts the responsibility of success and failure toward the individuals themselves and only themselves. Accordingly, when people accept the neoliberal rationality, they take upon themselves the responsibility for their success and failure. Moreover, Maman and Rosenhek (2019) suggest that many financial education programs play an important role in formulating and disseminating this rationality by which people's well-being and economic independence are factors that depend on their own financial decisions.

The idea of meritocracy gives this logic a name; it legitimizes emerging inequalities and provides an explanation why the losers can only blame themselves. Therefore, it provides a tool to deal with Stiglitz's dissonance between ideology and the experience of people.

Meritocracy Explains It All

Michael Young created the term in his book *The rise of the meritocracy* in 1958, cautioning against justification and the legitimization of class differences and the fact that the belief in meritocracy functions as a kind of legitimating myth. Trying repeatedly to clarify that his book was intended to warn against and not endorse meritocracy, he maintained that if success is considered the result of effort and ability, it becomes apparently well deserved, notwithstanding the fact that often it is only luck that led to having talent and the opportunity to use it. Young (2006) further maintains that people who do not succeed are made to believe that failure is their own fault since they are either not talented, lazy or both. Importantly, in the context of neoliberalism and entrepreneurship, meritocracy suggests that success is not related to Bourdieu's notions of one's social, cultural and economic capital, which are surely inherited, but to willpower, an enterprising spirit and hard work (Bal & Dóci, 2018). Although empirical findings largely expose the myth of meritocracy (Littler, 2017; van Dijk et al., 2020), interwoven with neoliberalism, meritocracy functions as a legitimation for the social position of the elites, assuming that the position was acquired due to talent and hard work, typically ignoring structural differences and social positionality.[2]

To sum up, it is important to recognize that the combination of the myth of meritocracy with the celebration of neoliberalism in general and competition in and for itself necessarily generates winners and losers (Davies, 2017). This dynamic mechanism occurs at the micro (individual), mezzo (organizational) and macro (international) levels. The competition narrative legitimizes the very existence of winners and losers, and since the losers—following the meritocracy argumentation—did not meet the competitive standards, they do not deserve access to support and protection from poverty (Harvey, 2005). Thus, the individual losers, those who did not manage to play the game and secure a reasonable income, are left to themselves.

Moving on from the individual to the organizational level of analysis, the following mechanisms can be identified: In the marketplace of the firms, the concentration of so-called "superstar firms" has produced winners and losers with returns divided extremely unequally and shared gains only for superstar firm employees. Thus, increasing inequalities and poverty are fundamentally defining the very essence of the neoliberal system, striking the very existence of the "losers."

At the macro level, neoliberalism ratified the perceived positive relation between entrepreneurship and economic growth. Technological changes and innovations interwoven within neoliberalism emerged as the material and ideational manifestation of growth (Heilbrunn & Iannone, 2019). The narrative of entrepreneurship generating job creation and growth has become standardized in the mainstream scholarly and public discourse (Smit & Pretorius, 2020). This link between entrepreneurship and economic growth is intuitively based on the assumption that if entrepreneurship is a source of innovation and will therefore convert ideas into economic opportunities, then it should lead to increased productivity and economic growth (Sanyang & Huang, 2010). In 2006, Schramm published his book titled *The Entrepreneurial Imperative: How America's Economic Miracle Will Reshape the World (and Change Your Life)* (Schramm, 2006). Entrepreneurship is the new imperative and, above all, is perceived as the source for economic growth. Or as Kuratko (2009) puts it, "The world is in the midst of a new wave of economic development, with entrepreneurship and innovation as the catalysts." In addition, he makes it very clear that companies can either be victims (or losers) of this entrepreneurial revolution "or they can join the revolution." There is—according to Kuratko—no other way.

George Monbiot explains these dynamics in a simple story:

> Never mind structural unemployment: if you don't have a job it's because you are unenterprising. Never mind the impossible costs of housing: if your credit card is maxed out, you're feckless and improvident. Never mind that your children no longer have a school playing field: if they get fat, it's your fault. In a world governed by competition, those who fall behind become defined and self-defined as losers.
>
> (Monbiot, 2016)

The Entrepreneurial Imperative in Practice

In the following paragraph, I discuss the manifestation of the entrepreneurial imperative at three levels of analysis—micro, mezzo and macro. I will start out with the organization (mezzo) level and then move on to the macro (inter)national level. The personal—micro—level is then discussed in a separate paragraph since it concerns the important issue of "heroization" of the entrepreneurial person.

Entrepreneurship has been contextually embedded within institutional frameworks. It has indeed come to be known as the new socioeconomic "common sense" (Lewis-Kraus, 2014; Baker & Welter, 2017; Szeman, 2015). This "common sense" has infiltrated the public and private spheres alike; thus, "we are all entrepreneurs now, or, at a minimum, we all live in a world in which unquestioned social value and legitimacy of entrepreneurship shapes public policy, social development, economic futures and cultural beliefs and expectations" (Szeman, 2015, p. 472). In the academic discourse, this "common sense" reflects the contextual embeddedness of entrepreneurship, fitting Scott's (1995) institutional framework with the regulatory, normative and cognitive pillars, each offering a different rationale for providing legitimacy—either by virtue of being legally sanctioned, morally authorized or culturally supported (Garud et al., 2007).

At this institutional mezzo level, a number of organizational developments exemplify the entrepreneurial imperative in practice. Thus, for example, the emerging gig economy composed of digital platforms created large-scale marketplaces for workers to connect with buyers of services. Consequently, smart technologies influence novel user-producer relationships, and asset-based platforms emerge. Uber is the classical example, using smartphone technology while outsourcing work to individual private drivers. Indeed, the transportation service for clients is improved, but at the same time, temporary and independent work patterns are promoted, which do not necessarily benefit the employees who have, in the process, become a form of freelancers, working in forms of nonstandard employment, usually without Social Security or pension schemes. Uber postulates to have originated a new future for taxi and transportation businesses, but there are winners and losers in this future, especially since many are no longer side-job drivers but eventually do it as their major employment. Uber came to be the "poster child for the gig economy" (Brooks, 2018), encouraging sharing economy at the individual level while promoting neoliberalism at the macro level and, at the same time, placing innovation as a "value-neutral process of supply and demand" (Papaioannou, 2020, p. 1).

At the macro level, we can more lately observe a widespread display of government policies that strengthen the promotion of entrepreneurship. Europe had an Entrepreneurship 2020 Action Plan,[3] and the Bologna Process includes policies on small and medium-sized enterprises (SMEs) and entrepreneurship. In 2000, the first OECD Ministerial Conference on SMEs took place in Bologna (14–15 June), titled "Enhancing the Competitiveness of SMEs in the Global Economy: Strategies and Policies," followed by its second, "Promoting Entrepreneurship and Innovative SMEs in a Global Economy," in Istanbul (3–5 June 2004) and third, "Better Financing for Entrepreneurship and SME Growth" (Brasilia, 27–29 March 2006). In the US, the Global Entrepreneurship Program (GEP), run by the Department of States, aimed to stimulate entrepreneurship ecosystems for scaling small businesses and PACE (Partnering to Accelerate Entrepreneurship), a USAID and private sector partnership, draws upon venture capital as well as US social investment funds to invest in new businesses nationally as well as internationally. In addition, funds from the US Department of Commerce are used to catalyze, foster and monetize new ideas through the Office of Innovation and Entrepreneurship as well as the Regional Innovation Strategies (RIS) Program. In Australia, the Innovation Policy Platform provides grants and assistance to entrepreneurs and entrepreneurship through non-formal training programs (Heilbrunn & Iannone, 2019). Entrepreneurship is fostered at conferences of international agencies (UN, 2018), and policy guidelines for the promotion of the entrepreneurship of a variety of groups are spread (OECD, 2019). Additionally, incubators, accelerators and a number of additional settings are globally endorsed, encompassing a wide arena of public and private spaces. These examples stand not for the promotion of entrepreneurship alone but are also advertised as the solution to the problem of economic growth via entrepreneurship. More indirectly but still following the same logic, entrepreneurship has been recruited by governments and NGOs as solutions for social problems. Entrepreneurship has been celebrated to decrease youth unemployment (Matlali, 2021) and to deal with social exclusion, especially of migrants and minorities, above and beyond the expectation that it is a tool to fight economic stagnation (OECD, 2015a, 2015b). Entrepreneurship education has infiltrated every corner at all educational levels, from kindergarten to MBAs (Bank & Almor, 2013), enabling youngsters to compete in tomorrow's world, cumulating in summer camps on child entrepreneurship (Kidspreneurship, 2022) in order to promote among small children that a "growth mind sets for a happy and fulfilling life."

Thus, globally, entrepreneurialism is fostered, and the paradigm of its lineal relationship with economic growth is seldom questioned. The neoliberal ethos is then intertwined with entrepreneurship praising competition, privatization, deregulation and marketplace dynamics in in private and public organizations alike (Osborne, 2010).

The Entrepreneurial Hero

To continue the previous discussion, driving these developments are neoliberalist ideals, evolving institutional practices that enact the vision of the "enterprise form," extending it "to all forms of conduct" (Burchell, 1993, p. 275) and to subjectivity itself (McNay, 2009; Scharff, 2016). Consequently, businesspeople who were former entrepreneurs are well regarded and celebrated, and business schools flourish, utilizing the life stories of Sloan, Iacocca, Jobs and others (Jørgense & Bager, 2020). "Today, the entrepreneur has become the neoliberal role model of social subjectivity" (Marttila, 2013, p. 5). Since the market is the very center of neoliberalism, the entrepreneur symbolizes the archetypal market actor; the aim is "to shape subjects to make them entrepreneurs capable of seizing opportunities for profit and ready to engage in the constant process of competition" (Dardot & Laval, 2014, p. 103). Likewise, Scharff explains how "entrepreneurial subjects relate to themselves as if they were a business, are active, embrace risks, capably manage difficulties and hide injuries" (Scharff, 2016, p. 108). Thus, "neoliberal subjects are market actors, standing alone and against their competitors, hoping that their risk-taking will pay off" (Murtola, 2020, p. 98). Thus, the entrepreneur is the classic actor for neoliberalism (Freeman, 2007).

Thus on, the micro (personal) level, neoliberalism has advanced individual entrepreneurial activities and freedom within an institutional framework promoting first and foremost private property rights, individual liberty, agile markets and free trade (Harvey, 2005). Consequently, the entrepreneur is addressed as a cultural hero, and self-employment has become an idealized aspiration—combining freedom and independence, wealth and hard work—while creating benefit for the economy and society. If the individual fails to succeed, it is their personal failure as an "entrepreneur of the self" (Harvey, 2005; Kalleberg, 2009, 2012).

In parallel and consequently, the entrepreneur hero as an archetype has arisen in popular culture, glorified as an iconic superhero. Television shows such as *Shark Tank* and *How I Made My Millions* glorify the riskiness of entrepreneurial behavior. *Planet of the Apps*, an Apple show centered on applications that started in 2017; *Silicon Valley*, a TV show of six seasons about a group of friends establishing a startup in Silicon Valley; and *New York Times* best sellers such as *The $100 Startup: Reinvent the Way You Make a Living, Do What You Love, and Create a New Future* by Chris Guillebeau (2012) and *The Lean Startup: How Today's Entrepreneurs use Continuous Innovation to Create Radically Successful Businesses* by Eric Ries (Reis, 2011) uphold the narrative that entrepreneurship can lead to gigantic success and that who wins is largely a democratic process for anyone with a little creativity who is willing to put in the persistent effort required. Following the popular narrative, the successful entrepreneur can meet all challenges and obstacles if he/she just invests enough effort and persistence.

Szeman (2015) describes the entrepreneurial hero logic as a closed-loop logic: the entrepreneur is hailed as a glorious hero, the "perfect figure" who "embodies the values and attributes that are celebrated as essential for the economy to operate smoothly and for the contemporary human being to flourish." Highlighted as the "common-sense way of navigating the inevitable, irreproachable, and apparently unchangeable reality of global capitalism" (Szeman, 2015, p. 473), the entrepreneur hero further legitimizes neoliberalism. Consequently, entrepreneurship has come to embody the principles of our modern socioeconomic society, in which markets synonymously denote societies and which then, following (Audretsch, 2009) contention, become entrepreneurial societies (Heilbrunn & Iannone, 2019) encompassing a political economic theory aimed at advancing entrepreneurial freedom within a governmental structure that include free markets, private property, and free trade (Regilme, 2019).

Despite being the cultural zeitgeist, the entrepreneur hero's typical business is hidden from popular discourse, as are many governmentally created opportunities for unproductive and unsuccessful entrepreneurship (Mitra, 2013). Gerpott and Kieser (Gerpott & Kieser, 2020) argue along the same line and state that the promises based on the overglorification of entrepreneurship are often not realized. Because most startups fail, entrepreneurial undertakings usually do not make people rich.

Nonetheless, those who are successful are celebrated as entrepreneurial role models. An atypical minority of extremely successful cases and their fetishization of certain entrepreneurial types, such as unicorns and college dropouts, have attracted the interest of the media, research and policy and have merged with the zeitgeist model. It is only lately that cases of fraud, deception and felony are discussed widely in the public discourse. Cases such Elizabeth Holmes' Theranos (Carreyrou, 2018) and Adam Neumann's WeWork (Thompson, 2019) focus on the founders and their behavior. Furthermore, cases such as NSO and Cellebrite (Rueckert, 2021; Rabat, 2020) reflect the questionable conduct of some gleaming startups and will be discussed in more detail in Chapter 14.

Concluding Thoughts

While entrepreneurship is mainstreamed and celebrated in neoliberal capitalism, it also uncovers new forms of precarity. The critical theory discourse on precarious work is based upon the assumption that the ongoing neoliberal transition toward flexible labor markets and economic and political deregulations imply higher risks for most participants in the labor market, including the self-employed. Following Gill and Pratt's (2008) precarious work arrangements are "atypical" or "nonstandard work," including temporary illegalized work, home working, piece working, freelancing (Gill & Pratt, 2008; Schmiz, 2013) and bogus or false self-employment (McKay et al., 2012; Vershinina et al., 2018). More so, the self-employed are the ones responsible for work-related benefits (Frade et al., 2004). Consequently, self-employment can be seen as precarious and associated with poor-quality work, resulting in low income, flexible (long) schedules and lack of security for the worker. Moreover, the International Labor Organization (ILO) suggests that job security must be understood and characterized by a salaried, stable and full-time job with rights and benefits. The processes of entrepreneurship and self-employment transfer the burden of job security and benefits from the employer and the state to the individual, which "is uncertain, unpredictable, and risky from the [worker's] point of view" (Kalleberg, 2009, p. 2). Following Schmiz (2013), the degree of the precariousness of entrepreneurship and self-employment is defined by control over work schedule and content, social insurance and retirement coverage, and adequacy of income and economic hardship. The preciousness of entrepreneurship and self-employment felt by the mainstream population has an even higher degree of impact on the vulnerabilities of migrants and minorities engaged in entrepreneurship and self-employment (Vershinina et al., 2018). Notwithstanding all these insights, entrepreneurship is utilized as a legitimizing argument for the rise of precarity, suggesting "human wellbeing can best be advanced by liberating individual entrepreneurial freedoms" (Harvey, 2005, p. 2) and promoting the tales of the modern world being built by the "self-made man" (Goffee & Scase, 2015).

The negative sides of entrepreneurship and innovation are often silenced in favor of overemphasizing the glorifications of success stories. It seems that entrepreneurship is here to stay and will be an alternative to employment in different economies for different reasons. Therefore, it is important to examine entrepreneurship's social and societal effects, in particular its potential impact on growing inequalities and imbalance of power (see Lippmann et al., 2005; Dey & Mason, 2018; Spinosa et al., 1995).

In Israel, entrepreneurship in general and technological entrepreneurship and innovation in particular are considered engines of national growth and competitiveness. At the center, there is a startup nation with a vibrant and successful high-tech entrepreneurial scene, accumulating resources and enabling constant growth, while at the geographical and social periphery, a parallel society has emerged, populated by often-marginalized groups not able to keep up. In one of the most unequal countries with extremely high rates of poverty, entrepreneurial heroes are celebrated at the center, promoting a myth that all could be self-made successes if they just tried hard enough. At the periphery, entrepreneurs are struggling to survive, often pushed into precarious working and living conditions. The glorious space of Israeli startups is far from meritocratic.

I believe that a critical perspective of the Israeli high-tech scene and its interrelationships with neoliberalist policies can facilitate a perception aiming not only at economic growth and financial wealth but also at shared prosperity, with technological entrepreneurs being potential agents for political and social change for society as a whole.

Notes

1. Neoliberalism has been widely discussed in the academic, public and political discourse. It is beyond the scope of this book to discuss the discourse more in detail. I decided to focus on Brown's governing rationality since it fits well in explaining the emergence of the entrepreneurial-hero figure.
2. Therefore, in this book, I rely on the positionality approach, which allows for the uncovering of structural disadvantages of various population groups. See chapter 5, pages XXX–XXX.
3. The Europe 2020 strategy recognizes entrepreneurship and self-employment as key for achieving smart, sustainable and inclusive growth (EU, 2013). In its support to entrepreneurship and self-employment, the European Commission focuses its efforts on business startups by the unemployed and people from disadvantaged groups; sustainability and quality of work of self-employed businesses and micro-entrepreneurs; and support for social entrepreneurs.

References

Adam Cobb, J. (2016). How firms shape income inequality: Stakeholder power, executive decision making, and the structuring of employment relationships. *Academy of Management Review, 41*(2), 324–348. https://doi.org/10.5465/amr.2013.0451

Audretsch, D. B. (2009). The entrepreneurial society. *The Journal of Technology Transfer, 34*(3), 245–254. https://doi.org/10.4337/9781783476923.00018

Baker, T., & Welter, F. (2017). Come on out of the ghetto, please!—Building the future of entrepreneurship research. *International Journal of Entrepreneurial Behavior & Research, 23*(2), 170–184. https://doi.org/10.1108/ijebr-02-2016-0065

Bal, P. M., & Dóci, E. (2018). Neoliberal ideology in work and organizational psychology. *European Journal of Work and Organizational Psychology*, 536–548. https://doi.org/10.1080/1359432x.2018.1449108

Bank, D., & Almor, T. (2013). The development of business education in a young, entrepreneurial country: The case of Israel. In I. Alon & V. Jones (Eds.), *Innovation in business education in emerging markets* (pp. 76–95). Palgrave Macmillan. https://doi.org/10.1057/9781137292964_6

Bergsteiner, H., & Avery, G. C. (2019). Misleading country rankings perpetuate destructive business practices. *Journal of Business Ethics, 159*(3), 863–881. https://doi.org/10.1007/s10551-018-3805-6

Bidwell, M., Briscoe, F., Fernandez-Mateo, I., & Sterling, A. (2013). The employment relationship and inequality: How and why changes in employment practices are reshaping rewards in organizations. *Academy of Management Annals*, 7(1), 61–121. https://doi.org/10.5465/19416520.2013.761403

Boas, T. C., & Gans-Morse, J. (2009). Neoliberalism: From new liberal philosophy to anti-liberal slogan. *Studies in Comparative International Development, 44*(2), 137–161. https://doi.org/10.1007/s12116-009-9040-5

Brooks, C. (2018, April 9). Uber's big lie. *jacobin*. Retrieved March 30, 2022, from www.jacobinmag.com/2018/09/uber-misclassification-gig-economy-taxi-workers-alliance

Brown, W. (2015). *Undoing the demos: Neoliberalism's stealth revolution*. Mit Press. https://doi.org/10.2307/j.ctt17kk9p8

Burchell, G. (1993). Liberal government and techniques of the self. *Economy and Society*, *22*(3), 267–282. https://doi.org/10.1080/03085149300000018

Carreyrou, J. (2018). *Bad blood: Secrets and lies in a silicon valley startup*. Knopf.

Dardot, P., & Laval, C. (2014). *The new way of the world: On neoliberal society*. Verso Books.

Davies, W. (2017). *The limits of neoliberalism: Authority, sovereignty and the logic of competition*. Sage. https://doi.org/10.4135/9781529793734

Dey, P., & Mason, C. (2018). Overcoming constraints of collective imagination: An inquiry into activist entrepreneuring, disruptive truth-telling and the creation of 'possible worlds'. *Journal of Business Venturing*, *33*(1), 84–99. https://doi.org/10.1016/j.jbusvent.2017.11.002

EU. (2013). Document 52012DC0795. *Communication from the commission to the European parliament, the council, the European economic and social committee and the committee of the regions entrepreneurship 2020 action plan reigniting the entrepreneurial spirit in Europe*. https://eur-lex.europa.eu/legal-content/EN/ALL/?uri=celex:52012DC0795

Frade, C., Darmon, E., & Laparra, M. (2004). *Precarious employment in Europe: A comparative study of labour market related risk in flexible economies*. European Commission, DG Research, Framework V Programme.

Freeman, C. (2007). The "reputation" of neoliberalism. *American Ethnologist*, *34*(2), 252–267. https://doi.org/10.1525/ae.2007.34.2.252

Galbraith, J. K. (2012). *Inequality and instability: A study of the world economy just before the great crisis*. Oxford University Press.

Garud, R., Hardy, C., & Maguire, S. (2007). Institutional entrepreneurship as embedded agency: An introduction to the special issue. *Organization Studies*, *28*(7), 957–969. https://doi.org/10.1177/0170840607078958

George, J. M. (2014). Compassion and capitalism: Implications for organizational studies. *Journal of Management*, *40*(1), 5–15. https://doi.org/10.1177/0149206313490028

Gerpott, F. H., & Kieser, A. (2020). The fairytale of the successful entrepreneur: Reasons and remedies for the prevalent ideology of entrepreneurship. In Springerlink (Ed.), *Against entrepreneurship: A critical examination* (pp. 133–151). Palgrave Macmillan. https://doi.org/10.1007/978-3-030-47937-4_8

Gill, R., & Pratt, A. (2008). In the social factory? Immaterial labour, precariousness and cultural work. *Theory, Culture & Society*, *25*(7–8), 1–30. https://doi.org/10.1177/0263276408097794

Goffee, R., & Scase, R. (2015). *Entrepreneurship in Europe (Routledge revivals): The social processes*. Routledge. https://doi.org/10.4324/9781315712925

Guillebeau, C. (2012). *The $100 startup: Reinvent the way you make a living, do what you love, and create a new future*. Currency.

Hackett, Y. (2021). *Who becomes a start-up innovator?* The Chief Economist Department.

Harvey, D. (2005). *The neoliberal state. In a brief history of neoliberalism*. Oxford University Press. https://doi.org/10.1093/oso/9780199283262.001.0001

Heilbrunn, S., & Iannone, R. L. (2019). Neoliberalist undercurrents in entrepreneurship policy. *Journal of Entrepreneurship and Innovation in Emerging Economies*, *5*(2), 149–162. https://doi.org/10.1177/2393957519861489

Jørgense, K. M., & Bager, A. S. (2020). Keep the machine running: Entrepreneurship as a practice of control in the neoliberal economy. In SpringerLink (Ed.), *Against entrepreneurship* (pp. 57–76). Palgrave Macmillan. https://doi.org/10.1007/978-3-030-47937-4_4

Kalleberg, A. L. (2009). Precarious work, insecure workers: Employment relations in transition. *American Sociological Review, 74*(1), 1–22. https://doi.org/10.1177/000312240907400101

Kalleberg, A. L. (2012). Job quality and precarious work: Clarifications, controversies, and challenges. *Work and Occupations, 39*(4), 427–448. https://doi.org/10.1177/0730888412460533

Kidspreneurship. (2022, March 22). *Kidspreneurship*. www.kidspreneurship.com/

Kuratko, D. F. (2009). The entrepreneurial imperative of the 21st century. *Business Horizons, 52*(5), 421–428. https://doi.org/10.1016/j.bushor.2009.04.006

Lazonick, W. (2014). Profits without prosperity. *Harvard Business Review, 92*(9), 46–55.

Lewis-Kraus, G. (2014, April 22). One startup's struggle to survive silicon valley's gold rush. *WIRED*. Retrieved March 30, 2022, from www.wired.com/2014/04/no-exit/

Lippmann, S., Davis, A., & Aldrich, H. E. (2005). Entrepreneurship and inequality. In L. A. Keister (Ed.), *Entrepreneurship* (Vol. 15, pp. 3–31). Emerald Group Publishing Limited. https://doi.org/10.1016/S0277-2833(05)15002-X

Littler, J. (2017). *Against meritocracy: Culture, power and myths of mobility*. Taylor & Francis. https://doi.org/10.4324/9781315712802

Maman, D., & Rosenhek, Z. (2019). The construction of Homo financius: Conventions, emotions and morals in financial education (Hebrew). *Israeli Sociology: A Journal for the Study of Israeli Society, 1*(20), 23–49.

Marttila, T. (2013). *The culture of enterprise in neoliberalism: Specters of entrepreneurship*. Routledge. https://doi.org/10.4324/9780203094693

Matlali, L. (2021, September 21). *Why entrepreneurship and innovation are key to addressing youth unemployment*. World Economic Forum. Retrieved March 30, 2022, from www.weforum.org/agenda/2021/09/the-role-of-entrepreneurship-and-innovation-in-tackling-unemployment-in-africa-youth-jobs-employment-education/

McGuigan, J. (2014). The neoliberal self. *Culture Unbound, 6*(1), 223–240. https://doi.org/10.3384/cu.2000.1525.146223

McKay, S., Jefferys, S., Paraksevopoulou, A., & Keles, J. (2012). *Study on precarious work and social rights* (pp. 72–74). Working Lives Research Institute, London Metropolitan University.

McNay, L. (2009). Self as enterprise: Dilemmas of control and resistance in Foucault's the birth of biopolitics. *Theory, Culture & Society, 26*(6), 55–77. https://doi.org/10.1177/0263276409347697

Mitra, J. (2013). *Entrepreneurship, innovation and regional development*. Routledge. https://doi.org/10.4324/9780203813782

Monbiot, G. (2016, April 15). Neoliberalism—The ideology at the root of all our problems. *The Guardian*. Retrieved March 30, 2022, from www.theguardian.com/books/2016/apr/15/neoliberalism-ideology-problem-george-monbiot

Murtola, A. M. (2020). Entrepreneurship ad absurdum. In A. Örtenblad (Ed.), *Against entrepreneurship: A critical examination* (pp. 93–110). Springer Nature. https://doi.org/10.1007/978-3-030-47937-4_6

OECD. (2015a). *Escaping the stagnation trap: Policy options for the Euro area and Japan*. OECD Publishers.

OECD. (2015b). *New approaches to SME and entrepreneurship financing: Broadening the range of instruments*. OECD Publishing. https://doi.org/10.1787/9789264240957-en

OECD. (2019). *OECD SME and entrepreneurship outlook 2019*. OECD Publishing. https://doi.org/10.1787/34907e9c-en.

Osborne, S. P. (2010). The (new) public governance: A suitable case for treatment? In S. P. Osborne (Ed.), *The new public governance?* (pp. 17–32). Routledge.

Papaioannou, T. (2020). Innovation, value-neutrality and the question of politics: Unmasking the rhetorical and ideological abuse of evolutionary theory. *Journal of Responsible Innovation*, 7(2), 238–255. https://doi.org/10.1080/23299460.2019.1605484

Peck, J., & Shu, S. B. (2009). The effect of mere touch on perceived ownership. *Journal of Consumer Research*, *36*(3), 434–447. https://doi.org/10.1086/598614

Porter, M. E. (2011, June 21). Creating shared value: Redefining capitalism and the role of the corporation in society. *HBR*. Retrieved March 30, 2022, from www.hbs.edu/faculty/Pages/item.aspx?num=46924

Rabat, H. (2020, September 1). Petition: Stop the export of celebrity Kong (Hebrew). *Calcalist*. Retrieved March 30, 2020, from www.calcalist.co.il/internet/articles/0,7340,L-3847533,00.html

Regilme, S. S., Jr. (2019). Constitutional order in oligarchic democracies: Neoliberal rights versus socio-economic right. *Law, Culture and the Humanities*. https://doi.org/10.1177/1743872119854142

Reis, E. (2011). *The lean startup*. Currency.

Rueckert, P. (2021, July 18). The Pegasus project | NSO's Pegasus: The Israeli cyber weapon oppressive regimes used against 180 journalists. *Haaretz*. Retrieved March 30, 2022, from www.haaretz.com/israel-news/tech-news/.premium-nso-s-pegasus-the-israeli-cyber-weapon-used-against-180-journalists-1.10010446

Sanyang, S. E., & Huang, W. C. (2010). Entrepreneurship and economic development: The EMPRETEC showcase. *International Entrepreneurship and Management Journal*, *6*(3), 317–329. https://doi.org/10.1007/s11365-008-0106-z

Scharff, C. (2016). The psychic life of neoliberalism: Mapping the contours of entrepreneurial subjectivity. *Theory, Culture & Society*, *33*(6), 107–122. https://doi.org/10.1177/0263276415590164

Schechter, A. (2018). Illiberal neoliberalism. *The Tel Aviv Review of Books*. Retrieved March 30, 2022, from www.tarb.co.il/illiberal-neoliberalism/

Schmiz, A. (2013). Migrant self-employment between precariousness and self-exploitation. *Ephemera: Theory & Politics in Organization*, *13*(1).

Schramm, C. J. (2006). *The entrepreneurial imperative: How America's economic miracle will reshape the world (and change your life)*. HarperCollins.

Scott, W. R. (1995). *Institutions and organizations*. Sage Publications.

Shenk, T. (2005, April 2). Booked #3: What exactly is neoliberalism? *Dissent*. Retrieved March 30, 2022, from www.dissentmagazine.org/blog/booked-3-what-exactly-is-neoliberalism-wendy-brown-undoing-the-demos

Smit, M., & Pretorius, M. (2020, December). "Un" trepreneurship. *African Journal of Business Ethics*, *14*(1). https://doi.org/10.15249/14-1-273

Spinosa, C., Flores, F., & Dreyfus, H. L. (1995). Disclosing new worlds: Entrepreneurship, democratic action, and the cultivation of solidarity. *An Interdisciplinary Journal of Philosophy*, *38*, 3–63. https://doi.org/10.1080/00201749508602373

Stiglitz, J. E. (2012). Macroeconomic fluctuations, inequality, and human development. *Journal of Human Development and Capabilities*, *13*(1), 31–58. https://doi.org/10.1080/19452829.2011.643098

Szeman, I. (2015). Entrepreneurship as the new common sense. *South Atlantic Quarterly*, *114*(3), 471–490. https://doi.org/10.1215/00382876-3130701

Thompson, D. (2019, October 25). WeWork's Adam Neumann is the most talented grifter of our time. *The Atlantic*. Retrieved March 30, 2022, from www.theatlantic.com/ideas/archive/2019/10/how-weworks-adam-neumann-became-billionaire/600607/

UN. (2018). *Trade and development report 2018*. United Nations.

van Dijk, H., Kooij, D., Karanika-Murray, M., De Vos, A., & Meyer, B. (2020). Meritocracy a myth? A multilevel perspective of how social inequality accumulates through wor. *Organizational Psychology Review*, *10*(3–4), 240–269. https://doi.org/10.1177/2041386620930063

Vershinina, N. A., Rodgers, P., Ram, M., Theodorakopoulos, N., & Rodionova, Y. (2018). False self-employment: The case of Ukrainian migrants in London's construction sector. *Industrial Relations Journal*, *49*(1), 2–18. https://doi.org/10.1111/irj.12199

Vitali, S., Glattfelder, J. B., & Battiston, S. (2011). The network of global corporate control. *PloS One*, *6*(10), e25995. https://doi.org/10.1371/journal.pone.0025995

Wisman, J. D. (2013). Wage stagnation, rising inequality and the financial crisis of 2008. *Cambridge Journal of Economics*, *37*(4), 921–945. https://doi.org/10.1093/cje/bes085

Young, M. (2006). Looking back on meritocracy. *The Political Quarterly*, 77, 73–77. https://doi.org/10.1111/j.1467-923x.2006.00782.x

2 National Neoliberalism and the Israeli Startup Nation

Introduction

In this chapter, I will attempt to describe and analyze the origins of the phenomenon labeled the *Israeli startup nation*. I will outline relevant underlying economic, social and political mechanisms that have contributed to its emergence.

Israel has labeled itself and is labeled by many as a "startup nation" (Senor & Singer, 2011). During the last decades, the country has undergone a process of transformation from being a developmental to a neoliberal model (Mandelkern & Shalev, 2018), configurating a specific version of national neoliberalism combining liberalization and strong national sentiments (Krampf, 2018a). The Israeli government has been using neoliberal tools to initiate technological entrepreneurship via the establishment of an institutional framework that is promoting this policy (Rosenberg, 2018). Throughout this process, Israel has been employing its innovation policy as a national strategic pillar to increase competitive advantage in the international arena.

One outcome of these processes has been the positioning of Tel Aviv's entrepreneurial high-tech ecosystem at the top of international competitive rankings (Isenberg, 2010). Innovation policy, alongside market-oriented policies initiated by the government, has brought about a stable and relatively high growth to the Israeli economy over the years. But the model of economic growth is based almost exclusively on the high-tech industry and has generated increasing economic inequalities: the fruits of the economic growth are very unevenly and unequally distributed (Zehavi & Breznitz, 2017), and the gap between center and periphery remains profound.

State-Initiated Innovation and Entrepreneurship

The exceptional economic performances of countries such as Japan, Taiwan and Singapore from the 1980s onward has driven a renewed academic and public interest in the role of politics in economic development. The relative success of these countries led to the questioning of the assumption of

DOI: 10.4324/9781003091042-3

the Washington Consensus[1] since the well-planned policy programs initiated by these countries' governments created economic transformation and competitiveness, not the "invisible hand" of the free market (Breznitz & Ornston, 2013). The role of the state in technological innovation has lately been discussed by innovation and political theorists (Block & Keller, State of innovation: the US government's role in technology development, 2011; Mazzucato, 2013; Mazzucato, 2016; Schot & Steinmueller, 2016; Papaioannou, 2020). The so-called entrepreneurial role of the state assumes "the existence of the state not only as a set of institutions that guarantees social evolution through protection of markets but also as an entity capable of creation of markets in risky areas of knowledge and technology" (Papaioannou, 2020, p. 200). Mazzucato's "The Entrepreneurial State: Debunking Public vs. Private Sector Myths" (2013) further fueled the argument that the state is a crucial partner of the private sector in fostering innovation. Therefore, according to Mazzucato (2013), instead of only fixing market failures, it is suggested that the state should be entrepreneurial and take risks, becoming the driving engine of technological innovations. In Mazzucato's terms, technological innovations themselves are not the aim of the entrepreneurial state but rather the tool to achieve societal missions. Innovation theorists such as Mazzucato (2013) and Block (2018) reject the capitalist view of the market as a self-regulating organism and stress the importance of governmental strategies in prioritizing technological innovation (Papaioannou, 2020). This necessarily contains risk-taking. For governments to impose risky technological innovation upon its citizens, the latter must account for the state's legitimacy requirements. According to Papaioannou (2020), in a liberal capitalist state, mission-oriented innovations should contribute to individual freedom and protect private property, whereas in a welfare state, mission-oriented investments for generating innovation and growth are conditional to the maximization of social welfare. In a neoliberal state, innovation policies would target growth by means of free competition among technology-based firms. Papaioannou sums up his line of argumentation by pointing to the fact that a neoliberal or libertarian state would be incompatible with any redistributive policies based on the returns of successful innovations (Papaioannou, 2020).

A major challenge of innovation policies in any form or type of state is the conflict of interests between private firms and the government. Breznitz and Zehavi (2010) have termed this phenomenon a "spillover problem." This problem concerns the location of innovation and production. More specifically, a spillover problem occurs when firms move R & D and/or production to new locations. The transition from "innovate here/produce here" to "innovate here/produce there" (where labor costs are low and regulations are lax) and, lately, also the possibility of "produce there/innovate there" constitute a major challenge for local economies (Maggor, 2021). The possibility of "produce there/innovate there" has been called in the literature of high-tech outsourcing/offshoring. It is a major concern for policy makers in developed economies since it may lead to reduction in employment, decreasing earnings and technological developments being pursued in other countries (Contractor et al., 2010; Hanafizadeh & Zare Ravasan, 2018; Pereira et al., 2019). Lately, new product design and R & D are increasingly outsourced and offshored as transportation-related constraints are fewer, and IT is now transferred electronically and relies on modern and reliable IT infrastructures (Temouri et al., 2010). In many countries, this "spillover problem" is addressed via policies aimed at keeping the outcomes of high-tech industries local.

The main challenge of the spillover problem is the commercialization of R & D (Maggor, 2021): at the commercialization stage, entrepreneurs must decide whether to "produce here" or sell their technology and thereby "produce there." Thus, policies aimed at keeping firms local, thereby realizing the broader social benefits for all citizens, need to address this challenge. Maggor (2021, p. 6) suggests two strategies to overcome the spillover problem: first, conditioning R & D funding in terms of manufacturing requirements, ownership requirements, and knowledge governance so that benefits remain local and, second, institutionalized disciplinary mechanisms to enforce these requirements.

In the remaining part of this chapter, I will outline the path of Israel from a historically low-technology economy and late developing country to a high-income country that effectively promoted rapid innovation-based growth, utilizing the strategies outlined previously (Breznitz & Ornston, 2013; Maggor, 2021).

How Did Israel Become the Startup Nation?

Mandelkern and Shalev (Mandelkern & Shalev, 2018) outline the main features of Israel's transformation to neoliberal capitalism[2]: rising inequality in the labor market and decline in the share of labor of the national income, massive decrease in welfare state spending and increasing industry monopolization. The Israeli government has used neoliberal policies tailored to their ambitions for economic growth (Nitzan & Bichler, 2002, p. 30), and this has become a national project (Charney, 2017; Krampf, 2018b). Maron and Shalev (2017) argue that four specific forms of governmental policies were instrumental in increasing neoliberalism in Israel. These include the privatization of both public and labor union-owned enterprises, the reduction of banks' dominant role in the economy, financial liberalization policies and changes in state subsidies for businesses. Rather than the habitual neoliberal conception of a free market with little to no state involvement, the Israeli government has continued to be directly involved in channeling direct and indirect financial aid to privately owned corporations. Before shifting toward neoliberalism, state support schemes generally went to financing big businesses with the motivation to increase jobs in the labor market. With the adaption of neoliberalism, the state's financial aid became much more selective and exclusive and has been targeted toward startups, innovation, and research and development (R & D) (Maron & Shalev, 2017). Policy was very much directed toward developing and benefitting the technological sector with investment grants and tax benefits to both local and foreign firms established in Israel. This was driven by the engaged and passionate role of state agencies. In short, the neoliberal agenda of Israel was aimed at creating opportunities and incentives for a heightened concentration of the high-tech sector (Dyduch & Olszewska, 2018; Krampf, 2018b; Mandelkern & Shalev, 2018), with neoliberalism enabling the country to become a destination for high-tech investors and a source of capital inflow (Nitzan & Bichler, 2002). Thus, in Israel, the state has been actively involved in enforcing market policies (Maman & Rosenhek, 2012), and "government bodies remain highly involved in the macroeconomic management of the economy and in regulating financial, labor and commodities markets" (Mandelkern & Shalev, 2018, p. 10).

In the following section, I will attempt to explain the emergence of Israel's innovation economy in more detail.

Israel's Innovation Policy

Israel is considered a late-developing country (Bareli & Elmaliach, 2021). Typically, these countries aim to govern their markets by creating links between the state and the market. This strategy is based on the assumption that without state intervention in the financial market, the country is predestined to a slow industrialization process that would result in it being placed low in the world-trade-system scale as well as in lower levels of social welfare for its citizens (Krampf, 2018a). For that aim, states build markets to advance their interests, and these endeavors are often legitimized by nationalistic narratives, values and identities (Dyduch & Olszewska, 2018).

In Israel, like in many countries globally, during the 1970s and 1980s, the traditional industrial economy was declining. This decline as well as additional global developments and local economic problems drove a group of political entrepreneurs from Israel's Ministry of Finance and the Bank of Israel to initiate a comprehensive stabilization plan in 1985—leading to institutional changes characterized by neoliberal reforms (Mandelkern & Shalev, 2018).

In order to restructure Israel's industry into a knowledge-based economy, a wide political coalition was designed by Israel's leading developmental agency. The coalition encompassed key figures of industry, finance and labor as well as former military elites and leading entrepreneurial scientists and engineers. Thus, an institutional body was established, called by Maggor (2021) as "institutional capacities." This goes along with what is often called a "mission mode" approach to organizing R & D (Brown, 2021). The established "institutional capacity" was composed of strong state commitment supported by appropriate resources, a politically convincing goal, centralized strong leadership with control over resources and a focus on a limited set of pointed tasks (Wilson et al., 2007).

Security needs have always been at the forefront of Israel's political strategies, and historically, a large share of resources has been allocated to defense purposes. There is no doubt that the defense industry accounts for a significant share of Israel's industrial capacity, and the security forces and associated industries were actively taking part in the coalition to foster a high-tech industry. In the military, innovative technologies were developed on a large scale led by the Israeli Aircraft Industry and Rafael, a government-owned company that develops and produces defense and combat systems. Rosenberg (2018) maintains that military technology was the first leader of the Israeli knowledge economy and until the 1990s—in the absence of a global market for Israeli technology and communication production—the main driver of innovation.

Nevertheless, the major innovation policies were composed by a civilian innovation agency, "the Office of the Chief Scientist" (later to become the Innovation Authority). Already in 1968, the Office of the Chief Scientist (OCS) in the Ministry of Trade and Industry received a budget targeting R & D in the private and public sectors. This was considered a turning point in the development of the Israeli high-tech industry.

Rosenberg (2018) explains that the startup economy in Israel emerged during the 1990s due to a number of developments—the previously mentioned reforms of 1985 and the cancellation of the Lavi[3] project, which led to the ejection of a large pool of highly qualified engineers of the security industry into the public and private sector (Sadan, 2017). Many of these engineers went on to establish the first wave of Israeli high-tech companies. In addition, like in the USA and later in Europe, the monopoly on telecommunication services came to an end, and at the same time, the need for information technologies increased. In the 1990s, Israel received a large immigration wave from the Former Soviet Union (FSU), and global and local political developments changed the geopolitical environment such that immediate threats from neighboring countries decreased dramatically. Finally, according to Rosenberg (2018), the emigration of many talented engineers from Israel to Silicon Valley led to the establishment of a network on which the Israeli high-tech scene definitely capitalized in the short and long run.

The OCS also established a political alliance of domestic elites whose economic interests aligned with the developmental priorities of the state. This partnership, led by the OCS, comprised bankers, industry leaders, labor leaders, entrepreneurs, scientists and the military. Similar to other cases of government or quasi government agencies promoting entrepreneurship and innovation, such as Enterprise Ireland (Enterprise-Ireland, 2022), Sitra (Sitra, 2022) in Finland and Sweden's Vinnova (Vinnova, 2022), the aim of the OCS was to promote strategic economic imperatives.

A main concern of the Israeli government was the spillover problem explained before; therefore, the aim of the upgrading the coalition led by the OCS was to promote the local commercialization of R & D.

The commercialization of technological innovation concerns the transformation process from R & D to market dissemination, including negotiations of intellectual property issues (Wonglimpiyarat, 2016a). Thus, it is a critical stage in terms of national interests. The policy promoted by the OCS was therefore directed at the ownership of intellectual property and manufacturing. More specifically, private enterprises would have ownership of the knowledge developed with R & D funded by the OCS but limited control over it. Entrepreneurs who reached the manufacturing stage were required to manufacture in Israel and forbidden to sell IPs to companies that were operating outside of Israel's borders. According to Lach (2000) and Meuleman and De Maeseneire (2012), government subsidies of R & D reduce financial liquidity constraints and produce a confirming effect to private funds. Thus, the OCS scheme explicitly gave an advantage to the public over private funding (Rosenberg, 2018).

During the first years after its establishment, OCS was granted enforcement mechanisms to control and discipline startups or firms that received state funding. Consequently, the commercialization of R & D stayed local, and holdings of multinational firms in Israel continued to operate from Israel. Thus, public investment in R & D translated into public rewards. According to Maggor (2021), these political mechanisms were successful since they included conditionality and a discipline-enforcing apparatus.

According to Avnimelech and Teubal (2006), the emergence of the Israeli venture capital industry has had a critical influence on the Israeli high-tech ecosystem. Over the years this industry gained power, to become a major player in the system. Naturally, the private venture capital industry promoted interests that were different from those of the OCS. Maggor (2021) states that policies initiated by the venture capital industry significantly reduced public rewards, which were a key pillar in the original strategy of the OCS. The main actor of this change was Yozma. The Yozma initiative—designed and administered by the OCS in cooperation with the Ministry of Finance—can be defined as the creator of the Israeli venture capital sector, a government policy that generates equity investments in technology startups (Yozma, 2022). The aim of Yozma was to acquaint Israeli technology industrial startups with the US financial and product market to help them become more commercially successful and competitive (Breznitz, 2007). Thus, Yozma provided direct investments to private venture funds on the condition that they invest in Israeli high-tech startups. It was the trigger for spreading the growth of venture capital and startups in Israel (Avnimelech, 2009) and, as such, enabled Israel's entry into the global technological market via government policy (Agmon & Messica, 2008). The purpose of the program was threefold: first, to encourage foreign venture capitalist firms to enter Israel; second, to contribute to the advancement of a local venture capital industry; and third, to integrate Israeli high-tech firms into international markets (Khavul & Deeds, 2016). The Yozma program therefore "mirrored the willingness of the Israeli government to take risks in VC investments" (Wonglimpiyarat, 2016b, p. 23) via private VC funds that invested directly in the technological enterprises.

Trajtenberg (2000) has defined Israel as a laboratory case for government intervention in a late-developing country. He has suggested that through Yozma, the government proceeded in a focused and fast manner to answer the need to catch up with global developments. Yozma was a neoliberal political tool (Maman & Rosenhek, 2012; Trajtenberg, 2000), creating a safety net for investors (Gold, 2018), intended to integrate Israel's venture capital industry within the global financial sphere world and opening the Israeli economy to the FDI by attracting foreign investors who brought along their expertise. Thus, the main target of Yozma were the investors. The program can be evaluated as a major success since the Israeli VCS became one of the largest in the world in relative terms. Venture capital gained power and influence in the high-tech industry and soon became the main capital source for startups to finance commercialization. The Israeli Venture Association (IVA), which was established in 1992, targeted the former policy tools of the OCS to keep the commercialization local: conditionality and the discipline to adhere to it.

The main arguments of the IVA to change the R & D law were obvious.[4] First, multinationals will not buy startups in Israel if they do not have full control over the IP; therefore, startups will experience difficulties to attract foreign investments. Second, in global economies, it makes no sense to try and control the transfer of knowledge. Third, the policy pursued by the OCS has been causing great damage to Israel. Typically, parallel to obliterating the constraints on commercialization of promising R & Ds, VCS wanted to keep the advantage of the OCSs funding schemes, taking over the risk during the development stage. As Chemi Peres, cofounder and partner of Pitango, states in an interview with Erez Maggor,

> Venture funds mostly invest at the stage where we can help firms become profitable. We do not want to bother too much with the development of the technology. There we cannot bring our investors the yield in the timeframe they expect it. We want to invest when a company already has a product and is about to penetrate the market.
>
> (2021, p. 123)

The reform demanded by the IVA was in line with Netanyahu's neoliberal reforms of that period (Maggor, 2021), which encompassed privatization, reduction in public employment, financial liberalization and implementation of welfare policies shifting responsibilities away from the state. The suggested reforms of the R & D law went along with and complimented these neoliberal trends, favoring the private over the public interest. The reformed R &

D law from 2005 allowed OCS-supported R & D to be transferred internationally, and over time, the redemption fee to be paid for internationalization would decrease. According to Maggor (2021), the rate of foreign investment in R & D has substantially increased between 2005 and 2017 (from 29% to 49.2%) mainly due to the relatively high number of multinational firms acting in the Israeli market as everywhere in the world. Maggor (2021) further maintains that since 2014, about 70% of R&D subsidiaries initiated by MNCs in Israel were based on the acquisition of Israeli startups. A study conducted by Getz et al. (2014) on the innovation of foreign R & D centers in Israel also revealed that the proportion of the transfer of innovative knowledge and ideas to foreign R & D has increased significantly over the last decade. The authors maintain that Israeli IPs are being bought, and those patents comprise a major part of the total patent portfolio of foreign R & D centers in Israel (Getz et al., 2014). This causes a potential loss to Israel's domestic economy since the investments of MNCs are usually intended at seizing control of local IPs. Whereas Getz et al. (2014) maintain that MNCs generate spillover effects to the local market and the economy in general, Maggor (2021) postulates that the dominance of foreign R & D in MNCs slows down job creation beyond the R & D centers. Additionally, he states, independent local startups could generate higher tax revenues, thereby sharing the rewards of innovation with the public rather than having them remain in private ownership.

The OCS was renamed the Israel Innovation Authority (IIA) in 2016. The Israeli Innovation Authority explicitly defines the objective of Israel's innovation policy as "maintaining Israel's position at the forefront of global innovation and elevating the entire community through technological innovation" (Israel Innovation Authority, 2018). Therefore, innovativeness and technological entrepreneurship has also become a diplomatic tool promoting the country's national and international interests (Dyduch & Olszewska, 2018). The latest policies concerned with the United Arab Emirates present an excellent example for this. As stated on the IIA's website,

> It seems that the two countries share a similar mindset on the necessity of innovation, research, and science and technology as the pillars of a knowledge-based, highly productive and competitive economy. . . . This means that Israel has a new partner for the journey to redefine and redesign the future through tech and innovation, and this partner opens up a whole new untapped market of Middle East North Africa (MENA) and Gulf Countries.
>
> (Israel Innovation Authority, 2022)

Concluding Thoughts

In sum, from the 1980s, the Israeli government has been applying neoliberal economic principles to realize their ambition for economic growth (Nitzan & Bichler, 2002). The innovation economy of technological advancement and high level of competitiveness were instrumental for the implementation of the country's strategic goals in the regional and global geopolitical arena. The fact that Israel is one of the global leaders in technological advancement is due to a government-led policy that shaped what has been called "national neoliberalism" (Krampf, 2018b). Within the logic of this national liberalism, the innovation paradigm was functional to construct an economic reality that compensates for and counters international pressure due to Israel's continued occupation of the Palestinian territories. The need to provide security rather than economic welfare and social justice to every citizen historically has gone along with the prioritization of the national over the social cause as the security narrative has not yet been challenged (Ben-Ephraim, 2020; Krampf, 2018b). It is only recently that the asymmetric distribution of the benefits of the technological advancement has been critically addressed in Israeli public discourse.

Notes

1. The Washington Consensus is a set of economic-policy recommendations for developing countries, Latin America in particular, that became popular during the 1980s. The term "Washington Consensus" usually refers to the level of agreement between the International Monetary Fund (IMF), World Bank and US Department of the Treasury on those policy recommendations. All shared the view, typically labelled neoliberal, that the operation of the free market and the reduction of state involvement were crucial to development in the global South (www.britannica.com/topic/Washington-consensus).
2. For a detailed description of the historical development, see Krampf (2018b).
3. The Lavi project was an Israeli initiative to build its own fighter jet. The project achieved the advanced stage of building two successful prototypes but did not proceed to the line-production phase due to political and economic issues. For further explanation, see Steinberg (1988).
4. Such claims were made, for example, in interviews with Chemi Peres, cofounder and partner of Pitango, and Yoram Oron, chairman of IVA.

References

Agmon, T., & Messica, A. (2008). Venture capital funds, financial foreign direct investment and the generation of local comparative advantage in the technology sector in Israel. *SSRN Electronic Journal*, *27*(1), 57–72. https://doi.org/10.2139/ssrn.1209988

Avnimelech, G. (2009). VC policy: Yozma program 15-years perspective. *Environment for Innovation EJournal*. https://doi.org/10.2139/ssrn.2758195

Avnimelech, G., & Teubal, M. (2006). Creating venture capital industries that co-evolve with high tech: Insights from an extended industry life cycle perspective of the Israeli experience. *Research Policy*, *35*(10), 1477–1498. https://doi.org/10.1016/j.respol.2006.09.017

Bareli, A., & Elmaliach, T. (2021). Israel as a case study in processes of nation-building. *Israel Studies Review*, *36*(2), 1–9. https://doi.org/10.3167/isr.2021.360202

Ben-Ephraim, S. (2020). From strategic narrative to strategic culture: Labor Zionism and the roots of Israeli strategic culture. *Comparative Strategy*, *39*(2), 145–161. https://doi.org/10.1080/01495933.2020.1718988

Block, F. L. (2018). *Capitalism: The future of an illusion*. University of California Press. https://doi.org/10.1525/california/9780520283220.001.0001

Block, F. L., & Keller, M. R. (2011). *State of innovation: The US government's role in technology development* (1st ed.). Routledge. https://doi.org/10.4324/9781315631905

Breznitz, D. (2007). Industrial R&D as a national policy: Horizontal technology policies and industry-state co-evolution in the growth of the Israeli software industr. *Research Policy, 36*(9), 1465–1482. https://doi.org/10.1016/j.respol.2007.06.006

Breznitz, D., & Ornston, D. (2013). The revolutionary power of peripheral agencies: Explaining radical policy innovation in Finland and Israel. *Comparative Political Studies, 46*(10), 1219–1245. https://doi.org/10.1177/0010414012472466

Breznitz, D., & Zehavi, A. (2010). The limits of capital: Transcending the public financer—Private producer split in industrial R&D. *Research Policy, 39*(2), 301–312. https://doi.org/10.1016/j.respol.2009.12.010

Brown, R. (2021). Mission-oriented or mission adrift? A critical examination of mission-oriented innovation policies. *European Planning Studies, 29*(4), 739–761. https://doi.org/10.1080/09654313.2020.1779189

Charney, I. (2017). A "supertanker" against bureaucracy in the wake of a housing crisis: Neoliberalizing planning in Netanyahu's Israel. *Antipode, 49*(5), 1223–1243. https://doi.org/10.1111/anti.12331

Contractor, F. J., Kumar, V., Kundu, S. K., & Pedersen, T. (2010). Reconceptualizing the firm in a world of outsourcing and offshoring: The organizational and geographical relocation of high-value company functions. *Journal of management studies, 47*(8), 1417–1433. https://doi.org/10.1111/j.1467-6486.2010.00945.x

Dyduch, J., & Olszewska, K. (2018). Israeli innovation policy: An important instrument of perusing political interest at the global stage. *Polish Political Science Yearbook*, (2). https://doi.org/10.15804/ppsy2018208

Enterprise-Ireland. (2022, March 19). *Enterprise-Ireland*. www.enterprise-ireland.com/en/

Getz, D., Leck, E., & Segal, V. (2014). *Innovation of foreign R&D centers in Israel: Evidence from patent and firm level data*. Samuel Neaman Institute for Advanced Studies in Science and Technology.

Gold, S. J. (2018). Israeli infotech migrants in silicon valley. *RSF: The Russell Sage Foundation Journal of the Social Sciences, 4*(1), 130–148. https://doi.org/10.7758/rsf.2018.4.1.08

Hanafizadeh, P., & Zare Ravasan, A. (2018). A model for selecting IT outsourcing strategy: The case of e-banking channels. *Journal of Global Information Technology Management, 21*(2), 111–138. https://doi.org/10.1080/1097198x.2018.1462070

Isenberg, D. J. (2010). The big idea: How to start an entrepreneurial revolution. *Harvard Business Review, 88*(6), 40–50. Retrieved March 30, 2022, from https://hbr.org/2010/06/the-big-idea-how-to-start-an-entrepreneurial-revolution

Israel Innovation Authority. (2018). *Innovation in Israel 2017 overview*. Israel Innovation Authority.

Israel Innovation Authority. (2022, March 19). *Innovationisrael*. https://innovationisrael.org.il/en/

Khavul, S., & Deeds, D. (2016). The evolution of initial co-investment syndications in an emerging venture capital market. *Journal of International Management, 22*(3), 280–293. https://doi.org/10.1016/j.intman.2016.03.006

Krampf, A. (2018a). Israel's neoliberal turn and its national security paradigm. *Polish Political Science Yearbook, 47*(2), 227–241. https://doi.org/10.15804/ppsy2018205

Krampf, A. (2018b). *The Israeli path to neoliberalism: The state, continuity and change.* Routledge. https://doi.org/10.4324/9781315193922

Lach, S. (2000). *Do R&D subsidies stimulate or displace private R&D? Evidence from Israel.* NBER Working Paper. https://doi.org/10.3386/w7943

Maggor, E. (2021). The politics of innovation policy: Building Israel's "neo-developmental" state. *Politics & Society, 49*(4), 451–487. https://doi.org/10.1177/0032329220945527

Maman, D., & Rosenhek, Z. (2012). The institutional dynamics of a developmental state: Change and continuity in state—Economy relations in Israel. *Studies in Comparative International Development, 47*(3), 342–363. https://doi.org/10.1007/s12116-012-9098-3

Mandelkern, R., & Shalev, M. (2018). *The political economy of Israeli neoliberalism* (pp. 353–672). Oxford University Press. https://doi.org/10.1093/oxfordhb/9780190675585.013.39

Maron, A., & Shalev, M. (2017). *Neoliberalism as a state project: Changing the political economy of Israel.* Oxford University Press. https://doi.org/10.1093/oso/9780198793021.001.0001

Mazzucato, M. (2013). *The entrepreneurial state: Debunking public vs. private sector myths.* Anthem Press.

Mazzucato, M. (2016). Innovation, the state and patient capital. In M. Jacobs & M. Mazzucato (Eds.), *Rethinking capitalism: Economics and policy for sustainable and inclusive growth* (pp. 98–118). John Wiley & Sons. https://doi.org/10.1111/1467-923X.12235

Meuleman, M., & De Maeseneire, W. (2012). Do R&D subsidies affect SMEs' access to external financing? *Research Policy, 41*(3), 580–591. https://doi.org/10.2139/ssrn.1099365

Nitzan, J., & Bichler, S. (2002). *The global political economy of Israel: From war profits to peace dividends.* Pluto Press.

Papaioannou, T. (2020). Reflections on the entrepreneurial state, innovation and social justice. *Review of Evolutionary Political Economy, 1*(2), 199–220. https://doi.org/10.1007/s43253-020-00018-z

Pereira, V., Munjal, S., & Ishizaka, A. (2019). Outsourcing and offshoring decision making and its implications for businesses-A synthesis of research pursuing five pertinent questions. *Journal of Business Research, 103*, 348–355. https://doi.org/10.1016/j.jbusres.2019.07.009

Rosenberg, D. (2018). *Israel's technology economy: Origins and impact.* Springer. https://doi.org/10.1007/978-3-319-76654-6

Sadan, N. (2017, September 2). 30 years since the abolition of "Lavi": At his death, he commanded us Israeli high-tech (Hebrew). *Calcalist.* Retrieved March 30, 2022, from www.calcalist.co.il/internet/articles/0,7340,L-3720135,00.html

Schot, J., & Steinmueller, W. E. (2016). *Framing innovation policy for transformative change: Innovation policy 3.0.* SPRU Science Policy Research Unit, University of Sussex.

Senor, D., & Singer, S. (2011). *Start-up nation: The story of Israel's economic miracle.* Random House Digital, Inc.

Sitra. (2022, March 19). *Sitra.* www.sitra.fi/en/

Steinberg, G. M. (1988). The politics of the Lavi project. *Newsletter (Association for Israel Studies), 4*(1), 8–10.

Temouri, Y., Driffield, N. L., & Higón, D. A. (2010). The futures of offshoring FDI in high-tech sectors. *Futures, 42*(9), 960–970. https://doi.org/10.1016/j.futures.2010.08.024

Trajtenberg, M. (2000). *R&D policy in Israel: An overview and reassessment*. Samuel Neaman Institute; Technion.

Vinnova. (2022, March 19). *Vinnova*. www.vinnova.se/en/

Wilson, P., Post, S., & Srinivas, S. (2007). *R&D models: Lessons from vaccine history*. International AIDS Vaccine Initiative, Columbia University. https://doi.org/10.2139/ssrn.1099495

Wonglimpiyarat, J. (2016a). Exploring strategic venture capital financing with Silicon Valley style. *Technological Forecasting and Social Change*, *102*, 80–89. https://doi.org/10.1016/j.techfore.2015.07.007

Wonglimpiyarat, J. (2016b). Government policies towards Israel's high-tech powerhouse. *Technovation*, *52*, 18–27. https://doi.org/10.1016/j.technovation.2016.02.001

Yozma. (2022, March 17). *Yozma*. www.yozma.com/

Zehavi, A., & Breznitz, D. (2017). Distribution sensitive innovation policies: Conceptualization and empirical examples. *Research Policy*, *46*(1), 327–333. https://doi.org/10.1016/j.respol.2016.11.007

3 Center and Periphery in Israel

Startup Nation and Parallel Economy

Introduction

In recent decades, socioeconomic inequalities have been increasingly apparent, and ongoing processes of polarization between dynamic metropolitan areas and rural former-industry areas portray many countries all over the world. Furthermore, large cities are believed to have many advantages over rural areas at the geographical periphery, and some argue that large cities are "innovation machines." Moreover, agglomeration economies (Duranton & Puga, 2004; Glaeser, 2011) are defined as a necessary precondition for innovative business development (Florida et al., 2017). Fritsch and Wyrwich (2021) review the literature on the assumption that successful innovation is more prevalent in large cities than in the rural periphery. They present four main reasons for this prevalence: (1) the existence of R & D facilities in universities, research institutes and innovative private firms; (2) ample input markets; (3) knowledge spillover due to geographic closeness and cooperation of R&D actors; and (4) attractiveness to creative and innovative people (Florida et al., 2017). Whereas the authors focus on the city's size as a main indicator, regional differences in innovation can also be explained by institutional conditions, the population-age structure, the sectorial composition of the local economy, the quantity and quality of available human and social capital, and regional cultures (Asheim et al., 2019; Crescenzi & Rodríguez-Pose, 2013; Fritsch & Wyrwich, 2021). An alternative but very overlapping approach to explain regional differences in innovation is the concept of entrepreneurial ecosystem, which accentuates that entrepreneurship happens within a community of interdependent actors. According to Stam (2015), the literature on entrepreneurial ecosystems emphasizes the role of the economic and social context in fostering or hindering entrepreneurship. The entrepreneurial ecosystem approach focuses on "high-growth startups" as an important source of innovation, productivity growth and employment (Stam, 2015; Foster et al., 2013). Like Fritsch and Wyrwich (2021), Stam (2015) maintains that elements of the entrepreneurial ecosystem concern network, leadership, finance, talent, knowledge and intermediary support services, framed by conditions such as formal institutions, culture, physical

DOI: 10.4324/9781003091042-4

infrastructure and demand. These conditions are more prevalent in large cities than in regional areas.

The Center-Periphery Nexus Explained

The center-periphery nexus is addressed in the Territorial Agenda 2020 of the European Union (EU). It relates to increasing inequality and its consequences: "the core-periphery division is still present" and it is important "to avoid polarization between capitals, metropolitan areas and medium-sized towns on the national scale" (European Commission, 2011). To follow up, innovation takes place mainly in the centers; therefore, the relation between innovation and the processes of peripheralization are important to consider.

Geographical peripheralization under globalization and neoliberalism and related governance and values has been addressed by social scientists (Harvey, 2003; Naumann & Reichert-Schick, 2013). Generally, the center periphery is theorized as a "particular socio-spatial configuration of power relations leading to uneven socio-spatial development" (Manfred & Matthias, 2013, p. 303); thus, it entails processes of centralization and polarization. Consequently, spatial centralization necessarily implies the peripheralization of other (noncentral) regions, thereby fostering immigration, localized economic productivity and infrastructural concentration. Hence, peripheralization describes social relations with spatial implications that often lead to polarization. According to Kühn (2015), peripheralization is closely related to marginalization, which, as a multidimensional process, includes lack of integration and development, as well as presenting economic, social, political and cultural disadvantages (Jones et al., 2007; Kühn, 2015).

Kühn (2015) reviews the theoretical approaches of peripheralization and points to three distinct perspectives: the economic perspective, the sociological perspective and the political perspective.

The economic perspective maintains that the growth of the "knowledge economy" is driven by business services mainly to be found in metropolitan centers (as outlined previously), attracting people and businesses (Herrschel, 2012). This results in a relative lack of innovation in periphery, which feeds into the economic process of peripheralization (Kühn, 2015).

Theories of marginality and poverty investigate the processes leading to sociospatial disadvantages. Kreckel (2004) explains that peripheral positions are the result of structurally embedded conditions disadvantaging individuals and groups as to accessibility of desirables and/or symbolic goods and the scope for autonomous action (Kreckel, 2004, p. 43). The *sociological view of peripheralization* thus emphasizes that peripheries are poorer than average sociospatial units and that this is caused by interplays of macrosocial, economic, political and spatial processes. In geographic peripheries, communities and households are suffering from impoverishment, often due to deindustrialization, demographic shrinkage, lack of investment and outmigration of higher-qualified workforce (Kühn, 2015).

The *political perspective* is reflected in political theories, which discuss the relation between center and periphery in terms of power and domination. Wallerstein's (1974) World-System-Theory is probably the most prominent global theory of power asymmetry between states. He divided countries into politically strong cores/centers with high productivity, politically and economically weak peripheries, and semiperipheries, located between these extremes and dialectically stabilizing the entire system. Kreckel defines a peripheral position as "exclusion from dominating resources of power and . . . insufficient possibilities, abilities or willingness to create counter power" (Kreckel, 2004, p. 44). Following the political-theory approach, peripheries are excluded from decision-making centers and from actor networks that also have decision-making power (Manfred & Matthias, 2013). Thus, the sociospatial processes of centralization and peripheralization lead to the core-periphery configuration of structural gaps within a country. The majority of the population and of political and economic power is located at the core center, increasingly gaining power over the periphery (Castree et al., 2013; Gren, 2003; Sharabi et al., 2020). Following polarization theories, growth processes in the centers are linked to shrinking growth in the periphery, with core regions characterized by technological, economic and social innovation (Friedmann, 1973). Moreover, core-periphery relations are manifested not only spatially and economically but also socially as populations that have a lower socioeconomic status and are otherwise marginalized tend to reside in the periphery (Borgatti & Everett, 2000; Castree et al., 2013). Neoliberalist policies, pushing toward the privatization of municipality services (former provided by the government), are contributing to social polarization and increasing inequality (Collins & Rothe, 2019; Harvey, 2003), with smaller peripheral municipalities more impacted by these trends of polarization, which are often presented as neutral "bottom-up" processes (Clarno, 2017; Tzfadia & Yacobi, 2015).

Summing up, political and economic power is usually located at the center, where populations with a higher socioeconomic status are concentrated, whereas the periphery is associated with socioeconomic deprivation. In short, wealth is concentrated in the center and poverty in the periphery. Cultural hegemony at the center often drives the stigmatization of population groups in the periphery, with the deconstruction of elements of the welfare state often occurring there, increasing processes of polarization.

Center and Periphery in Israel

Historically, the center-periphery construct has been used to explain the social construct of Israeli society (Kimmerling, 2001; Tzfadia & Yacobi, 2015; Yiftachel & Tzfadia, 2004). According to this view, a sociopolitical elite of Jewish Eastern European origin, inspired by national-secular Zionism and a socialist welfare state ideology, established Israel. Consequently, a variety of "others" perceived as marginal to the Zionist project constituted and still constitute the periphery in Israel. These "others" included all non-Jewish population groups—immigrants from the Middle East, North Africa and the former USSR and the ultra-Orthodox community.

The peripheralization and marginalization of these groups is largely the outcome of spatial policies, the absence of public investment and planning, unequal public-budget allocations and expenditures, and stereotyping on the basis of ethnic descent (Shdema et al., 2021; Smooha, 1978; Tzfadia & Yacobi, 2015). Discussing the intentionality of these processes goes beyond the scope of the present chapter, which intends to show their outcomes as the basis for the various groups of technological entrepreneurs discussed in Chapters 6 through 12.

What Characterizes Peripheral Areas in Israel?

First, Israel is a knowledge economy characterized by the need for knowledge services such as banking, consulting, legal services, marketing and so on. Knowledge economies in general tend to centralize because they attract high-skilled individuals who then produce higher economic profitability. Knowledge centers often generate better infrastructure than peripheries. In addition, in Israel the majority of international companies are located in Tel Aviv, with a vibrant commercial-services sector around them.

Second, in Israel, like in many other countries, the center coincides with the main metropolitan core, and geographic and ethnic, social, and cultural boundaries partly overlap. This fact provides the basis for the saying that Israel contains the "Tel Aviv country" and "the rest." "Tel Aviv country" is located between Hadera and Gedera and contains about 70% of the Israeli population today. "The rest" at the geographic periphery are municipalities with a high concentration of minorities and overall lower socioeconomic profiles.

Thirdly, and more specifically, Israeli municipalities are usually divided along community, ethnic and religious lines, therefore separating Palestinian Israeli from Jewish Israeli populations and Jewish ultra-Orthodox from the Jewish religious and secular population. While there are many lines of conflict in Israel, the one between the Jewish dominant majority and Palestinian (mainly (Muslim minority concerns a major, if not the major, segregation characteristic, with Palestinian Israelis still composing a marginalized minority located in the spatial, political and social periphery.

In the following, I will present an overall picture of Israeli society in terms of the center and periphery divide. The particularities of the population groups introduced in Chapters 6 to 13 in this book will be discussed in the respective chapters.

Income. As Israel's GDP per capita grew significantly during the past decade—31,706 in 2012; 37,806 in 2016; and 42,912 in 2019, all in US dollars (OECD, 2021)—not all groups of society enjoyed the rapid growth, which is apparent via income inequality measured by the Gini coefficient, which stood at 0.348 in 2018 (OECD, 2022), compared to the OECD average of 0.316 (OECD, 2011).

Residents of municipalities located at the social and geographical periphery of Israel often receive lower wages than the Israeli average. In 2018, the share of employees earning minimum wage or below in Jewish urban municipalities was 33.7%, compared to 46.5% in Arab urban municipalities (Rozrenberg, 2020). In 2017, 55% of the residents of the ultra-Orthodox settlements, 45% of residents in Arab municipalities and 37% of residents of development towns earned up to the minimum wage. In comparison, only 26% of residents of prosperous municipalities earned up to the minimum wage (Swirsky et al., 2020). Additionally, in 2018, the percentage of employees earning less than minimum wage significantly varied between geographical regions. Whereas in Jerusalem (46.3%) and in the Northern (45.3%) and Southern periphery (41%) of the country, more than 40% of the employees earned less than minimum wages; in the Tel-Aviv district and center district, the percentage was significantly lower (34.2% in Tel Aviv and 35% at the center). Importantly, these percentages are high in comparison to the OECD average. The same accounts for monthly wages, with an average of 7,963 NIS wage in Jerusalem; 8026 NIS in the northern periphery; 8,661 NIS in the southern periphery; 10,955 in Tel Aviv; and 11,114 NIS in the center district (Butush, 2020). Table 3.1 depicts the data.

Income inequality also occurs along ethnic and gender lines. In 2018, the average income for Israeli women was 8,546 NIS and 12,498 NIS for men. Reviewing the data along ethnic lines brings up a more complex picture: while the average monthly income for an Israeli Jewish female was 8,923 NIS, Israeli Palestinian females earned an average of 5,722 NIS. The same tendency occurs for men: while Israeli Jewish men earned an average of 13,558 NIS, Israeli Palestinian men earned only 8,190. Income gaps are also evident within the Israeli Jewish society, with Jews immigrated from Europe

Table 3.1 Average monthly wage and percentage of employees earning less than the minimum wage, by district, for the year 2018.

District	*Average monthly wage*	*Percentage of employees earning less than the minimum wage*
Jerusalem[1]	7,963	46.3%
North	8,026	45.3%
Beer Sheva	8,502	42.3%
South	8,661	41.0%
Haifa	9,456	40.3%
Tel Aviv	10,955	35.5%
Center	11,114	34.2%
National average	9,634	39.4%

Source: Butush (2020)

or North America at the top of the income pyramid (women 11,918 NIS and men 18,772 NIS), followed by second-generation female and male Ashkenazi (Israeli born with Europe-/America-born father), earning 10,470 and 16,483 NIS, respectively. Second-generation Mizrachi (with an Asia-/Africa-born father) and first-generation Mizrachi (immigrated from Asia/Africa before 1989) men earned 14,153 NIS and 13,578 NIS, respectively. Men immigrated from Europe and America after 1990, a group comprised mostly with immigrants from the USSR, earned 13,179 NIS. Finally, men that immigrated from Asia/Africa from 1990 onward (mostly from Ethiopia) were earning 7,193 NIS on average (Swirsky et al., 2020). Rates of earning also vary significantly by type of municipality and for the year 2017 amounted to 55% in ultra-Orthodox settlements, 45% in Arab municipalities, 37% in development towns, 31% in non-ultra-Orthodox Jewish municipalities and 26% in prosperous municipalities. In 2018, overall, 35.1% of employees earned the minimum wage or less for a month's work. In Jewish urban municipalities, the share of employees earning up to the minimum wage was 33.7%, compared to 46.5% in Arab urban municipalities (Rozenberg, 2020). Table 3.2 depicts average gross monthly income for wage earners in Israel by ethnic origin and gender.

Table 3.2 reveals average gross monthly income differences for wage earners between the ethnic groups and within all groups between men and women. Women have substantially lower wage incomes in all groups.

For representing the difference between groups, I chose to define the Ashkenazi Jewish Israelis as a benchmark. All other groups earn less in comparison, as can be seen in Table 3.3.

The data show that all groups generate a lower monthly gross income than the Ashkenazi Jewish Israelis. For the Palestinian Israelis and the Ethiopian community, the difference amounts to more than 30%. It seems safe to state that in the last three years (2018–2021), no significant change occurred, and

Table 3.2 Average gross monthly income for wage earners in New Israeli Shekel (NIS), by ethnic origin and gender, 2018.

Ethnic origin	*Average*	*Female*	*Male*	*Percentage compared*
Total	10,522	8,546	12,498	18.8%
Jewish Israelis	11,241	8,923	13,558	20.6%
Ashkenazi Jewish Israelis	13,477	10,470	16,483	22.3%
Mizrachi Jewish Israelis	12,026	9,899	14,153	17.7%
Immigrants from the FSU* (after 1990)	10,768	8,357	13,179	22.4%
Ethiopians**	6,766	5,619	7,913	17.0%
Palestinian Israelis	6,956	5,722	8,190	17.7%

* Jews, Europe-/America-born, immigrated from 1990 on (mostly from the former Soviet Union)
** Jews, Africa-/Asia-born, immigrated from 1990 (mostly Ethiopian Jews)
Source: Swirsky et al. (2020)

Table 3.3 Benchmarked average gross monthly income for wage earners in NIS, by ethnic origin, 2018.

Group	*Average income*	*Percentage compared to benchmark*
Ashkenazi Jewish Israelis (Benchmark)	13,477	n/r
Jewish Israelis	11,241	9%
Mizrachi Jewish Israelis	12,026	6%
Immigrants from the FSU* (after 1990)	10,768	11%
Ethiopians**	6,766	33%
Palestinian Israelis	6,956	31%

Source: Swirsky et al. (2020)

Table 3.4 Rate of families below the poverty line, by district, 2017–2020.

District	*Haifa (district)*	*North*	*South*	*Center*	*Tel-Aviv (district)*	*Jerusalem (district)*
2017	18.8	27	22.7	9.9	11	34
2018	18.1	26.7	22.2	9.4	11.2	30.9
2019	19.6	24.2	24.5	14.7	16.0	36.2
2020	18.4	22.8	23.4	14.0	15.5	36.4

Source: Bituach Leumi (2019; 2021)

the social periphery remains to be mostly characterized along ethnic and national/religious lines.

There is also evidence of socioeconomic inequalities in the number of families living in poverty for different groups of the Israeli society. In the year 2018, the rate of families in poverty in the general population was 18%; the rate of families in poverty among the Jewish ultra-Orthodox population was 42.3% and 45.3% among Israeli Palestinian families (Bituaj Leumi, 2019). When analyzed in geographical terms, data reveal that 30.9% of families in poverty live in Jerusalem, 26.7% live in the North, 22.2% in the South, and 18.1% in Haifa District. Only 11.2% and 9.4% of poor families live in Tel Aviv District and the Center District, respectively (Bituach Leumi, 2019, 2021). Table 3.4 depicts this distribution over time.

Table 3.5 illustrates poverty distribution by disposable income along ethnic group affiliation over three years.

Accordingly, the number of welfare recipients in general and people receiving unemployment benefits in particular is 30% higher in the periphery than in the center. The Bank of Israel recently estimated that for every 100 kilometers one travels from Tel Aviv, the average income drops by 15% (Atmor & Friedberg, 2019).

Table 3.5 Rate of families below the poverty line by group 2018–2020.

Year	*General population*	*Israeli Jewish*	*Ultra-Orthodox*	*Israeli Palestinian*
2018	18.0	13.4	42.3	45.3
2019	21.7	18.6	43.7	36.6
2020	20.8	17.9	42.1	35.2

Source: Bituach Leumi (2019)

In sum, income disparities between the richest and the poorest areas in Israel continue to expand (Machlica, 2020), and the growth of income over the last years has occurred in wealthier regions. Thus, the overall growth of the economy over the last couple of years has not benefited all sections of the Israeli population.

Employment. Israel's labor market exemplifies a dual labor market. The high-tech sector is highly productive and is mainly located at the country's geographic center, with lower-productivity industries and jobs located at the periphery (Brand & Regev, 2015). As in many other countries, distance from the center is therefore negatively correlated with the rate of employment, and the percentage of job seekers in the periphery is higher than in the center. This is due to an overall job shortage in peripheral areas, particularly in high-paying positions (Cohen & Aharon-Gutman, 2016). Low employment rates have a negative effect on living standards and on the volume of production and enlarges the dimensions of poverty and inequality (Cingano, 2014).

In 2001, Flug and Kasir (2003) found that lack of employment is the major factor affecting the likelihood of being poor in Israel; this has not changed, as evidenced in the State of the Nation Report published in 2019 (Gal & Bleikh, 2019). Following the OECD Economic Survey of Israel (2018), the chances of being poor are four times higher in families without breadwinners than in families in which one of the adults works. Additionally, persons who stay for a relatively long period out of work often lose work skills and experience difficulties to return employment. These phenomena occur much more in the Israeli periphery than in the center. Overall, labor market participation in the periphery is lower than in the center of the country, and this accounts for the social and geographical periphery. Typically, the rate of workers in the center of Israel is much closer to the OECD average and significantly lower in the periphery. The high tech are located around Tel Aviv, in the geographical and social center of Israel. Eighty percent of all high-tech companies are located there, which employ more than 60% of all high-tech jobs. Over the years, the tendency of centralization is increasing rather than decreasing.

Infrastructure. Israel suffers from a general low level of infrastructure due to a chronic underinvestment that lasted for two decades (OECD, 2020). The country's core infrastructure lags significantly behind in comparison to the OECD average. Although public transport is known to be a vital factor in countering centralization processes and connecting populations from the geographical periphery to the center, the public transport system in Israel is inefficient, and the accessibility to public transport is weak, especially in peripheral areas (Machlica, 2020). Since Israel's population is constantly growing and traffic intensity is extremely high, the investment in infrastructure in general and public transport in particular is of major importance (OECD, 2013).

Social infrastructure. Israel's social infrastructure depends to a high degree upon local authorities and municipalities, and its differential funding increases regional differences. In poorer municipalities, local authorities' revenues are much lower, making them unable to invest in social services for the citizens. Service provisions in terms of housing, education, health and the like are therefore much lower in poor municipalities. Additionally, housing costs are high for poor households, with social housing and rent subsidies very low in comparison to other countries (Machlica, 2020). Also, the provision of health services is much better in the center in comparison to the periphery, with significantly fewer hospital beds in the periphery, less surgical units and less presence of medical staff. Data show that mortality rates are higher and average life expectancy is lower in the periphery (Chernichovsky et al., 2017). In conclusion, there is substantial disparity between the scope of healthcare services available in the periphery compared to central Israel (Chernichovsky et al., 2017).

Education. The Israeli education system is divided into four different subsystems/subsectors: the official education system made out of three different sectors (the Jewish secular system, the Jewish religious [state] system and the Arab system) and the recognized but unofficial education system, comprising mainly the Jewish ultra-Orthodox system (and a few exempt "private" schools of the other three sectors). Each of the first three systems share their core curriculum with variability based on culture, language and religion. The ultra-Orthodox system operates based on a different curriculum, almost entirely made of religious studies. While government funding and budgets should, on paper, be allocated equally between the four segments, the government expenditure per student is significantly higher for the Jewish education system than the parallel expenditure on students in the Arab education system. Out of the three official systems, the Jewish religious (state) system receives the largest allocations. This is also the case when comparing government expenditures by students' socioeconomic background: the Jewish religious (state) education system is budgeted at the highest level and the Arab education system at the lowest level (Blass, 2018; Blass & Bleikh, 2020).

While the share of Israeli Palestinian high school students in technological-vocational educational tracks has increased significantly over the past few years (with over 45% of students in the Arab education system enrolled in such tracks compared to 37% of students in the Jewish system), the overall scholastic level of Arab students' matriculation diploma is lower on average compared to the Jewish education system average. Compared to Israeli Jewish students, fewer Israeli Palestinian students are enrolled in math and English at the highest proficiency level. As explained by The Taub Center, "In general, the lower level of English (and Hebrew, which is also studied as an additional language) proficiency in the Israeli Palestinian sector harms their ability to integrate into high wage employment. Improving their proficiency in these languages is central to narrowing labor market gaps." (Taub Center Staff, 2019) Exemplifying the overlap of population groups as well as center and periphery, the overall per-student investment is lower in the periphery than in the center; therefore, the proportion of diploma eligibility and enrollment in higher education is lower in the geographic periphery. Educational spending is much lower in poorer localities, and therefore, less skilled labor is available (Machlica, 2020).

Following the OECD 2020 criteria, Israel can be defined as having large income disparities among localities, which are divided along community, ethnic and religious lines with highly significant spatial segregation. Overall, Arab and ultra-Orthodox cities are the poorest, and both populations have a high share of marginalization on different grounds.

Conclusion

Israel is a classic example for the intensification of polarization, a result of the emergence of the knowledge economy. Innovation, technological advancement and development occur in the geographic and social center of the country, with entire population groups at the periphery excluded. As the data presented previously shows, there are substantial disparities between different communities in Israel. The Palestinian Israelis and the ultra-Orthodox Jews compose the largest of these segregated communities and go along social and geographical lines of peripheralization. These population groups have separated school systems and lower labor market participation and, due to cultural preference, usually rely on one family member engaged in work—for the Israeli Palestinian population, mainly men, and for the ultra-Orthodox Jewish population, mainly women (OECD Economic Surveys, 2018). The segregation of these two large groups is part of the overall inequality between center and periphery in Israel concerning many aspects of people's life, such as employment, education, welfare and transportation. Therefore, the geographical location of communities profoundly impacts people's lives in terms of socioeconomic status, access to high-quality education, labor market participation and quality of social services. As shown previously, in Israel, education and income components are the key features of the gaps between the center and the periphery, impacting opportunities for following generations. Overall, populations in the social and geographical periphery of Israel are disadvantaged in numerous areas. Since financial activities, strategic employment decisions, education and health service-related policies, the media and most cultural production are mainly located in the center of the country, peripheral agencies have much less influence over these sectors and are usually deprived of fair and proportional allocation of resources (Kühn, 2015). These tendencies reinforce the polarization between "Tel-Aviv and all the rest," with the "rest" hardly playing a part in shaping Israeli society. On the background of Israel's generally low public investment in education, healthcare, infrastructure and transportation per capita and considering the diminishing of the welfare state, gaps increase rather than decrease over time, and the periphery is left behind.

Spatial gaps are recognized as potentially dangerous to political stability and economic development (Iammarino et al., 2019). Tensions resulting from economic inequalities and perceived social injustice between center and periphery are higher, when peripheral population contrasts from the population in the center along ethnic, religious or national lines such as in Israel (Johnston et al., 2014; Massey & Tannen, 2015). While many countries adopt a spatial policy in an attempt to narrow existing spatial gaps, Israeli policy makers did not yet add the issue to the priority list. The outstanding success of the Israeli high-tech ecosystem during the last decades generated a dual structure with an extremely high level of technological advancement, but that does not benefit all populations equally. Geographic and social distance from the metropolitan center of Tel Aviv, where the ecosystem is located, consequently has decisive and enduring implications for economic, social and educational opportunities for people, perpetuating inequalities.

Data provided by the Innovation Authority shows that 77% of all startups have been established in the center and that more than 60% of all high-tech jobs in Israel are located in Tel Aviv and central regions of the country. Similar gaps can be observed for non-high-tech entrepreneurship and self-employment competing within the national space. One manifestation of this phenomenon is the fact that minority populations in Israel are very under-represented in Tel Aviv's entrepreneurial ecosystem: Israeli Palestinians, who make up about 20% of the Israeli population, account for less than 3% of the tech workforce, and ultra-Orthodox populations account for just 1% of the tech workforce. Lately, policy makers and official agencies such as the Israeli Innovation Authority have acknowledged that incorporating marginalized sections of the population into the technological labor market is crucial in order to provide its future development and ensure competitiveness.

Note

1. Jerusalem has a very high percentage of the ultra-Orthodox population, which ranks high on poverty due to lifestyle.

References

Asheim, B. T., Isaksen, A., & Trippl, M. (2019). *Advanced introduction to regional innovation systems*. Edward Elgar Publishing Limited.

Atmor, N., & Friedberg, C. (2019). Gender gaps in the center versus the periphery: Evidence from the Israeli elections. *Israel Studies Review, 34*(2), 92–113. https://doi.org/10.3167/isr.2019.340206

Bituach Leumi. (2019). *Dimensions of poverty and social disparities—annual report 2018 (Hebrew)*. Bituach Leumi.

Bituach Leumi. (2021). *Poverty and Income Inequality - Administrative Data Report*. Bituach Leumi.

Blass, B. (2018). *The Israeli education system: An overview (Hebrew)*. Taub Center for Social Policy Stidies in Iseael.

Blass, N., & Bleikh, H. (2020). *Expenditure per class and per student in the primary school education system*. Taub Center for Social Policy Studies in Israel.

Borgatti, S. P., & Everett, M. G. (2000). Models of core/periphery structures. *Social Networks, 21*(4), 375–395. https://doi.org/10.1016/s0378-8733(99)00019-2

Brand, G., & Regev, E. (2015). The dual labor market: Trends in productivity, wages and human capital in the economy. *State of the Nation Report, 48*.

Butush, N. (2020). *Employment and wage disparities between the periphery and the center—Data and possible policy tools*. The Knesset—Departement of Research and Knowledge. Retrieved March 24, 2022, from https://fs.knesset.gov.il/globaldocs/MMM/64f30c05-0b0e-eb11-811a-00155d0af32a/2_64f30c05-0b0e-eb11-811a-00155d0af32a_11_16406.pdf

Castree, N., Kitchin, R., & Rogers, A. (2013). *A dictionary of human geography*. Oxford University Press. https://doi.org/10.1093/acref/9780199599868.001.0001

Chernichovsky, D., Bisharat, B., Bowers, L., Brill, A., & Sharony, C. (2017). *The health of the Arab Israeli population* (pp. 325–368). The Taub Center; State of the Nation Report.

Cingano, F. (2014). Trends in income inequality and its impact on economic growth. *OECD Social, Employment and Migration Working Papers, OECD Publishing*. https://doi.org/10.1787/5jxrjncwxv6j-en.

Clarno, A. (2017). *Neoliberal apartheid: Palestine/Israel and South Africa after 1994*. University of Chicago Press. https://doi.org/10.7208/chicago/9780226430126.001.0001

Cohen, N., & Aharon-Gutman, M. (2016). Labor agencies and the temporality of struggles: A comparative study in the Israeli periphery. *Geoforum, 74*(1), 98–107. https://doi.org/10.1016/j.geoforum.2016.06.004

Collins, V. E., & Rothe, D. L. (2019). *The violence of neoliberalism: Crime, harm and inequality*. Routledge. https://doi.org/10.4324/9780429505768

Crescenzi, R., & Rodríguez-Pose, A. (2013). R & D, socio-economic conditions, and regional innovation in the U. S. *Growth and Change, 44*(2), 287–320. https://doi.org/10.1111/grow.12011

Duranton, G., & Puga, D. (2004). Micro-foundations of urban agglomeration economies. In V. Henderson & J. F. Thisse (Eds.), *Handbook of regional and urban economics* (Vol. 4, pp. 2063–2117). Elsevier. https://doi.org/10.3386/w9931

European Commission. (2011). *Territorial agenda of the European Union 2020 — Towards an inclusive, smart and sustainable Europe of diverse regions*. European Commission.

Florida, R., Adler, P., & Mellander, C. (2017). The city as innovation machine. *Regional Studies, 51*(1), 86–96. https://doi.org/10.1080/00343404.2016.1255324

Flug, K., & Kasir, N. (2003). Poverty and employment, and the gulf between them. *Israel Economic Review, 1*(1), 55–80.

Foster, G., Shimizu, C., Ciesinski, S., Davila, A., Hassan, S., Jia, N., & Morris, R. (2013). *Entrepreneurial ecosystems around the globe and company growth dynamics*. World Economic Forum.

Friedmann, J. (1973). The spatial organization of power in the development of urban systems. *Development and Change*, *4*(3), 12–50. https://doi.org/10.1111/j.1467-7660.1973.tb00643.x

Fritsch, M., & Wyrwich, M. (2021). Is innovation (increasingly) concentrated in large cities? An international comparison. *Research Policy*, *50*(6), 104237. https://doi.org/10.1016/j.respol.2021.104237

Gal, J., & Bleikh, H. (2019). *The welfare system: An overview*. The State of the Nation Report; The Taub Center.

Glaeser, E. (2011). *Triumph of the city: How urban spaces make us human*. Pan Macmillan.

Gren, J. (2003). Reaching the peripheral regional growth centre: Centre-periphery convergence through the structural funds' transport infrastructure actions and the evolution of the centre-periphery paradigm. *European Journal of Spatial Development*, *1*(3), 22–22.

Harvey, D. (2003). *The new imperialism*. Oxford University Press. https://doi.org/10.1093/oso/9780199264315.001.0001

Herrschel, T. (2012). Regionalisation and marginalisation: Bridging old and new divisions in regional governance. In M. Danson & P. de Souza (Eds.), *Regional development in Northern Europe* (pp. 48–66). Routledge. https://doi.org/10.4324/9780203127247-9

Iammarino, S., Rodriguez-Pose, A., & Storper, M. (2019). Regional inequality in Europe: Evidence, theory and policy implications. *Journal of Economic Geography*, *19*(2), 273–298. https://doi.org/10.1093/jeg/lby021

Johnston, R., Poulsen, M., & Forrest, J. (2014). Segregation matters, measurement matters. In C. D. Lloyd, I. G. Shuttleworth, & D. W. Wong (Eds.), *Social-spatial segregation: Concepts, processes and outcomes* (pp. 13–44). Bristol University Press. https://doi.org/10.2307/j.ctt17rw5cs.6

Jones, G., Leimgruber, W., & Nel, E. (2007). *Issues in geographical marginality*. Rhodes University.

Kimmerling, B. (2001). *The invention and decline of Israeliness*. University of California Press. https://doi.org/10.1525/9780520939301

Kreckel, R. (2004). *Politische Soziologie der sozialen Ungleichheit (German)* (Vol. 3). Campus.

Kühn, M. (2015). Peripheralization: Theoretical concepts explaining socio-spatial inequalities. *European Planning Studies*, *23*(2), 367–378. https://doi.org/10.1080/09654313.2013.862518

Machlica, G. (2020). *"Reducing socio-economic differences between municipalities in Israel," OECD Economics Department Working Papers*. OECD Publishing. https://doi.org/10.1787/4a8ada63-en

Manfred, K., & Matthias, B. (2013). Peripheralization and power—theoretical debates. In M. Naumann & A. Fischer-Tahir (Eds.), *Peripheralization* (pp. 302–317). Springer VS. https://doi-org.ezprimo1.idc.ac.il/10.1007/978-3-531-19018-1

Massey, D. S., & Tannen, J. (2015). A research note on trends in black hypersegregation. *Demography*, *52*(3), 1025–1034. https://doi.org/10.1007/s13524-015-0381-6

Naumann, M., & Reichert-Schick, A. (2013). Infrastructure and peripheralization: Empirical evidence from North-Eastern Germany. In M. Naumann & A. Fischer-Tahir (Eds.), *Peripheralization* (pp. 145–167). Springer VS. https://doi.org/10.1007/978-3-531-19018-1_7

OECD. (2011). *An overview of growing income inequalities in OECD countries: Main findings*. OECD. https://doi.org/10.1787/9789264119536-3-en

OECD. (2013). *"Preface," in environment at a glance 2013: OECD indicators*. OECD Publishin. https://doi.org/10.1787/9789264185715-en

OECD. (2020). *"Public investment in Israel," in Accelerating climate action in Israel: Refocusing mitigation policies for the electricity, residential and transport sectors.* OECD Publishing. https://doi.org/10.1787/fb32aabd-en

OECD. (2021). *Country statistical profile: Israel 2021/1.* OECD Publishing. https://doi.org/10.1787/g2g9eb3a-en

OECD. (2022). *OECD (2022), Income inequality (indicator).* OECD DATA. Retrieved March 21, 2022, from https://doi.org/10.1787/459aa7f1-en

OECD Economic Surveys. (2018). *Overview of national and regional labour markets, Israel.* OECD Publishing. https://doi.org/10.1787/job_local_dev-2018-table89-en

Rozenberg, M. (2020). *Wages and income from work by locality and various economic variables (Hebrew).* Bituach Leumi, Research and Planning Administration.

Sharabi, M., Shdema, I., & Abboud-Armaly, O. (2020). Nonfinancial employment commitment among Muslims and Jews in Israel: Examination of the core—periphery model on majority and minority groups. *Employee Relations: The International Journal.* https://doi.org/10.1108/er-12-2019-0486

Shdema, I., Martin, D. G., & Abu-Asbeh, K. (2021). Exposure to the majority social space and residential place identity among minorities: Evidence from Arabs in Israel. *Urban Geography, 42*(4), 507–527. https://doi.org/10.1080/02723638.2020.1727118

Smooha, S. (1978). *Israel: Pluralism and conflict.* University of California Press.

Stam, E. (2015). Entrepreneurial ecosystems and regional policy: A sympathetic critique. *European Planning Studies, 23*(9), 1759–1769. https://doi.org/10.1080/09654313.2015.1061484

Swirsky, S., Konor-Attias, E., & Lieberman, A. (2020). *Israel: A social report 2020: The public interest needs to return to center stage.* Adva Center.

Taub Center Staff. (2019). *REALITY CHECK*—Arab Israelis: From education through employment.* Taub Center for Social Policy Studies in Israel.

Tzfadia, E., & Yacobi, H. (2015). The privatization of space. In I. Galnoor, A. Paz-Fuchs, & N. Zion (Eds.), *Privatization policy in Israel: State responsibility and the boundaries between the public and the private* (pp. 405–444). Van Leer Jerusalem Institute.

Wallerstein, I. (1974). *The modern world-system: Capitalist agriculture and the origins of the European world-economy in the sixteenth century* (Vol. 974). Academic Press.

Yiftachel, O., & Tzfadia, E. (2004). Between periphery and 'third space': Identity of Mizrahim in Israel's development towns. In A. Kemp, U. Ram, D. Newman, & O. Yiftachel (Eds.), *Israelis in conflict: Hegemonies, identities and challenges* (pp. 203–235). Ben Gurion University.

4 Maybe Not *the* Startup Nation but Definitely *a* Startup Nation

Introduction

The current chapter introduces and presents the Israeli high-tech ecosystem based on data available in 2021. The fact that Israel is one of 13 developing countries escaping the "middle income trap"[1] and managed to transform into a high-income status (Doner & Schneider, 2016) is largely due to its technological industry, the origins of which have been explained in Chapter 2 of this book. The country has an impressive record of economic growth and success, and following the OECD outlook published in 2021 relating to Covid-19 crisis, the Israeli economy has largely reopened, and the GDP of the country is projected to grow robustly by around 6.3% (OECD, 2020). In the following part of this chapter, I will discuss the Israeli high-tech ecosystem in international comparison. Furthermore, I will briefly introduce the Israeli Innovation Authority, which is the main government-funded public player in the high-tech scene. I will then present the current data describing the ecosystem in terms of numbers and types of startups, investments and funding, the presence of multinational companies, and employment and conclude with some critical thoughts.

The Israeli High-Tech Ecosystem in Comparison

On the 16th of September 2021, the management of the World Bank announced to discontinue the famous *Doing Business* report due to claims of fixing data to favor Saudi Arabia and China. The indicator ranks 190 countries on the ease of doing business and is widely used by policy makers and academics alike, and the accusation of data manipulation has done great harm to the reputation of the World Bank research. In addition, Robert Picciotto and Vinod Thomas, both former high-ranked World Bank employees and academics, claimed in a critical article published on *devex* in October 2021 (Picciotto & Thomas, 2021), that the indicator for the *Ease of Doing Business* is based on the questionable assumption that government deregulation will positively influence short-term GDP growth. Indeed, ranking economies and countries by indicators is deeply embedded within

DOI: 10.4324/9781003091042-5

the neoliberal paradigm discussed in Chapter 1 of this book. Rankings and indicators necessarily apply evaluative assumptions, based on a worldview, on power relations and on cultural beliefs. Bergsteiner and Avery (Bergsteiner & Avery, 2019), for example, maintain that the World Economic Forum's *Global Competitiveness Report* (GCR) has been criticized "for containing multiple methodological, conceptual, and logical flaws that bias competitiveness rankings toward countries that favor neoliberalism" (Bergsteiner & Avery, 2019, p. 863), thereby perpetuating competition toward goals that do not include societal and environmental aspects and so endanger sustainable future developments. Davis et al. (2012) devote an entire edited volume to the subject of governance by indicators, discussing global power through quantification and rankings from a variety of perspectives, making it clear that indicators and rankings affect governance itself, decision-making and power relations.

In spite of the previous and additional criticisms, nonetheless, rankings are widespread and very often applied for comparing between economies and countries, and nowadays many public and private organizations provide rankings on a vast variety of issues.

Israel is an interesting example to showcase the problematics of ranking, first since there is a relatively large gap between the self-image and the actual data and second since there are large inconsistencies between the rank of the country in various indices, some of them provided by organizations and institutions not necessarily neutral in their opinion toward Israel.[2]

Israel's startup-nation image has been cherished widely and often been accepted uncritically, without actually checking the data.

> Few people in the fields of business and technology today are unaware of Israel's reputation as a world leader in innovation and entrepreneurship. The 2009 New York Times Best Seller Startup Nation put Israel on the map as a force to be reckoned with for the disproportionate number of Startups churned out by a country that is barely the size of New Jersey. Israel consistently appears at the top of international rankings and reports, such as the World Intellectual Property Organization (WIPO) Global Innovation Index (GII) and the World Economic Forum (WEF) Global Competitiveness Report.
>
> (Daniely, 2020, p. 165)

When looking closer at the rankings mentioned by Daniely (2020), it is noticeable that on the World Intellectual Property Organization (WIPO) provided by the Global Innovation Index (GII), Israel is ranked 15 in 2021 (WIPO, 2021). The Global Competitiveness Report of the World Economic Forum (WEF) includes a "Transformation Readiness Performance" index composing 11 categories (Schwab & Zahidi, 2020: 72-75). Israel ranks fifth in two categories ("facilitate the creation of markets of tomorrow" and "incentivize and expand patient investments in research, innovation and invention"). In all the others categories, it ranks lower or significantly lower (Schwab & Zahidi, 2020). In other words, in both rankings that Daniely (2020) provides in order to verify his statement that "Israel consistently appears at the top of international rankings and reports," Israel is not among the top countries. Accordingly, although useful for comparisons, rankings should be taken cautiously. Within the framework of this book and in order to place Israel within the international context, I will relate to three rankings concerning entrepreneurship, innovation and competitiveness.

After reviewing many of the available relevant rankings (among others, Startup Blink, Startup Genome, Global Entrepreneurship Index, Global Entrepreneurship Monitor, Global Innovation Index and World Competitiveness Ranking, and Global Competitiveness Report), I decided to choose three research institute based rankings concerning entrepreneurship, innovation and competitiveness.

The "Global Entrepreneurship Index"—first published in 2009—developed by the Global Entrepreneurship and Development Initiative, is a Washington, DC–based policy development organization established by and working in collaboration with leading researchers in the field such as Zoltan Acs and David Baumal. In 2019 Israel ranked 16th on the *The Global Entrepreneurship Index* based on 2018 data (Ács et al., 2018). The countries with the highest ranking on this index are the USA, Switzerland and Canada. The methodology of the GEI contains three blocks of subjects, namely entrepreneurial attitudes, entrepreneurial abilities and entrepreneurial aspiration. These three blocks stand on 14 pillars,[3] encompassing an individual and an institutional variable corresponding to the micro- and the macrolevel aspects of entrepreneurship. Thus, data on entrepreneurial attitudes, abilities and aspirations are weighted against the prevailing social and economic infrastructure. Country-specific institutional variables constitute the strength of this index, which balances individual perceptions and attitudes with inherent system features of the institutional environment.

The Global Innovation Index (GII) Ranking is conducted by the World Intellectual Property Association, and it was first established in 2007. The index is published by the World Intellectual Property Organization (WIPO), an agency of the United Nations. The methodology of this index concerns innovation based on criteria divided into innovation input and innovation output. Table 4.1 presents the criteria included in the GII, and Table 4.2 describes Israel's ranking in the GII over time.

Relating to the data of 2021, Israel ranks 15th among the 132 countries participating in the 2021 report. Israel ranks 12th in innovation outputs and 18th in innovation inputs, and the country performs better in innovation outputs than in innovation inputs from 2011 till 2021. It was only in 2010 that Israel received a higher input than output rank. The input-output relationship concerns the translation of innovation investments into more quantity and higher quality of outputs. Israel produces somewhat more outputs in relation to its input investment into innovation. The data of the

Table 4.1 Criteria of the Global Innovation Index divided into innovation input and innovation output.

Innovation	*Criteria*	*Within each criterion*
Input	Institutions	Political environment; Regulatory Environment; Business Environment
	Human Capital and Research	Education; Tertiary Education; R&D
	Infrastructure	Information and Communication Technologies; General Infrastructure; Ecological Sustainability
	Market Sophistication	Credit, Investment; Trade; Diversification; Market scale
	Business Sophistication	Knowledge Workers; Innovation Linkage; Knowledge Absorption
Output	Knowledge and Technological	Knowledge Creation; Knowledge Impact; Knowledge Diffusion
	Creative	Intangible Assets, Creative Goods and Services, Online Creativity

Source: WIPO (2020)

Table 4.2 Israel's rank in the Global Innovation Index between 2010 and 2021.

Year	*Overall rank*	*Innovation inputs rank*	*Innovation outputs rank*
2010	23	22	23
2011	17	17	13
2012	14	20	8
2013	14	19	9
2014	15	17	13
2015	22	21	16
2016	21	21	16
2017	17	20	14
2018	10	19	11
2019	10	17	8
2020	13	17	13
2021	15	18	12

Source: WIPO (2022)

index further reveal that relative to its GDP, Israel's innovation performance is above expectations. In comparison to other high-income countries, Israel performs higher in human capital and research, market and business sophistication, and knowledge and technological output. In 2021 Israel's performance in institutions and infrastructure was weak. Notably, the 2021 scores of these two indicators are weaker than in 2019, pointing to a relative decrease in investment in infrastructure and institutional stability. The index provides a list of main strengths and weaknesses of the indicators. Israel's

Table 4.3 The Institute of Management Development World Competitiveness Ranking of Israel.

	2017	*2018*	*2019*	*2020*	*2021*
Overall	22	21	24	26	27
Economic performance	31	37	40	39	36
Government efficiency	24	20	30	27	33
Business efficiency	22	18	21	26	29
Infrastructure	16	13	18	20	21

Source: IMD (2022)

strengths concern, for example, gross expenditure on R & D, venture capital investors and recipients, percentage of gross domestic expenditure on R & D by business and from abroad, innovation linkages, and so on. The main weaknesses of Israel in the GII are related to political and operational stability, cost of redundancy dismissal and additional measures that relate directly or indirectly to educational achievements and infrastructures.

The Institute for Management Development (IMD) World Competitiveness Yearbook (WCY) was first published in 1989 and is conducted by the International Institute for Management and Development, located in Lausanne. Based on a wide variety of data, it analyzes and ranks countries according to how they manage their competencies to achieve long-term value creation. The IMD World Competitiveness Rankings accentuate long-term trends. The ranking includes 334 competitiveness criteria selected based on academic research and dialog with the business community, government agencies and academics. The following table indicates the rank of Israel in comparison to 64 countries.

A closer look at the criteria reveal that among the 64 participating countries in this index, Israel's economic performance is within the upper half since 2017 but continuously declined in comparison to other countries. Israel managed to improve neither its government efficiency over the years nor its business efficiency. In addition, the country's infrastructure rank has declined between 2017 and 2021.

Summing up, the data presented previously show that Israel's high tech is exposed to intense global competition from innovation trends accompanied by huge investments by other countries as well as global corporations. Relatively to its size and geopolitical complexity, the country data in the presented indices show that Israel is not the startup nation but definitely a startup nation.

The Innovation Authority

Israel's flagship organization to promote innovation and entrepreneurship is the government-funded Israel Innovation Authority (Israel Innovation Authority, 2022). The Authority has an approximate yearly budget of

$500 million and plays an important role in supporting early and growth stages in startups as well as promoting policies that target specific support areas. The Israel Innovation Authority has six major divisions:

The Startup Division offers unique tools to support the early development stages of technological enterprises. Target audiences include entrepreneurs with innovative technological ideas and startup companies. The Growth Division contains a number of programs that support technological innovation for mature companies. Target audiences are high-technology companies in sales or presale growth stages, as well as mature high-technology companies that employ growth channels based on technological innovation and look for support in funding innovative research and development.

The Technological Infrastructure Division focuses on the advancement and development of generic technologies and R & D infrastructure. Integrating academia and industry, the proposed incentive programs address academic applied knowledge. Therefore, the main audiences are researchers and research institutions as well as industrial companies.

The International Collaboration Division proposes a variety of international cooperation and incentive programs through international frameworks such as Horizon 2020. Additionally, there are a number of binational funds providing finance for joint projects of Israeli and foreign companies. Target audiences comprise Israeli and foreign agencies, companies and researchers. The Division of Collaboration of the Israeli Innovation Authority works in close collaboration with the Israeli government to develop and maintain bilateral and multilateral cooperation in the field of technological innovation. The activities of the Advanced Manufacturing Division encompass promotion and implementation of R & D and innovation processes in manufacturing firms. Owners of small and medium-size factories and manufacturing sights are supported in the initiation and development of technologically innovative products, particularly in low and medium-low technologic sectors. The Societal Challenge Division aims at coupling technological innovation to solve substantial problems in society and in the public sector. The division develops supporting training programs for excluded populations such as ultra-Orthodox Jews, minorities and women. Thus, it addresses the persistent lack of skilled workers in the Israeli high-technology industry and attempts to assist underrepresented groups to enter the industry.

The Innovation Authority is the main government-funded public player in the Israeli high-tech ecosystem.

Mapping the Scene

Israel is a leading technology and innovation power worldwide. According to PWC's The State of Innovation 2019 report, Israel is the number one globally in VC investment dollars per capita, number one in R & D spending as a percent of GDP and number two globally in the number of cybersecurity companies. In 2018, VCs' investment per capita in Israel was $674. For comparison, the USA comes second with $401 per person. Israel has over 6,600 startups—one startup per 1,350 people in population compared to one startup per 20,000 people in Europe (PWC Israel, 2019). In the third quarter of 2019, VC investment per capita in Israel was $414.2 on average, compared to $282.1 is the US (IVC, 2021).

Following the 2020–2021 report of the Israeli Innovation Authority, about 10% of Israeli employees work in high tech, 15% of Israel's GDP is created in high-tech companies, 43% of Israel's export is attributed to high-tech companies and high-tech employees pay 25% of all income taxes. Whereas the OECD average on investment in R & D as percentage of the GDP was 2.4%, for Israel it was 4.94% (Israel Innovation Authority, 2021).

Different data sources present different numbers as to the actual number of startups in Israel. The data provided by the Central Bureau of Statistics (CBS) in Table 4.4 present the trend over time of the number of startups operating, number of startups launched and number of startup shutdowns. These data are available for the years 2011–2019.

The Innovation Authority also provides data concerning launches and closures of technological startups. For the year 2014, there is a rather large gap between the two databases (780 CBS and 1404 IIA). Since the Innovation Authority does not provide the same years as the CBS, no further comparison is possible. Nonetheless, the important point of similarity is that both reveal a decrease in startup launches: The CBS data show the decrease between 2018 and 2019 (from 689 to 473). The data provided by the Israeli Innovation Authority show that in 2014, the number of startups launched was 1,404 in comparison to 520 in 2020.

The platform of Start-Up Nation Central, an independent nonprofit that "builds bridges to Israeli innovation," reports on its innovation discovery platform that there are currently 7,121 companies (Start-Up Nation Central, 2022), whereas Deloitte describes Israel as a powerhouse of innovation and maintains that there are over 6,000 active startups in Israel today. In an

Table 4.4 Number of startups operating, number of startups launched and number of startup shutdowns from 2011 to 2019.

	2011	*2012*	*2013*	*2014*	*2015*	*2016*	*2017*	*2018*	*2019*	*Total*
Total operating startups	3,217	3,667	4,059	4,370	4,723	4,943	4,975	4,907	4,685	-
No. of startups launched	601	701	744	780	859	791	688	689	473	6,326
No. of startup shutdowns	140	194	174	243	296	364	406	578	527	2,922

Source: CBS (2021b)

attempt to deal with the data inconsistencies that probably are due to different definitions of a startup, I would sum up and state that there are currently between 5,000 and 7,000 startup companies active in Israel.

In investigating the data in line with clusters, it can be seen that the total number of active Israeli corporate venture capital–backed tech companies by leading clusters during the years 2015–2020 amounted to 1,052, with 193 in AI (artificial intelligence), 124 in machine learning, 107 in IoT (internet of things), 84 in big data, and 75 in cybersecurity (IVC, 2021). There are estimates that Israel accounts for 10% of all turnovers in the global cybersecurity industry.

For the purpose of the book, it is important to relate to the location of the Israeli startups.

In 2017, Tel-Aviv alone had 2,198 startup companies operating within the city boundaries, compared to 425 startups in Jerusalem that year. Next in line were several cities in the center district of Israel: Herzliya (439), Petah-Tikva (271), Ramat Gan (258), Ra'anana (188), Netanya (182), Kfar Saba (156), Rehovot (142). In the north of Israel, Haifa had 225 startups and the Arab city of Nazareth had 24. "The capital of the southern district," Be'er Sheva, had 68 startups operating in 2017.

In 2018, 225 startups were launched in Tel Aviv and 135 in the Central District, compared to less than 50 startups launched in other parts of Israel that year (Levi, 2020). This trend is stable over the years, and following the data of the CBS for 2019, 73% of all startups were located in Tel Aviv, altogether 236 startups (Anselman, 2020). These data again reflect the notion of "Tel Aviv and all the rest" and the question of whether the startup nation is not a startup city. Table 4.5 depicts this gap between center and periphery in terms of high-tech positions.

The presented data reveal the centralization of the Israeli high tech in and around Tel Aviv.

Table 4.5 High-tech companies and positions in the Israeli periphery, measured as share of positions in R & D companies and share of R & D positions, by district, for the year 2017.

District	*Share of positions in companies that have R & D departments*	*Share of R & D positions only*
Jerusalem	5.1%	4.5%
North	14.2%	7.8%
Haifa	14.2%	14.5%
Center	34.8%	33.8%
Tel Aviv	21.6%	35%
South	10%	4.4%

Source: Butush (2020)

Funding and Investments

The history of the Israeli venture capital industry goes back to the early 1980s and was initiated by a government policy providing seed capital to banks and venture capitalists who wanted to invest in the emerging high-tech industry (Avnimelech & Teubal, 2008). The latter and additional policy mechanisms of the Israeli government, in combination with the availability of global capital, nurtured the beginning of the venture capital industry, which strengthened the high-tech industry.

Since 2010, 2,503 investors, 406 accelerators and incubators, and 389 active multinational companies (MNCs) are operating in the funding scene of the Israeli high-tech ecosystem. Following the Central Bureau of Statistics (CBS), the frequency of investments and amount of dollars raised by startups companies increased immensely over the last years (CBS, 2021b). In 2017, 767 investments amounted to more than $5.5 million; in 2018, 819 investments amounted to a total of about $7.4 million, and in 2019, 658 investments amounted to about $8.3 million. Venture capital investment per capita dollars in 2021[4] amounted in Israel to $959, in the USA to $808, in Sweden to $700, UK $472, in France to $178 and in Germany to $202 (Glasner, 2021). Thus, the presence of venture capital in Israel is extremely high in international comparison. Table 4.6 presents the numbers for corporate-backed exits and investments over the years.

Indeed, Israel enjoys an uncommon source of risk capital, ranking high in the world for venture capital availability. As discussed in Chapter 2 of this book, originally, venture capital availability was encouraged and supported by public resources. More recently though, private actors encouraged by the establishment of many local R & D centers by multinational corporations (MNCs), such as Facebook, Google, Amazon, and others, are increasingly stepping into the venture capital market. Table 4.7 provides information as to exit deals between 2011 and 2020.

Table 4.6 Corporate-backed exits and corporate-backed investments from 2015 to 2020.

	Corporate-backed exits					
	2015	*2016*	*2017*	*2018*	*2019*	*2020*
Number of deals	27	24	20	27	20	23
$M	2624	1802	2030	780	2449	2879
	Corporate-backed investments					
	2015	*2016*	*2017*	*2018*	*2019*	*2020*
Number of deals	135	147	147	191	129	154
$M	1173	1724	1714	2445	2067	2917

Source: IVC (2021)

Table 4.7 Exit deals (both mergers and acquisitions and initial public offerings) from 2011 to 2020.

	2011	*2012*	*2013*	*2014*	*2015*	*2016*	*2017*	*2018*	*2019*	*2020*
No. of exits	63	50	45	70	70	55	70	61	80	60
Total amount in $M	5,078	5,567	7,643	14,850	10,695	3,531	7,442	4,944	9,917	15,429
Average deal size in $M	81	111	170	212	153	64	106	81	124	257

Source: PWC Israel (2020)

The data presented in the table show an increase of exit deals and the financial value of the deals. In short, the venture capital scene in the high-tech ecosystem of Israel is strong and getting stronger over the years.

Multinational Companies

The number of multinationals operating in Israel is estimated to be close to 400. In 2020, 387 multinational technology companies (MNCs) were active in Israel (compared to 220 MNCs in the year 2010), employing approximately 68,000 employees throughout Israel. The leading sector of MNCs was IT and enterprise software. Other prominent clusters of MNCs operating in Israel in 2020 were enterprise applications, security, industrial technologies and mobile applications. The majority of MNCs operating in Israel (over 41%) are located in Tel Aviv-Yafo, Herzliya, Petach Tikva and Haifa. However, in terms of number of employees, Kiryat Gat in southern Israel, with its Intel and HP manufacturing facilities, is a significant location concerning employment. Foreign corporate investments in Israel reached $900 million in 2020, spanning over 251 deals (IVC, 2020). 7Seventy percent of all M&A (merges & acquisitions) activities in Israel during the years 2014–2019 were performed by foreign companies. Most of the MNCs acquiring Israeli startups are USA-based companies, with an average of more than 50 exit deals performed by American MNCs in Israel per year. The most active American companies in M&A activity in Israel in the past years are Google and Microsoft (IVC; GKH; ITAI, 2019).

High-Tech Employment

Around 324,000 Israelis were employed in high-tech companies in 2020, standing for 9.6% out of the Israeli workforce (in 2019 323,400 and 8.64%, respectively).

The growing demand for tech employees (with an increase of 4,500 recruitments in the first half of 2019 alone) goes hand in hand with a shortage of engineers and other skilled technological employees, both

Table 4.8 Number of employees in the high-tech sector from 2016 to 2020.

	2016	*2017*	*2018*	*2019*	*2020*
All employees	3,493,800 (100%)	3,592,500 (100%)	3,675,000 (100%)	3,742,300 (100%)	3,371,400 (100%)
Employees in high tech (all)	290,100 (8.3%)	302,500 (8.42%)	314,800 (8.57%)	323,400 (8.64%)	324,000 (9.61%)
Manufacturing in HT	94,100 (32.44% within HT)	95,900 (31.7% within HT)	96,400 (30.7% within HT)	96,200 (29.75% within HT)	9,4500 (29.17% within HT)
Knowledge intensive in HT	196,000 (67.56% within HT)	206,600 (68.3% within HT)	218,400 (69.3% within HT)	227,200 (70.25% within HT)	229,500 (70.83% within HT)
Other industries	320,3800 (91.7%)	328,9900 (91.58%)	336,0300 (91.43%)	341,8900 (91.36%)	304,7400 (90.39%)

Source: CBS (2021a)

Table 4.9 Average wages in NIS in the high-tech sector from 2016 to 2020.

	2016	*2017*	*2018*	*2019*	*2020*
All employees	9,799	10,109	10,470	10,782	11,510
Employees in high tech (all)	21,083	21,542	22,479	23,545	28,872
Manufacturing in HT	20,155	20,660	20,861	21,706	22,657
Knowledge intensive HT	21,529	21,951	23,193	24,324	25,784
Other industries	8,778	9,058	9,345	9,575	10,089

Source: CBS (2021a)

reflecting the growth of the Israeli high-tech industry (Israel Innovation Authority, 2019).

The chronic shortage of skilled high-tech personnel has continued in 2021 as well. Following Dr. Ami Appelbaum, chairman of the board of the Israeli Innovation Authority, there are currently about 13,000 technological job openings for which companies have difficulties to find adequate candidates (Israel Innovation Authority, 2020). This shortage is astonishing when taking into account the salaries in high-tech in Israel.

The average salary for an employee in a startup in 2019 was 23,545 NIS. There was a substantial differentiation in the average employee salary between startups located in Tel-Aviv (22,200 NIS in average) and startups located elsewhere: Jerusalem 17,449 NIS; Northern district 18,811 NIS; Haifa district 19,892; NIS, Central District 20,869; Southern district 18,521 NIS. In comparison, the Israeli average monthly salary for an employee in 2019 was 10,482 (CBS, 2021b), meaning that the average pay is double

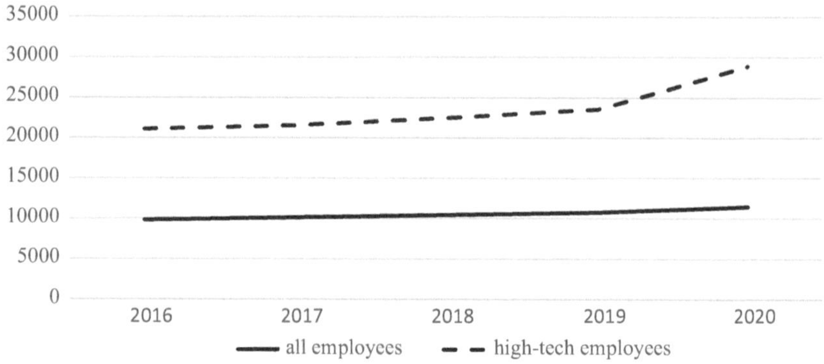

Figure 4.1 Average wages over the years 2016–2020 in New Israeli Shekel (NIS) of all employees and employees in the high-tech industry.

Source: CBS (2021a)

in high tech. The average salary for an employee in a startup in 2020 was around 28,872 NIS.

According to an estimation made by financial newspaper *TheMarker* comparing the income of a high-tech employee to a tech entrepreneur, by the third year of working after completing their university degree, an employee will have total earnings of 624,000 NIS, compared to 274,000 made on average by tech entrepreneurs during the same period. Thus, it pays more to enter the ecosystem as an employee rather than an entrepreneur. It should also be noted that majority of startups shut down after only three years, and only a few continue to operate longer. By the fifth-year markdown, a tech employee will have total earnings of 1.15 million NIS, compared to the 650,000 income from salary and benefits of the tech entrepreneur. In the rare case of accomplishing an exit, the tech entrepreneur will make a total average earning of 1.4 million NIS, comprising both salary and exit revenues (Zarhovitz, 2017).

In line with the situation described in Chapter 3, there are groups who are underrepresented in the Israeli high-tech industry. Probably due to the Covid-19 pandemic, 2020 marked a slowdown in the upward trend of engagement of underrepresented populations in the Israeli high-tech scene, namely women, Arabs and ultra-Orthodox (Israel Innovation Authority, 2020).

Following the 2020 High-Tech Human Capital Report (Israel Innovation Authority, 2020), the total share of women in high-tech companies did not change considerably during 2020 and was 28% (compared to 29% in 2019). Among those women employed in high tech, women held only 23% of the tech positions and 19% of the tech management positions, and they are concentrated in the HR and marketing managerial positions and much less in the technology-oriented positions. Following the report, the rate of women entrepreneurs rose significantly from 7% in 2010 to almost 14% in 2019 but dropped back to 10.9% during 2020. Only 4.5% of the tech companies founded in 2020 were led by a woman; 84.5% of the companies were founded by a male founder, and 11% of companies founded that year had a both female and male founders. At the same time, women's share in undergraduate students of mathematics, statistics and computer science rose by 5% from 28.7% in 2010 to 33.7% in 2020.

The share of Palestinian Israelis employed in high-tech companies fluctuated during the past decade (2010–2020), with a very modest overall increase. In 2018, their share of high-tech employees was 3% (while their share in the general population was 21%). In 2020, that number dropped to 2.3%. The share of Palestinian Israelis in innovation-development positions in high tech, which generate the highest salary, tech was estimated in the report to be about 1.4%—even lower than their total share of high-tech employees. Following the data presented in the report, Palestinian Israeli women were 20%–30% of all Palestinian Israelis employed in the high-tech ecosystem and increased to 42% in 2019. Following the report, it dropped back to 31.8% in 2020.

The share of Jewish ultra-Orthodox among high-tech employees in 2019 was around 3%, while their share in technological positions was even lower. Over 70% of the ultra-Orthodox employed in high tech were women. In the foreword to the report, it is mentioned that in 2020, the former upward trend of the integration of underrepresented populations such as women, Palestinian Israelis and the ultra-Orthodox has been halted and even slightly reversed, which could most probably be due to the Covid-19 pandemic.

Nonetheless, the demand for employees outpaces the supply, and in spite of the fact that, for example, the share of Palestinian Israeli students enrolled in technological fields of study more than doubled between 2012–2020, female students of this population even tripled during these years. Eugene Kandel, a well-known Israeli economist, the CEO of the Start-Up Nation Central, and an Emil Spyer, professor of economics and finance at the Hebrew University of Jerusalem sum up the important issue of making the high-tech workforce in Israel more inclusive:

> The fact that the demand of human capital in high-tech remains high even in a year of global crisis suggests that the shortage is chronic. . . . Apart from the social aspect of integrating of these populations, they represent the main potential for increasing the supply of high-tech employees. Without the large-scale integration of women, Arabs and the ultra-Orthodox population in high-tech, the primary growth engine of the Israeli economy will be without fuel, and the negative impact will far exceed the tech industry's relative size in the economy.
>
> (Israel Innovation Authority, 2020, p. 4)

Impact of Covid-19 on the High-Tech Industry

Following the pandemic, general unemployment in Israel is still rather high, but labor demand has strengthened, especially in high-tech-related fields. The Israeli labor market is highly segregated—with a tremendous gap between a highly educated group with outstanding skills and a large share of people who lack the basic skills enabling them to achieve decent work. The mismatches of demand and supply in the Israeli labor market are higher than in other OECD countries, which do not have such a high-level skill dispersion. The pandemic damaged the weaker sectors of the Israeli labor market much more than high tech, where work from home and flexibility was easier to achieve. Thus, the pandemic widened the productivity gap between high tech and all the other sectors, which have lower productivity rates in comparison with the other high-performing OECD countries. The Social Report 2021 published by the Adva Center titled "Corona: Epidemic of Inequality" relates explicitly to the fact that high tech in Israel was adversely affected by the pandemic and benefited from generous state assistance. The authors of the report suggested reconsidering the identification between what is good for the country and what is good for high tech.

> This is especially relevant because most of the investments in hi-tech come from foreign sources, about a fourth of hi-tech investments go to the R&D centers of foreign corporations, and most of the profits from the hi-tech sector end up in the hands of these same corporations.
>
> (Swirski et al., 2021, p. 9)

The authors of the report disagree with the statement that the high-tech sector is the engine that drives the Israeli economy and maintain that an employment rate of 9%–10% is not impressive if compared with other historical engines.

Accordingly, overall, the Israeli high-tech ecosystem dealt well with the Covid-19 pandemic and its consequences, and the demand for technology development and advancement remains high. Nonetheless, small technological companies have had a more difficult time to hold on to experienced employees than larger companies have. Software-based and internet companies continued to grow during the crisis and reported a continuously high demand for highly qualified employees, and the multinational companies in the ecosystem overcame the pandemic easier than local companies, probably also due to their size. The MNCs were less likely to send their employees on leaves of absence, and there are some indications that more experienced employees replaced less experienced ones, with the former dropping out of smaller startups.

Concluding Thoughts—Not Scaling Up?

The Israeli Innovation Authority measures the success of the Israeli high-tech industry with the following factors: raised capital, scope of exits, contribution of sector to export and contribution of sector to employment. Accordingly, for 2020–2021 the report of the Authority summarizes the contribution of the high-tech sector to the Israeli economy accordingly: 40% of the value of all TA-35 Index companies belongs to high-tech companies; 10% of Israeli employees work in high tech; 15% of Israel's GDP is created in high-tech companies; 43% of Israeli export is attributed to high-tech companies; and 25% of all income tax is paid by high-tech employees.

But then, these success indicators are completely financial driven and rather abstract. In other words, success is measured in terms of abstract economic growth with no consideration as to the essence of what is produced (cyberweapons or tomatoes) and what the overall potential impact is. The indicators reflect only the amount of money generated by the high-tech industry. In addition, there is no consideration of the status of ownership. Time and again, the public discourse on the Israeli high-tech ecosystem points to the fact that Israel has few large industry-leading global companies. Check Point and TEVA employ less than 10,000 people locally together, and Check Point is the only Israeli tech company on the *Forbes* Global 2000 list, ranking the world's 2,000 largest publicly traded companies (Murphy et al., 2019). One explanation of this relative lack of big companies is the so-called "exit culture" that emerged in the Israeli ecosystem, aiming at being purchased rather than establishing a company. The purchase then often happened by big international companies. Whereas the profits of these exit deals could be translated into launching new startups, they also export the technological knowledge. Importantly, the success indicators of the Innovation Authority do not account for the ownership question or whether the technology actually stayed and materialized in Israel.

Some maintain that the exit culture will increase the divide between Tel Aviv and all the rest since if there is no establishment of local companies, then there will be no influx of tax payments (needed in order to strengthen the social and physical infrastructure) and less available jobs.

Lately, the future challenges of the Israeli high-tech industry are discussed more openly in the media and in the political realm by the Innovation Authority and the high-tech entrepreneurs themselves.

Talent shortage is discussed widely and consistently, and reports of the Bank of Israel and Start-Up Nation Central show that over the years, the demand for tech employees is increasing and matched by the supply of programmers, engineers and scientists. Uri Gabai, a co–general manager at Start-Up Nation Central, claims that the 2020 report—produced jointly by Start-Up Nation Central and the Innovation Authority—shows that the fact that 13,000 positions in high-tech are still open points to a chronic shortage. Companies are increasingly offshoring development teams to locations where the supply of employees is available and salaries lower.

Indeed, the wage inflation leading to extremely high salaries in the high-tech ecosystem are a second concern. Benny Landa, a tech entrepreneur and one of the founders of the Israeli high-tech ecosystem, was interviewed in a daily Israeli newspaper in September 2021 (Wolman, 2021). He predicts that the so-called high-tech bubble will blow up since the salaries are too high. He blames this on the multinationals and the shortage of skilled employees, which is linked to the decline in the level of education. In addition, the hybrid work models encourage companies to hire much cheaper employees from Ukraine and India.

This goes along with the claim that foreign multinationals and firms do not benefit the Israeli economy. Rosenberg (2018) explains that R & D centers, which were former Israeli startup companies that have been bought by multinationals, are businesses but not in the conventional understanding. Whereas for each employee of an Israeli high-tech manufacturer, such as Intel for example, two more local jobs are created, the spin-off factor of R & D centers of foreign companies is minimal. Also, Eugene Kandel (former head of Israel's National Economic Council) maintains that whereas growing companies create circles of production, services and jobs, an R & D center does not.

Benny Landa adds a historical perspective and explains that in Israel, initially, high tech developed both software and hardware but has recently focused on software only. Producing hardware helps employ people in wider circles and therefore has more societal impact than software-only companies.

Talent shortage, high wages and too little overall economic reward has been slowing down the Israeli startup ecosystem, as indicated by the fact that the number of startups founded each year in Israel is decreasing while the number of startups that close is increasing. While the amount of capital has risen over the years, the number of deals has fallen.

The paradox of the apparent success in terms of the measures applied by the Innovation Authority discussed previously is now obvious. While experts observing the Israeli ecosystem are anxious because of skill mismatch, wages that drive companies to hire in foreign countries and the excessive control of multinationals, the Innovation Authority's success indicators are financially driven and reflect only the amount of money generated by the high-tech industry. This is obviously not a very sustainable approach.

In sum, while Israel has a very good startup ecosystem, is not yet "scaling-up" (Daniely, 2020). The excellent R & D infrastructure and the presence of extensive venture capital do not yet generate a local high-tech industry and downgrades, in a way, Israel as a part of the USA ecosystem. In the meantime, Tel Aviv has recently been ranked as the most expensive city in the world, making one wonder about the overall impact for the entire Israeli society.

Notes

1. The term "middle-income trap" (MIT) usually refers to countries that have experienced rapid growth and thus quickly reached middle-income status but then failed to overcome that income range to further catch up to the developed countries.

2. In 2019 the startup Blink and *CEOWORLD Magazine* ranked Israel fourth, and in Startup Genome, Israel received place 6–7. This does not describe/respond to what it is related to prior. Yes, there is a difference between magazines, which can be normal, but that is the phrase before the reference to here. This does not explain the issue that the data comes from sources that are not neutral about Israel.
3. The 14 pillars include Opportunity Perception, Startup Skills, Risk Acceptance, Networking, Cultural Support, Opportunity, Startup Technology, Absorption, Human Capital, Competition, Product Innovation, Process Innovation, High Growth, Internationalization and Risk Capital. Further details can be found in "GEI 2018: Technical Annex."
4. From November 2020 to October 2021.

References

Ács, Z., Szerb, L., Lafuente, E., & Lloyd, A. (2018). *Global entrepreneurship and development index 2018*. Springer. https://doi.org/10.1007/978-3-030-03279-1

Anselman, T. (2020). *A note to the press: Srartups in Israel 2019–2021 (Hebrew)*. Central Bureau of Statistics. Retrieved March 24, 2022, from www.cbs.gov.il/he/mediarelease/DocLib/2020/436/29_20_436b.pdf

Avnimelech, G., & Teubal, M. (2008). From direct support of business sector R&D/innovation to targeting venture capital/private equity: A catching-up innovation and technology policy life cycle perspective. *Economics of Innovation and New Technology*, *17*(1–2), 153–172. https://doi.org/10.1080/10438590701279417

Bergsteiner, H., & Avery, G. C. (2019). Misleading country rankings perpetuate destructive business practices. *Journal of Business Ethics*, *159*(3), 863–881. https://doi.org/10.1007/s10551-018-3805-6

Butush, N. (2020). *Employment and wage disparities between the periphery and the center—Data and possible policy tools*. The Knesset—Departement of Research and Knowledge. Retrieved March 24, 2022, from https://fs.knesset.gov.il/globaldocs/MMM/64f30c05-0b0e-eb11-811a-00155d0af32a/2_64f30c05-0b0e-eb11–811a-00155d0af32a_11_16406.pdf

CBS. (2021a). *Employee Jobas and average wages per employee job in the high-tech sector, by industry*. Central Bureau of Statistics.

CBS. (2021b). *Startups in Israel 2019–2021: Findings from the CBS database on start-up companies in Israel*. Central Bureau of Statistics. Retrieved March 24, 2022, from www.cbs.gov.il/he/mediarelease/DocLib/2020/436/29_20_436b.pdf

Daniely, Y. (2020). Israel's challenging transformation from start-up nation to scale-up nation. In S. Dutta, B. Lanvin, & S. Wunsch-Vincent (Eds.), *Global innovation index 2020*. Johnson Cornell University.

Davis, K. E., Kingsbury, B., & Merry, S. E. (2012). Introduction: Global governance by indicators. In K. Davis, A. Fisher, B. Kingsbury, & S. E. Merry (Eds.), *Governance by indicators: Global power through classification and rankings*. Oxford University Press. https://doi.org/10.1093/acprof:oso/9780199658244.003.0001

Doner, R. F., & Schneider, B. R. (2016). The middle-income trap: More politics than economics. *World Politics*, *68*(4), 608–644. https://doi.org/10.1017/s0043887116000095

Glasner, J. (2021, November 2). These countries have the most startup investment for their size. *Crunchbase News*. Retrieved March 24, 2022, from https://news.crunchbase.com/news/countries-most-startup-investment/

IMD. (2022, March 31). *Competitiveness ranking Isreal—Rank 2021*. Worldcompetitiveness. https://worldcompetitiveness.imd.org/countryprofile/IL/wcy

Israel Innovation Authority. (2019). *High-tech human capital report 2019*. Israel Innovation Authority. Retrieved March 24, 2022, from https://innovationisrael.org.il/sites/default/files/High%20Tech%20Human%20Capital%20Report%202019%20-%20English%20Version_25.02_1.pdf

Israel Innovation Authority. (2020). *2020 High-tech human capital report*. Israel Innovation Authority. Retrieved March 24, 2022, from https://startupnationcentral.org/wp-content/uploads/2021/04/2020-Human-Capital-Report-Eng.pdf

Israel Innovation Authority. (2021). *Israel innovation authority's 2021 innovation report*. Israel Innovation Authority—Economics and Research Division.

Israel Innovation Authority. (2022, March 23). *Innovationisrael*. https://innovationisrael.org.il/en/

IVC. (2020). *Multinational corporations—Contribution to the Israeli tech eco-system*. IVC Research Center. Retrieved March 24, 2022, from www.iati.co.il/files/files/IATI%20MNC%202020.pdf

IVC. (2021). *Israeli tech echosystem*. IVC. Retrieved March 24, 2022, from www.ivc-online.com/Portals/0/RC/POSTS/IVC_Israeli_Entrepreneurial___FEB_2021_Final.pdf?ver=2021-02-07-115759-273&timestamp=1612691886497

IVC; GKH; ITAI. (2019). *Multinational companies (MNC)—Contribution to the Israeli tech ecosystem*. IVC; GKH; ITAI. Retrieved March 24, 2022, from www.ivc-online.com/Portals/0/MNC%20Report/MNCs_Report_Dec_2019_Final.pdf

Levi, R. (2020, December 27). Corona effect: A start-up from Binyamina manages to recruit talent from the center (Hebrew). *The Marker*. Retrieved March 24, 2022, from www.themarker.com/technation/.premium-1.9403353

Murphy, A., Ponciano, J., Hansen, S., & Touryalai, H. (2019, May 15). Global 2000-The world's largest public companies. *Forbes*.

OECD. (2020). *OECD SME and entrepreneurship outlook 2021*. OECD Publishing. https://doi.org/10.1787/97a5bbfe-en

Picciotto, R., & Thomas, V. (2021, November 19). Opinion: The real problem in the world bank's doing business indicator. *DEVEX*.

PWC Israel. (2019). *The state of innovation*. PWX Israel & Start-Up Nation Central.

PWC Israel. (2020). *PWC Israel high-tech exit report 2020*. PWX Israel. Retrieved March 24, 2022, from www.pwc.com/il/en/assets/pdf-files/2020/exit_report_2020-english.pdf

Rosenberg, D. (2018). *Israel's technology economy: Origins and impact*. Palgrave Macmillan. https://doi.org/10.1007/978-3-319-76654-6

Schwab, K., & Zahidi, S. (2020). *Global competitiveness report: Special edition 2020*. World Economic Forum.

Start-Up Nation Central. (2022). *Start-Up Nation Central*. https://startupnationcentral.org/

Swirski, S., Konor-Attias, E., Swirski, B., Hoffmann-Dishon, Y., Lieberman, A., & Livnat, M. (2021). *Social Report 2021—Corona: Epidemic of inequality*. Adva Center.

WIPO. (2020). *THE global innovation index (GII) conceptual framework (Appendix 1)*. World Intellectual Property Organization.

WIPO. (2021). *Global innovation index 2021*. World Intellectual Property Organization.

WIPO. (2022, May 1). *Global innovation index (GII)*. WIPO. www.wipo.int/global_innovation_index/en/

Wolman, Y. (2021, September 17). The warnings of the Israeli high-tech veterans (Hebrew). *Ynet*. Retrieved March 23, 2022, from www.ynet.co.il/economy/article/hjyvtptgt

Zarhovitz, O. (2017, May 30). Start-up employee or entrepreneur—who earns more? (Hebrew). *The Marker*. Retrieved March 24, 2022, from www.themarker.com/technation/startup/1.4138216

5 Introducing the Theoretical Framework

Contexts, Fields, Norm Circles and Positionality

The Importance of Context

Entrepreneurship is embedded within a variety of contexts (Baker & Welter, 2018; McAdam & Cunningham, 2019), and scholarly work accentuating the importance of context argues that it encompasses the effects of social, spatial and institutional factors on entrepreneurship (Villares-Varela & Essers, 2019). Following institutional theory, contexts can be homogeneous or heterogeneous, fostering or hindering, enabling or challenging entrepreneurship. In any case, context is acknowledged as a critical factor in explaining the situatedness of entrepreneurs and their ventures (McKeever et al., 2015).

Dy and Agwunobi (2019) present an overview of three prominent conceptualizations of context, namely that of Autio et al. (2014), Zahra and Wright (2011) and Welter (2011). Autio et al. (2014) focus on the social context, which is given a similar theoretical weight as other contexts such as the institutional, policy and cultural contexts. Zahra and Wright (2011) focus on practice, merging context into a sociocultural, economic and political entity. Welter (2011) refers primarily to social networks, family contexts and households. Whereas the call for context has definitely emphasized the significance of social, institutional and spatial factors, Dy and Agwunobi (2019) claim that although these understandings of context are useful and important, they fail to incorporate a very central aspect, namely multiple social hierarchies rooted in unequal distribution of power. Often overlooked, however, is the question of power relations within these contexts, or in other words, who has access to critical resources and who has not and, more importantly, why. Here I account for power and hierarchies in context via the conceptual lens of social positioning, informed by and expanding the notion of intersectionality. The intersectional perspective recognizes the interconnectedness of social categorization in the production of hierarchical relationships of power, social marginality, exclusion and inequality (Acker, 2006; Cho et al., 2013; Hancock, 2007). It simultaneously accounts for the individual, the group and the wider societal level (Collins, 2000; Dhamoon, 2011). It explains complex social divisions that emerge, in "particular social

DOI: 10.4324/9781003091042-6

locations in particular historical moments, within particular social, economic and political contexts in which some social divisions have more saliency and effect" (Yuval-Davis, 2015, p. 95). Accordingly, Anthias maintains that intersectionality is a "social process related to practices and arrangements" that gives rise to particular forms of positionality (Anthias, 2006, p. 27). Therefore, positionality happens in context, and in the following, I will outline the line of argumentation for analyzing the contexts of technological entrepreneurship in Israel.

As I have hinted at before, there is a tendency to describe the technological-entrepreneurship scene and the Israeli labor market as "the high-tech and all the rest." The data provided in the previous chapter largely confirm this statement, in terms of the labor market, geographic dispersion and socio-economic status. Nevertheless, the homogenization of the members of the "rest" or the "others" as all disadvantaged is misleading. While demographic characteristics and structural positions make members of the groups different from the hegemonic ideal of "the entrepreneur"—a straight white Jewish adult male (Ogbor, 2000)—these are in fact extremely diverse groups.

In order to set the scene for analyzing the groups addressed in this book and elaborating on the difference between them and the distances among them in relation to the technological high-tech ecosystem perceived here as the dominant center, I will recruit the Bourdieuian approach to entrepreneurship based on the concept of Bourdieu's theory of "field" and Elder-Vass' (2012) idea of the "norm circle" in critical realism. The use of these two theoretical concepts allows for analyzing and explaining the social positionality of the entrepreneurs of the various groups.

Fields, Habitus, Capitals and Norm Circles

Bourdieu (1977) defined "fields" as historically produced social spaces of rules, traditions and power relations (Spigel, 2013). Fields are institutional arenas where people express their dispositions and where they compete for the distribution of different kinds of capital (Gaventa, 2003). Actors in the field agree obliquely to follow the rules of the field and thereby enable social interaction. Bourdieu (1977) terms these rules doxa "because they are not only unquestioned by those who follow them, but they also appear to be so natural and unremarkable that they are unquestionable" (Spigel, 2013, p. 808). Doxa, in the form of unchallenged, taken-for-granted assumptions, is a source and a manifestation of power. Fields are also networks and structures, sets of a variety of kinds of relationships (Navarro, 2006). People experience power in accordance with the field they are in, and therefore, the concept of "field" considers tensions and contradictions occurring when people are confronted with different contexts.

People give interpretation to fields via internalized intentions and dispositions, referred to as *habitus* (Bourdieu, 1980). Habitus is "the way society becomes deposited in persons in the form of lasting dispositions, or trained capacities and structured propensities to think, feel and act in determinant ways, which then guide them" (Wacquant, 2005, p. 318). Thus, people internalize rules, structures and hierarchies of a field as well as the evaluation of their own position within the field. By that, they generate an imbedded knowledge of how the rules, structures and hierarchies apply to them considering their own status and position in the field. Through their habitus, actors not only generate an understanding of the rules of the field but also develop an implicit knowledge of how those rules apply to them given their status or position within the field. The habitus is best understood as the internalization of the rules, structures and hierarchies of a field as well as a simultaneous knowledge of one's position within the field (Swartz, 2013).

The position and power of people within a field are determined by their stocks of capital. Bourdieu (1986) maintained that forms of capital can be accumulated and are transferrable: material capital is the traditional economic form, social capital includes the value of resources accessible through one's social network and cultural capital concerns the knowledge of specific social rules and normative expectations. It acts as a source of social class stratification through a complex interaction of cultural capital with social capital and human capital (Bourdieu, 1986). Finally, symbolic capital is defined as "the form that the various species of capital assume when they are perceived and recognized as legitimate" (Bourdieu, 1987, p. 4). The value of these forms of capital depends on the nature and structure of the field (Spigel, 2013).

"A norm circle is the group of people that is committed to endorsing and enforcing a particular norm" (Elder-Vass, 2012, p. 22). Elder-Vass explains norm circles as overlapping social collectives encouraging, endorsing and enforcing certain practices. In a dialectic dynamic, these circles produce a synergy evolving a certain interpretation of circle members' normative environment. Thus, norm circles have causal powers to influence their members by the virtue of the ways in which those members interact in them. These powers are founded on the commitment that members of the circle have to endorse and enforce practices that are congruent with the norm in question (Elder-Vass, 2012, p. 122).

> They may support the norm by advocating the practice, by praising or rewarding those who enact it, by criticizing or punishing those who fail to enact it, or even just by ostentatiously enacting it themselves. The consequence of such endorsement and enforcement is that the members of the circle know they face a systematic incentive to enact the practice.
>
> (Elder-Vass, 2012, p. 124)

The concept of norm circles overlaps to a certain extent with Bourdieu's concept of "social fields." The empirical representation of a social field includes firstly the estimation of the location of the field in relation to the dominant elite class's "field of power" (Wacquant, 1993). Secondly, it includes the mapping of agents and institutions, their respective positions and relations between them. Finally, the empirical representation of a social field comprises the examination of the habitus of the agents of the field (Bourdieu & Wacquant, 1992). Therefore, a social field can be considered as encompassing overlapping "circles" that produce and reproduce the particular dynamics in context. Accordingly, norm circle theory maintains that social groups will be linked with a number of overlapping norm circles described by Elder-Vass as "clustered circles" (Elder-Vass, 2012).

According to Anthias (2008), positionality "combines a reference to social position (as a set of effectivities: as outcome) and social positioning (as a set of practices, actions and meanings: as process)" (in Martinez Dy & Marlow, 2017, p. 12). Therefore, positionality is located at the intersection of structure and agency, at the intersection of the outcome of social position and the process of action and meaning within fields and norm circles. It accounts for resource allocation and accumulation and the potential inequality in access due to existing social hierarchies (Dy & Agwunobi, 2019, p. 1735).

In the following, I will elaborate on how to apply the theoretical concepts to the empirical part of the book.

Technological Entrepreneurship, Fields, Norm Circles and Social Positionality

Entrepreneurial practices occur within Bourdieuian fields. Leaning upon Willig's (2013) metaphorical explanation of Bourdieu's field, analyzing the entrepreneurial high-tech ecosystem could be argued as follows: Looking at the field as a game (Bourdieu & Wacquant, 1992), the high-tech ecosystem has its own logic of practice and values and norms. The ecosystem's doxa is the implicit, unquestioned, taken-for granted understanding of the high-tech game, the undisputable conviction that the game is worth playing and the elementary beliefs managing its practices. The high-tech habitus is the way the game is played, the dispositions of the players (agents) for positioning himself/herself in the game. High-tech capitals comprise the resources the entrepreneurs, investors, policy makers, etc. are investing in the game, and these resources are recognized as valuable in the field and by the other agents in the field (Willig, 2013). More specifically and following Spigel (2013), for technological entrepreneurs, their human capital (technical skills and knowledge) is valuable if combined with material capital (savings and investments) and the capability to sell their vision to customers and investors (cultural capital), which is facilitated by prior entrepreneurial successes or degrees from particular universities (symbolic capital). Power in the field of the entrepreneurial high-tech ecosystem means to have the ability to control the value of different forms of capital. In the norm circle of the high-tech ecosystem, practices that promote the high-tech habitus are constantly endorsed and enforced, and therefore, the members of the circle know they face a systematic incentive to enact the practice. In the reminder of this book, I will explain in detail how that happens. When applying this line of argumentation, it becomes obvious that entrepreneurship is entrenched within persistent social hierarchies in which some entrepreneurs have access to critical capitals and others do not. Consequently, following Anthias (2001), a marginal positionality constraining the accumulation of human, social and economic capital and will therefore likely generate structural barriers to entrepreneurial activity (Dy et al., 2017). Accounting for positionality therefore challenges the assumption that entrepreneurship is neutral or meritocratic (Dy, 2022) and awareness of positionality is crucial for contextualizing entrepreneurship while focusing on the accessibility of resources and the criteria for gaining accessibility, or in Bourdieu's terms, on the power of the habitus and control of capitals in the field. Additionally, belonging to the dominant norm circle is of critical importance for high-tech entrepreneurs to succeed.

This book is about the winners and losers of technological advancement and entrepreneurship in Israel. Utilizing the concepts discussed previously, I intend to display the distance of various groups of technological entrepreneurs from the center, try to understand and explain the reasons for the distance from the center and deal with the consequences of the distance in terms of the technological entrepreneurs themselves, the group they belong to and society as a whole.

Importantly, the assumption that all entrepreneurs have equal access to resources, participation and support, as well as an equal chance to develop a successful venture startup (McAdam et al., 2019), must be questioned concerning disadvantaged entrepreneurs. Thus, in terms of the OECD agenda, missing entrepreneurs are groups of people who need to receive support and access to equal opportunities and resources in order to create successful sustainable businesses (OECD & European Union, 2019; OECD & European Commission, 2021). Next to seniors, immigrants and young people, women are among the key target groups of the OECD's agenda of an inclusive entrepreneurship policy, aimed at expanding entrepreneurship in order to create jobs, leverage technological development and meet economic and social challenges (OECD & European Union, 2019).

Introducing the Groups

For each of the following chapters, I will locate the respective groups analyzed within the sociospatial processes of centralization and peripheralization along economic, social and political lines, as outlined in Chapter 3. Additionally, I will present the most updated available data as to the group characteristics as well as the technological entrepreneurial activities of these groups. Importantly, I would like to clarify that the groups discussed in the following chapters are not homogenous but include a variety of subgroups. It was beyond the scope of this book to specifically relate to the subgroups.

Furthermore, I will introduce case studies for each group. Entrepreneurs will be located within the analytical framework of positionality according to the following criteria: availability of employment opportunities; access to business owners' networks; knowledge of "doing business"; access to financial and material resources (personal or within networks); support or lack of support of family and friends; cultural particularities (i.e., perceptions of desirability and feasibility of starting a business, perception of appropriateness of starting a business); and precarity in terms of occupational and social security or the lack of them. In addition, I will use the methodology of constructing "persona" in order to exemplify typical generalized members of each group (Fergnani, 2019).

The composition of the groups chosen reflect the theoretical postulate that class, gender, race and ethnicity are social structures that have historically shaped the struggle over resources and hierarchies (Anthias, 2001; Martinez Dy, 2020). More specifically, causes for disadvantage in accessing resources necessary for entrepreneurship in general and technological entrepreneurship in particular can be various and may include national identity, disabilities, sexual orientation, age, religion or political affiliation. Importantly, the assumption that all entrepreneurs have equal access to resources, participation and support as well as an equal chance to develop a successful venture startup (McAdam et al., 2019) must be questioned when considering disadvantaged entrepreneurs (Maalaoui et al., 2020).

When investigating the respective groups of technological entrepreneurs, I assume that social class, nationality, gender, race and ethnicity, potential intersections and additional country-specific hierarchies impact the space in which entrepreneurs act and their potential to accumulate the necessary resources for setting up technological ventures. The various groups addressed in this book exemplify all of the relevant classifications, as detailed earlier in this chapter.

The Ethiopian community in Israel represents an ethnic and visible minority of people who immigrated to Israel from Ethiopia in two waves (1984 and 1991). The Israeli government initiated their immigration on the basis of Jewish origin. Nonetheless, Ethiopian community members live mostly in the socioeconomic periphery and are underrepresented in the public space. The only high-tech entrepreneur of this group that I found for the purpose of interview for this book highlights the intersection of ethnic minority and social periphery.

Women are severely underrepresented in the Israeli high-tech scene. They amount to 5% only among startups, and this in spite of a variety of former and current programs aimed at formative action. They represent the gender lenses and highlight the intersection of gender and technology.

The Palestinian Arab minority in Israel constitutes about 20% of the Israeli population. Their minority status concerns religion and nationality and is complicated by the fact that about 90% are of Muslim religion and are therefore often identified by the Jewish majority as attached to neighboring

Muslim countries—Israel's long-standing enemies. They highlight the national minority lens and the intersections of religion, national identity and peripherality.

Kibbutzim—collective communities—symbolize Jewish settlement in Palestine and Israel since the first Kibbutz, Degania, was established in 1907. For many years, Kibbutzim were at the very political, economic, social and cultural center of Israeli society. During the last decades, they have lost this position due to changing political constellations. Since most of the Kibbutzim are located in the geographic periphery of Israel, technological entrepreneurs discussed here represent the geographic periphery combined with a high socio-economic status and belonging to the dominant majority of Israeli society.

Since the beginning of the 1990s, more than one million immigrated from the Former Soviet Union (FSU) to Israel. Today they compose about 20% of the Israeli population. Although many of the FSU community are already Israeli-born, the majority hold on to language and cultural particularities and are sometimes considered as a Russian-speaking enclave. Technological entrepreneurs of this group highlight the intersection of migration status and ethnic and cultural particularity.

The ultra-Orthodox Jewish community in Israel constitutes around 12.5% of the Israeli population today and is constantly growing. This population group is growing exponentially and is expected to make up about a 25% the Israeli population in 2050. Their lifestyle separates them in many aspects from mainstream society. A main characteristic of this group is their low labor market participation. Therefore, they are targeted by many state schemes in order to increase their ability to earn a living and not rely on state subsidies only. Their representation in the high-tech ecosystem is extremely low, with more women than men among the few participants in a number of initiatives. The high-tech entrepreneurs of this group highlight the intersection of religiosity and being a minority group within Jewish dominant mainstream of Israeli society.

In the following chapters, I will set the scene of the groups presented previously to account for the particular context. In this analytical process, I will present interview data, policy documents, population statistics and media material with the goal of capturing the particularities of the contexts in line with the social positionality approach. The overall goal is to identify patterns of social structures that assist in explaining the underrepresentation of these groups in the Israeli high-tech ecosystem.

References

Acker, J. (2006). Inequality regimes: Gender, class, and race in organizations. *Gender & Society*, *20*(4), 441–464. https://doi.org/10.1177/0891243206289499

Anthias, F. (2001). The material and the symbolic in theorizing social stratification: Issues of gender, ethnicity and class. *British Journal of Sociology*, *52*(3), 367–339. https://doi.org/10.1080/00071310120071106

Anthias, F. (2006). Belongings in a globalising and unequal world: Rethinking translocations. *The Situated Politics of Belonging*, 17–31. https://doi.org/10.4135/9781446213490.n2

Anthias, F. (2008). Thinking through the lens of translocational positionality: An intersectionality frame for understanding identity and belonging. *Translocations: Migration and Social Change*, *4*(1), 5–20.

Autio, E., Kenney, M., Mustar, P., Siegel, D., & Wright, M. (2014). Entrepreneurial innovation: The importance of context. *Research policy*, *43*(7), 1097–1108. https://doi.org/10.1016/j.respol.2014.01.015

Baker, T., & Welter, F. (2018). *Contextual entrepreneurship: An interdisciplinary perspective* (Vol. 14). Now Publishers Inc. http://dx.doi.org/10.1561/0300000078

Bourdieu, P. (1977). *Outline of a theory of practice*. Cambridge University Press. https://doi.org/10.1017/CBO9780511812507

Bourdieu, P. (1980). *The logic of practice*. Stanford University Press. https://doi.org/10.1515/9781503621749

Bourdieu, P. (1986). The forms of capital. In J. Richardson (Ed.), *Handbook of theory and research for the sociology of education* (pp. 241–258). Greenwood Press.

Bourdieu, P. (1987). What makes a social class? On the theoretical and practical existence of groups. *Berkeley Journal of Sociology*, *32*, 1–17.

Bourdieu, P., & Wacquant, L. J. (1992). *An invitation to reflexive sociology*. University of Chicago Press.

Cho, S., Crenshaw, K. W., & McCall, L. (2013). Toward a field of intersectionality studies: Theory, applications, and praxis. *Signs: Journal of Women in Culture and Society*, *38*(4), 785–810. https://doi.org/10.1086/669608

Collins, P. H. (2000). *Black feminist thought: Knowledge, consciousness, and the politics of empowerment* (2nd ed.). Routledge. https://doi.org/10.4324/9780203900055

Dhamoon, R. K. (2011). Considerations on mainstreaming intersectionality. *Political Research Quarterly*, *64*(1), 230–243. https://doi.org/10.1177/1065912910379227

Dy, A. M. (2022). Levelling the playing field? Towards a critical-social perspective on digital entrepreneurship. *Futures*, *135*. https://doi.org/10.1016/j.futures.2019.102438

Dy, A. M., & Agwunobi, A. J. (2019). Intersectionality and mixed methods for social context in entrepreneurship. *International Journal of Entrepreneurial Behavior & Research*, *25*(8), 1727–1747. https://doi.org/10.1108/ijebr-12-2017-0498

Dy, A. M., Marlow, S., & Martin, L. (2017). A web of opportunity or the same old story? Women digital entrepreneurs and intersectionality theory. *Human Relations*, *70*(3), 286–311. https://doi.org/10.1177/0018726716650730

Elder-Vass, D. (2012). *The reality of social construction*. Cambridge University Press. https://doi.org/10.1017/CBO9781139169202

Fergnani, A. (2019). The future persona: A futures method to let your scenarios come to life. *Foresight*, *21*(4), 445–466. https://doi.org/10.1108/fs-10-2018-0086

Gaventa, J. (2003). *Power after Lukes: An overview of theories of power since Lukes and their application to development* (pp. 3–18). Participation Group, Institute of Development Studies.

Hancock, A. M. (2007). When multiplication doesn't equal quick addition: Examining intersectionality as a research paradigm. *Perspectives on Politics*, *5*(1), 63–79. https://doi.org/10.1017/s1537592707070065

Maalaoui, A., Ratten, V., Heilbrunn, S., Brannback, M., & Kraus, S. (2020). Disadvantage entrepreneurship: Decoding a new area of research. *European Management Review*, *17*(3), 663–668. https://doi.org/10.1111/emre.12424

Martinez Dy, A. (2020). Not all entrepreneurship is created equal: Theorising entrepreneurial disadvantage through social positionality. *European Management Review, 17*(3), 687–699. https://doi.org/10.1111/emre.12390

Martinez Dy, A., & Marlow, S. (2017). Women entrepreneurs and their ventures: Complicating categories and contextualizing gender. In C. N. Henry (Ed.), *The Routledge companion to global female entrepreneurship* (pp. 15–29). Routledge. https://doi.org/10.4324/9781315794570-2

McAdam, M., & Cunningham, J. (2019). *Entrepreneurial behaviour—Individual, contextual and microfoundational perspectives*. Palgrave Macmillan. https://doi.org/10.1007/978-3-030-04402-2

McAdam, M., Harrison, R. T., & Leitch, C. M. (2019). Stories from the field: Women's networking as gender capital in entrepreneurial ecosystems. *Small Business Economics, 53*(2), 459–474. https://doi.org/10.1007/s11187-018-9995-6

McKeever, E., Jack, S., & Anderson, A. (2015). Embedded entrepreneurship in the creative re-construction of place. *Journal of Business Venturing, 30*(1), 50–65. https://doi.org/10.1016/j.jbusvent.2014.07.002

Navarro, Z. (2006). In search of cultural interpretation of power. *IDS Bulletin, 37*(6), 11–22. https://doi.org/10.1111/j.1759-5436.2006.tb00319.x

OECD & European Commission. (2021). *The missing entrepreneurs 2021: Policies for inclusive entrepreneurship and self-employment*. OECD Publishing. https://doi.org/10.1787/71b7a9bb-en

OECD & European Union. (2019). *The missing entrepreneurs 2019: Policies for Inclusive entrepreneurship*. OECD Publishing. https://doi.org/10.1787/3ed84801-en

Ogbor, J. O. (2000). Mythicizing and reification in entrepreneurial discourse: Ideology-critique of entrepreneurial studies. *Journal of Management Studies, 37*(5), 605–635. https://doi.org/10.1111/1467-6486.00196

Spigel, B. (2013). Bourdieuian approaches to the geography of entrepreneurial culture. *Entrepreneurship & Regional Development, 25*(9–10), 804–818. https://doi.org/10.1080/08985626.2013.862974

Swartz, D. L. (2013). *Symbolic power, politics, and intellectuals: The political sociology of Pierre Bourdieu*. University of Chicago Press. https://doi.org/10.7208/chicago/9780226925028.001.0001

Villares-Varela, M., & Essers, C. (2019). Women in the migrant economy. A positional approach to contextualize gendered transnational trajectories. *Entrepreneurship & Regional Development, 31*(3–4), 213–225. https://doi.org/10.1080/08985626.2018.1551789

Wacquant, L. J. (1993). From ruling class to field of power: An interview with Pierre Bourdieu on La Noblesse d'Etat. *Theory, Culture & Society, 10*(3), 19–44. https://doi.org/10.1177/026327693010003002

Wacquant, L. J. (2005). Habitus. In J. Beckert & M. Zafirovski (Eds.), *International encyclopedia of economic sociology* (pp. 317–321). Routledge. https://doi.org/10.4324/9780203824214

Welter, F. (2011). Contextualizing entrepreneurship—Conceptual challenges and ways forward. *Entrepreneurship Theory and Practice, 35*(1), 165–184. https://doi.org/10.1111/j.1540-6520.2010.00427.x

Willig, I. (2013). Newsroom ethnography in a field perspective. *Journalism, 14*(3), 372–387. https://doi.org/10.1177/1464884912442638

Yuval-Davis, N. (2015). Situated intersectionality and social inequality. *Raisons Politiques*, *2*, 91–100. https://doi.org/10.3917/rai.058.0091

Zahra, S. A., & Wright, M. (2011). Entrepreneurship's next act. *Academy of Management Perspectives*, *25*(4), 67–83.

6 What You Look Like Is Important

Technological Entrepreneurs of the Ethiopian Community

Introduction

Within the kaleidoscope of populations in Israel, the Ethiopian community constitutes an interesting case: Ethiopians arrived from Africa to Israel under the Law of Return. According to the Law of Return, Jews are entitled to request Israel citizenship, assuming they posed no imminent danger to public health, state security, or the Jewish people as a whole. Thus, essentially, all Jews everywhere are Israeli citizens by right (The Jewish Agency for Israel, 2022).

Therefore, as part of the Jewish majority and especially as Jewish migrants, the Ethiopian immigrants are entitled to institutional arrangements that foster integration in general and labor market integration in particular. However, upon arrival, their Jewishness was questioned by part of the religious establishment, a fact that deeply influenced the relationship between the Ethiopian community and the Israeli society in general and the religious establishment in particular.

Ethiopians in Israel make up about 2% of the population, and their "blackness" positions them as the most visible among the Jewish Israeli populations. Businesses established by members of the Ethiopian community are mainly located in the informal economy, reflecting their double disadvantage of being a migrant community and of being black. Although Israel is part of the Global Entrepreneurship Monitor (GEM) Project, there is no systematic track record of the level and nature of entrepreneurial activity of the Ethiopian community in Israel; expert estimate is significantly lower than that of the overall Israeli population. No data as to the participation of community members in the technological ecosystem could be found. Additionally, the interview partner, which will be presented in the following pages of this chapter, was the only high-tech entrepreneur I was able to locate. Thus, members of the Ethiopian community are underrepresented in the high-tech scene in Tel Aviv.

The Ethiopian Community in Israel

By the end of 2019, some 155,300 of Israeli citizens were of Ethiopian origin, 87,500 of them born in Ethiopia. They migrated to Israel in two mass

DOI: 10.4324/9781003091042-7

migration operations in the 1980s ("Operation Moses") and early 1990s ("Operation Solomon"). In addition, 67,800 community members resided in the country who were born in Israel to Ethiopia-born parents (CBS, 2020, p. 1).

Concerning *residence distribution* of the community, 38% of Ethiopian Jews reside in the center district and 25% in the southern district, mainly in the development towns of Kiryat Gat (10.2% of the town's population) and Kiryat Malachi (16% of the town's population). Often, community members are concentrated in marginalized neighborhoods, comprising 30%–50% of those neighborhoods' populations (CBS, 2020, p. 1; Shishon, 2015).

Overall, and in relation to the population of Israel, members of the Ethiopian community are in a *poor economic situation*. The net financial income for a household of Ethiopian Jews in 2019 was 14,027 NIS, compared to the national average of 17,276 NIS (CBS, 2020, pp. 2–6). Ethiopian Jews are the poorest group of the Jewish part of Israeli society: 31.8% were near poverty and 22.8% in poverty (Svirsky et al., 2019, p. 21). The net financial expenditure (7,037 NIS) is also lower than the national average (12,792 NIS) per month. Interestingly, the Ethiopian community imported a circle saving system bypassing the formal banking framework in order to mutually support members of extended families (Kotler, 2017).

In 2019, 30,000 Ethiopian-born Jews were maintained by the welfare authorities, which is 2.5 times more than the number of all non-Israeli-born Jewish citizens. The number stands for a situation in which one out of three Ethiopians are in contact with the welfare authorities. Additionally, 19,500 people of Ethiopian origin who were born in Israel were maintained by the welfare system—3 times higher than the parallel number among the general Israel-born Jewish population (CBS, 2020, p. 16). When adding up all these data, one can conclude that about a third of the Ethiopian community in Israel were in need for support by governmental welfare agencies.

Also concerning the *participation of community members in the labor market*, the picture is rather distressing. Nonacademic Ethiopian immigrants are overrepresented in five of the industries that pay the lowest wages. Ethiopian academics, on the other hand, are integrated into major industries in the private sector, even those who pay high wages, but still suffer from very high wage gaps, receiving only 42% of the salaries of their non-Ethiopian counterparts. Ethiopian academics earn 55% of the salaries of the other academic Jews in the industry. Semyonov et al. (2015) investigated labor force participation, occupational status and earnings of immigrant groups in Israel, and the results of their study revealed that overall the Ethiopians are located at the bottom of an ethnic hierarchy.

In 2019, almost 43% of students of Ethiopian origin attended schools of the Jewish religious state education system (compared to 55.4% a decade ago), and 52.2% attended the Jewish secular state education system (compared to 42.3% last decade). A small but growing share of Ethiopian students attended the ultra-Orthodox education system (4.9% as of 2019)

(CBS, 2020, p. 9). The rate of high school students eligible for a matriculation diploma among students of Ethiopian origins, although on the rise in recent years, is still significantly lower than the average in the Hebrew (Jewish) education system—64.3% compared to 80.5%. 49.2% of Ethiopia-originated high school students attended vocational schools, tracking them to blue-collar occupations, compared to only 34.7% of Jewish high school students who are not of Ethiopian origin (CBS, 2020, pp. 10–11).

Only 21.7% of high school graduates from Ethiopian origin acquired academic education within eight years after graduating from high school, compared to 47.2% of all graduates in the Hebrew-speaking educational system of Israel. Moreover, this is after a significantly higher dropout rate from academia among the Ethiopian students, which can get up to twice higher compared to the total average of the whole Jewish population (Knesset, 2015; Ilan, 2019). Out of the Ethiopian-originated high school graduates who did continue to acquire an academic degree, only 26.5% did so in universities, which constitute the highest level of academic education. Half of the Ethiopian students (51%) acquired their bachelor degree from an academic college, compared to 35.8% (university) and 40.4% (college) of all graduates from the Jewish education system, respectively (CBS, 2020, p. 12). Those Ethiopian university students who study toward a PhD degree (0.2%) in 2018/2019 are enrolled in programs of business administration, social sciences and education, not in those academic disciplines potentially generating high income.

Over the years, a number of programs to support the integration of the Ethiopian community and the empowerment of the community members have been initiated by NGOs and governmental agencies, often in cooperation with each other and Jewish confederations in the USA. The "Farah" program concerns professional training in 12 Israeli cities and is aimed at placement in high-paying jobs. The Ethiopian National Project (ENP) was established in 2004 in partnership with the government promoting the advancement of the integration of Ethiopian Israeli Jews into Israeli society (Ethiopian National Project, 2022). "Telem" (Employment and Study for Adults) is an educational program operated in cooperation of the Ministry of Aliyah and Integration with the Kibbutz Movement. It focuses on personal empowerment of Ethiopian youth. "Tene Briut" is an NGO providing workshops and lectures on health topics to groups of Ethiopian immigrants and the National Council for the Child funded programs designed to deal with education issues of children as well as providing workshops for parents (Ministry of Aliyah and Integration, 2020).

Already in 2013, the state comptroller at the time, Yosef Shapira, determined that the state failed to implement a program to enable the absorption of Ethiopian Israelis into society and that there were considerable gaps between the Ethiopians and the rest of the Israel population (State Comptroller, 2013). In addition, the comptroller noted that 65 percent of Ethiopian children live below the poverty line, and there are significant deficiencies in programs formulated to address gaps in education, military service, higher education, employment and housing. Based on a research project conducted in 2020/2021, Grotlüschen and colleagues (2021) found that in addition to difficulties experienced by all members of other low-achieving groups, Ethiopian Israelis experience racist reactions to their skin color. It is not surprising that the state comptroller's 2021 report determines that the statistics indicate racial bias by the police and prosecution (State Comptroller, 2021). One—although not the only—expression of the racialization is the fact that Ethiopians are more often arrested and incarcerated (Yaron, 2018), and in "August 2016, Israel's police commissioner claimed it was 'natural' for officers to suspect Israelis of Ethiopian origin-as well as Arabs-of being more involved in crime. He admitted Ethiopians had been over policed" (Trujillo-Pagán, 2019, p. 67).

In sum, the integration of the Ethiopian community into the Israeli society and economy cannot be evaluated as successful. Very recent findings show that Israeli Ethiopians still report a sense of discrimination and racism due to their origins and skin color (Shouach & Ben-Eliezer, 2021; Walsh et al., 2019). The diversity index (Ministry of Economy and Industry, 2021) reveals systematic and structural discrimination of the community in the labor market, with an extremely low occupational status in comparison to all other groups (Saabneh & Tesfai, 2019). CBS data and the comptroller's report indeed disclose that Ethiopian Israelis earn less, suffer from ethnic segregation and find it extremely difficult to break the glass ceiling. A number of researchers foresee that the Ethiopian community in Israel is in danger of experiencing more ghettoization in the future (Ben-Eliezer, 2004; Kaplan & Salamon, 2004; Kimmerling, 2001; Offer, 2007).

Reasons for Lack of Integration

Following Ben-Eliezer (2008), there are a number of reasons for the fact that among the second generation of Israeli-born Ethiopians, their situation as a group also has not improved significantly. The failure of the government agencies responsible for the absorption (Kaplan, 2010), which applied "dual assimilationist-separationist treatment" (Yakhnich et al., 2021), is one main reason. This policy included mechanisms such as suggestion to change Ethiopian names into Hebrew Israeli names and sending children to boarding schools in an effort to assimilate them. But at the same time, the Ethiopian community was provided with housing in socially peripheral areas. Thus, separation in the education system was indirectly promoted. An additional reason for the lack of integration is the relatively low level of human, social and financial capital. Furthermore, the Jewishness of the community was questioned by the religious establishment. There was and still is a rather profound cultural distance from the mainstream Israeli society, and the number of single-parent families is relatively high (Ben-Eliezer,

2008; Kaplan & Salamon, 2004; Kimmerling, 2001; Swirski & Yosef, 2005; Yonah, 2005). The Ethiopian community is a visible minority. Ben-Eliezer maintains that the combination of these factors caused their marginalization, which was further reinforced by growing patterns of racism. The transition of Israeli society toward a neoliberal model, as discussed in the first chapter of this book, increased cultural exclusionary racism according to Ben-Eliezer (2008, p. 956):

> The young generation of the immigrants, who tried to avoid discrimination and institutional racism by developing a distinctive style and a hybrid identity, found itself excluded, marginalized and segregated. Cultural racism has not disappeared but changed its form, from institutional racism to everyday racism, which appears to be inherent in Israel's multicultural group classification along the color line.

Ethiopian Entrepreneurship in Israel

There is only a small number of empirical studies on entrepreneurship by members of the Ethiopian community in Israel. A comparative study conducted in 2015 by Heilbrunn and Kushnirovich investigated problems experienced by entrepreneurs when obtaining finance to set up and promote their business. Immigrants from Ethiopia experienced the overall problems (85.0%) in comparison to all the other groups (Palestinian Israelis, immigrants from the Former Soviet Union and Jewish Israelis). They reported that problems related to their bank account (overdraft, large credit commitments, etc.) and prejudice are the two prominent reasons for not receiving loans. The study revealed that problems accessing bank loans are affected by the affiliation of entrepreneurs to ethnic and immigrant groups, and minority entrepreneurs are disadvantaged when seeking bank loans. In the case of the Ethiopian entrepreneurs, the results of the study represent a classic case of resource disadvantage (Heilbrunn & Kushnirovich, 2015). In the same year, Kushnirovich (2015) published an article on the economic integration of immigrant entrepreneurs, but Ethiopian immigrants—although a very distinct group—were included within the Africa/Asia immigrant group since that is where they are located in most of the Israeli national statistical databases. Interestingly, this can be inferred to as another reflection of their invisibility. The Ethiopian Jewish immigrants are the only group of African origin immigrants who are black. They are distinct from Jewish immigrants from Morocco, Tunisia and other African countries by their color. The inclusion into the group named "Africa/Asia" does not account for their particularity in Israel, where next to them, only asylum seekers and refugees from Africa are black. Thus, in many databases, such as the social survey of the CBS, which is the database Kushnirovich used for her study, Ethiopians cannot be identified.

Fanta-Vagenshtein and Anteby-Yemini (2016), in their study on Ethiopian Israeli women's narratives of career trajectories, introduce a group of women entrepreneurs who own stores and companies. The women and their businesses are very much concentrated within the ethnic enclave of the Ethiopian community, some commuting between Ethiopia and Israel, importing and exporting ethnic products. In some neighborhoods, all-women credit associations based on Ethiopian tradition have been established (Salamon et al., 2009) to enable funding for the shops and businesses established by the women (Fanta-Vagenshtein & Anteby-Yemini, 2016). In 2019 Heilbrunn conducted a comparative study on women entrepreneurs and their inclination to enter the formal or informal economy. The results of the study revealed that businesses in the formal sector of the economy were mostly established by women from the Former Soviet Union, belonging to a migration group with more human, social and cultural capital, being less discriminated against and being able to better cope with obstacles and barriers. Those businesses located in the informal economy were established by Ethiopian migrant women belonging to the most marginalized group of Israeli society, triple disadvantaged as being women, migrants and black. These women were not able to cope with barriers and obstacles and were exposed to a high degree of precariousness (Heilbrunn, 2019).

The Israeli government has promoted a niche entrepreneurship policy toward a number of groups identified as weakened and marginalized for various reasons. One of these programs was directed at the Ethiopian community. In 2016 Heilbrunn and Rodrigues published an article evaluating a program initiated by one of the Israeli Centres for the Promotion of Entrepreneurship (CPE) in one of the major cities of Israel, with a relatively large percentage of Ethiopian citizens. The program intended to train Ethiopian unemployed academics to become mentors for Ethiopian small business owners. The idea was to help Ethiopian academics out of unemployment in such a way that they would receive some kind of professional experience and, at the same time, assist Ethiopian small business owners. The evaluative study by Heilbrunn and Rodriguez (2016) revealed that the program failed due to a number of reasons, such as lack of intercultural sensitivity, lack of embeddedness within existing community structures and networks and lack of networking activities of the CPE.

Till today, the Ministry of Aliyah and Integration of the Israeli government provides assistance for immigrants and returning residents through five business centers located all over the country. Those interested to get assistance can receive a preliminary business consultation at no charge and an ongoing consultation program at subsidized prices. For the Ethiopian community members, many of whom are no longer immigrants but Israeli citizens, a dedicated state scheme exists to assist potential entrepreneurs throughout the process of setting up their business.

The Case Studies

Salomon Mangiest—the Only Ethiopian Tech Entrepreneur to Be Found

At the time of the interview, Salomon Mangiest was 36 years old, married and father to a small son. He was born in Kiryat Gat, where he spent his youth in a family of six brothers and sisters. In 1983, his parents migrated from Ethiopia via Sudan to Israel. Salomon was raised in a religious environment until the age of 17. After he finished his compulsory military service of three years, Salomon joined Techcareer and spent eight months of training in high-tech-related skills in the laboratory of Kibbutz Nahshon. He then joined John Brice—a private provider of computer and programming courses—as a QI lecturer. Since 2008 Salomon has been teaching and working at the same time. He worked in bigger and smaller companies, in both management and "hands-on" roles. In parallel, he enrolled for a BA in business administration and information systems at one of the private colleges in Israel. During that period, he ran an ice cream shop on a franchise basis, which he purchased with the money he earned at his high-tech jobs. Thus, Salomon gathered quite some experience in running a small business and in high-tech companies.

Salomon met his wife when he was already in his third job, while she still serving in a military tech unit. After the army service his wife took a number of professional courses and is since working in high-tech companies. Salomon received interview invitations from Amazon and Facebook and a job offer from Apple including relocation to Ireland. "I was in a dilemma then. Personally, I am very interested to get to know other cultures, but then, getting up every morning doing something I do not really like? I decided against it." After working for some time in a big company in Israel, he felt "swallowed up" and less in the spotlight. He explained that working in a big company with a lot of managers above and around him was not his "cup of tea" and although he did appreciate the social security, this "day to day is not what" he wants. Therefore, he decided to go and work for smaller companies with more familiarity: "I still want to do what I love despite abandoning the financial security." His wife and some of his friends see things differently and do not really understand his decision. He pointed out that he is confident that he will be able to leverage his experience and succeed as a tech entrepreneur in Israel; that is what he really wants to be. Before starting his current startup, Salomon worked at Fast—an online supermarket. He became good friends with Simon, the founder and CEO of the supermarket. Approximately 18 months after Simon left the supermarket, he contacted Salomon—"Call me if you're interested"—and offered him partnership in a new startup related to data analysis. Salomon said, "It was exactly that time that I felt the urge to do something on my own, to tread a new path, so I told Simon that I am in." For the last two years, Salomon has been working in the startup. At the beginning, the salary Salomon generated from the startup was very low since he was an active partner and owns shares. Therefore, until recently he taught courses in the afternoon but will soon be able to invest all his time in the startup and earn a decent salary since negotiations with an investor are proceeding well, and Simon and Salomon hope to be able to close the deal for funding the growth of their startup soon. The main focus of their business is data gathering and analysis for businesses—it is a business-to-business concept aimed at increasing the effectiveness and efficiency of small and medium-size businesses. Up to the date of the interview, Salomon and his partner managed to generate one meaningful client, a chain of coffee shops. Today they employ four people in their business, two of them from the Ethiopian community and former students of Tech-Career—an NGO promoting the inclusion of young people from the Ethiopian community into high-tech professions (explained in detail following). Salomon stressed that it is personally important for him to support the Ethiopian community. By volunteering for Tech-Career, he stays in close contact with the organization ever since he himself graduated from the program.

Salomon complains about the lack of support from his wife, who is "not entrepreneurial" and more security oriented. The fact that they have a child is challenging according to Salomon, but they are managing the problems rather well. His parents are very proud of him, especially since an article about him and his startup has been published in a national news channel. Salomon explains that he is not sure that his parents understand what tech entrepreneurship is all about, but they are proud of him.

The Covid-19 pandemic hit Salomon and Simon during the beginning stages of the startup. Initially, they were not sure how to handle the new situation since they were in the process of elaborating the foundations of the business and developing it further. In the first weeks, the employees had to take unpaid vacation; however, they quickly realized the opportunity of working from home. So they gave up the office and managed to hold on to the clients they already had. Salomon explained, "During the first lockdown periods of the pandemic, we did not recruit new clients, but we managed to keep the business going. The period gave us some time to rethink and reconsider some of our features and concepts." Salomon maintained that new opportunities came around and that there was a dialog with the clients about needs and business processes that did not exist before.

Now the company needs to raise funding for the next stage of development and growth. Simon was the one who invested initially in the startup, and Salomon invested time, knowledge and technological skills. "I would have a really hard time would I have to do the fundraising by myself. Really a gap there—I have no connection to investors." He went on explaining that he had no family members or friends of family members who even knew about the existence of the high-tech industry, let alone having any connections to relevant networks.

Also, getting business credit at banks is a major hurdle for people from the Ethiopian community. "You know, when we [the Ethiopians] ask for credit, we are first of all turned down. The bank people often do not even look into the requests. I know that from some cousins who set up small businesses in the service sector such as shops and hairdressing studios and who had really a hard time." Although reluctantly, Salomon did imply the stigmatization of the Ethiopian community. "Setting up a business needs support—never mind a tech startup or a shop. We do not easily get this support, which is a shame." Ultimately, says Salomon, entrepreneurs have to connect with money. "That is a pretty serious hurdle."

Salomon wants to succeed as a tech entrepreneur and have an impact on the retail sector in Israel. His dream is also to integrate as many community members as possible into the high-tech scene, "not in minor roles but as managers."

Tech-Career—a Game-Changer?

Takele Mekonen is the CEO of Tech-Career, an NGO "offering young adults a game-changing opportunity to break the cycle of low-wage employment and poverty through technological training, career preparation and placement and pursue rewarding careers in high tech" (Tech-Career, 2022). Tech-Career's main vision is to create a strong group, financially speaking, in the Ethiopian community, and "shatter the glass ceiling," influencing and empowering the community through high tech.

The NGO was established by Asher Elias, who is of Ethiopian descent and was the first Ethiopian software engineer. He worked in a tech startup in Jerusalem and wondered why there were no other Ethiopians around him. After some intensive searching, he managed to detect only five Ethiopians in high tech. Importantly, all got their university degrees from a university in Addis Ababa or had a good high school diploma from there. They were not alumni of the Israeli education system. Elias himself was born in Israel; his parents came in the 1970s as refugees with no permits. He grew up facing racism and discrimination and was constantly looking for models to integrate populations from the social and geographical periphery. While establishing a tech career, Elias adopted the American boot camps model, teaching underprivileged populations how to code, which only requires learning skills, the willingness to work hard and basic English. So Asher copied this model, adapted it to the Israeli environment, found an adequate location in Kibbutz Nachshon, and recruited the first students, serving as their teacher, social entrepreneur and CEO of the NGO. Today, more than 800 graduates of Tech-Career are working in the Israeli high-tech industry, and usually, about 200 students yearly are taking the courses. The courses focus on technical skills—coding mostly—as well as integration into the industry during the course of studies.

Today the NGO is located in Lod, a city at the periphery of Tel Aviv with a low socioeconomic profile. The initiators of the NGO decided that the former location (Kibbutz Nachshon) was too remote. Lod was chosen purposefully in order to be close to Ethiopian communities. The NGO rented a building, and the students rent apartments and volunteer in schools building websites. The concept is based on a boarding school model, to enable the youngsters to study in a friendly environment, which they usually do not have at home. The payment for the course amounts to $600–$900 for the entire program, and 70–80 of the Ethiopian youngsters live together in the apartments rented by Tech-Career. About seven to eight students stay in the same apartment sleeping in bunk beds. They have keys to the venue where the courses take place so that they can practice after class hours. They are responsible for the maintenance and cleaning of the dorms and the study spaces so that they treat them as their homes. The goal of the NGO's concept is to bypass bureaucracy, bypass obstacles, minimize financial burdens and make it relatively easy for the students to concentrate on the studies. The boarding school environment gives them this opportunity.

Mekonen highlights how universities are too focused on theoretical knowledge, which serves—according to his opinion—as a discriminatory tool against disadvantaged communities. He maintains that "the academy and high-tech industry have both started to understand that introductory courses that have massive syllabi do not work anymore." He postulates that in order to get a job in the high-tech industry, one needs practice and needs to know how to code. According to his opinion, the high dropout rate of students is also due to the fact that the first years in academia are not praxis oriented and teach too many theoretical courses. The model of Tech-Career is incorporating extensive mentoring and integrating the students into the industry—opening up doors.

It is all about opening the doors—the 24/7 open lab with the computers and programs, the mentoring by people from the high-tech industry, touring the industry so that the students can see and get a feeling for themselves of how things look and work, doing a graduation project within the industry. Mekonen explains, "Those who excel with their projects always get 'snatched' by the companies, and it also opens up doors for more opportunities." In addition, Mekonen is very enthusiastic about the graduates, like Salomon, who come back to Tech-Career and teach and mentor and thereby provide role models. "They are the examples for breaking the glass ceiling, which can be a steal ceiling for Ethiopians in Israel." Mekonen believes that the NGO will make a long-lasting difference in the Ethiopian community, and although Salomon is currently the only high-tech entrepreneur of Ethiopian origin, many of the Tech-Career alumni are working in the high-tech industry by now.

Mekonen has very clear visions about the reasons of lack of integration of the members of the Ethiopian community in society in general and in the high-tech ecosystem in particular. First, he explains that tracking in the Israeli education system is a major reason for the lack of integration of members of the Ethiopian community into society in general and a major barrier for their integration into the high-tech ecosystem in particular. "Schools are automatically tracking Ethiopian students to the lower levels of mathematics. For Ethiopian pupils to enter the high levels of mathematics classes in high school is unimaginable." Many academic articles based on empirical research have been published on this problem (Knesset, 2017; Kashti, 2021), and it is related directly to the underrepresentation of Ethiopian young people in the Israeli high-tech ecosystem. A high school diploma with a good grade in the highest level of mathematics classes is a precondition for studying high-tech-related disciplines in higher education and is extremely important in order to enter military units in the field of technology. Thus, tracking in the schools in disciplines such as mathematics, physics and English has an immense impact of future opportunities. Salomon explains, "I have a friend who works as a tutor in a boarding school. One of his pupils is really gifted and able to attend the high-level math courses. But the teacher disagreed on the basis of the pupil being Ethiopian. Then the tutor goes to the teacher and tries to convince her to put the student in the high-level math class. She has been working there for 30 years, she is tired and she does not really care. But for that child, it really matters. This boy just passed his high-level math exam with a 95 grade." He also tells about his own experience when he was in school: "When I was 10 or 11 years old, they took me and the other Ethiopian kid in my class and put us in a separate English class for low achievers, without having us take a placement test. When I came home, my dad asked me, as he did every day, how school was. So I told him that the teacher took me, Hanna and Nathan out of the regular English class. The next day, my father went to the school principal and demanded to return us to our classmates. He said he would make a fuss and bring in the media. I think my father did not really know what the media was at that time, but he had a clue how to use it." Fortunately, Salomon's father was successful, but this is yet an additional and disturbing example for the phenomenon educational tracking based on being of Ethiopian origin.

Mekonen maintained that another important reason for the underrepresentation of Ethiopians in high tech is the fact that there are "no meeting points between the populations." There can be no integration between the Ethiopian and the high-tech communities since they are physically segregated. "Where should they meet?" Geographic segregation and educational tracking prevents meeting in elementary or high schools, and also, the military tech units were for a long time very exclusive. "When I graduated from high school," explains Salomon, "I didn't have anyone to tell me try to get into one of highly reputed tech military units." However, for his younger sister, things were different.

> When she went to the army, she was told, "Listen, you did five units of computer studies, so you should go to Maram" (Center of Computing

> and Information Systems). When she arrived at the recruitment center of the military, she was told she was not fit for it. She had all necessary preconditions and paperwork, test results and a recommendation from the school headmaster. Luckily, she insisted and opposed the decision and did end up in Maram.

Today she works in a high-tech company. Salomon further explains that "two or three non-Ethiopian classmates of my sister from wealthy neighborhoods got exceptional offers from the army to join Maram. She did not although her grades and quality ranking was better. How can you explain this?"

Mekonen perceives the lack of representation of entrepreneurs from the Ethiopian community also, and in addition to the reasons discussed previously as stemming from their lack of representation in military tech units, it is itself a result of a lack of encounters and integration between the Ethiopian community and stronger populations. So it is a kind of "vicious circle," he maintains.

"Most high-tech startups in Israel originated somehow in the relevant military units. The high-tech entrepreneurs 'grew up' there. It's a sort of close members' club. If you're not there, you're not there." Mekonen explains that as the CEO of Tech-Career, it is his job to approach high-tech firms as potential employers of the alumni of the courses the Ethiopian students took at Tech-Career.

> When we meet a new high-tech company, they are completely astonished—they haven't had any contact with the Ethiopian community, they didn't serve in the military with them, didn't serve in the elite units with them, not in the 8200 unit, have never met them.

Mekonen further maintains that once the contact is established, things usually work well, and the rate of placement of the course alumni in the high-tech industry is high. Tech-Career did pick up on the army matter and introduced a pilot course for young software developers before their military service. Participation in the course essentially increased the rate of young Ethiopian soldiers who pass the exam to enter the military in technological development and cybersecurity. In a way, Tech-Career compensates for the lack of opportunities young Ethiopians face in the educational system and also for the lack of the possibility their parents could pay for preparatory courses, as is common in the richer neighborhoods of Tel Aviv.

He does complain though about a lack of state support on the national level. The main problem is to break the vicious circle of "invisibility" of the community—starting in the educational framework, the army, universities and the labor market. To break this circle requires a lot of work. Unfortunately, according to Mekonen, gaps in Israel have been widening in the last years and thereby also the communication between the groups. The disadvantaged populations—like many members of the Ethiopian community—stay in the weaker neighborhoods of cities such as Ramle and Lod; those who are more successful leave the neighborhoods. Therefore, the weak neighborhoods stay isolated, and their populations do not integrate.

Consequently, Mekonen explains, for many Ethiopian youngsters, there are few employment opportunities once they leave the army after finishing the three years' compulsory service. Tech-Career therefore provides an opportunity to acquire important skills and open doors to the labor market. Salomon also understood that his opportunities after the army would have been limited if he had not either studied in academia or enrolled in professional courses. Therefore, he is still very much involved in Tech-Career and believes that he affects the community of Ethiopians. "Even before our business started to grow, some of the youngsters at Tech-Career would tell me, 'That's where I want to be,'" and he stresses the importance for Ethiopian youngsters to believe they also may be able to get there. Salomon is volunteering in the disadvantaged neighborhoods in order to recruit more youngsters who are "hanging around bored in the streets" to join Tech-Career courses. He explains that "there are big gaps as to very basic understanding of what a computer is all about" between these youngsters and the kids growing up in well-to-do households in Tel Aviv.

Tech-Career is currently funded mainly by donations from the United States, family donations (about a third of the yearly budget) and by the Israeli government. Mekonen manages to recruit about 40,000–50,000 NIS per year from the banks, and some additional money comes from a few private donors in Israel, but most of the funding comes from the USA. He explains that the NGO did not yet approach funding schemes in the UK or Germany, and since Covid-19 makes things more difficult, the main target for recruiting more funds is the Israeli government. Mekonen continues and explains that he and the fellow management people of Tech-Career have made efforts to open up an incubator for high-tech entrepreneurs inside Tech-Career but that the Israeli government is reluctant to invest in pilot projects that don not have a private donor matching. Mekonen is approaching embassies in Israel (USA, UK and Germany) and the European Union to find matching—he is optimistic and hopes to be able to eventually establish the incubator that would expand the scope of the aim of the NGO from high-tech employment only to also include high-tech entrepreneurship.

Entrepreneurial Culture

When asked about the general attitude of the Ethiopian community in Israel toward entrepreneurship, both Salomon and Mekonen agree that overall risk aversion and the search for security in terms of employment are dominant. The community, as a community, does not encourage challenges, they maintain. However, due to barriers in the labor market, in recent years, there are more attempts to set up small businesses. Salomon talks about some older women who started selling products and services from home.

The findings of the research I conducted a couple of years ago on women entrepreneurs in the formal or informal economy of Israel confirm this statement. The data that I gathered revealed that small businesses located in the informal economy of Israel were established mostly by Ethiopian women belonging to the most marginalized group of Israeli society. These women are in a triple-disadvantage trap—they are women, they belong to a migrant community and they are black (Heilbrunn, 2019). The women were not able to cope with the bureaucratic requirements and additional barriers and obstacles of the formal economy. The fact that their businesses were located in the informal sector also exposed them to a high degree of precariousness since they did not accumulate any social security rights, as is required of self-employed business owners in the formal economy of Israel since a couple of years.

"Taking a loan from the bank was not something people of the community would do some years ago," maintains Mekonen, but now things are bit different. But still, he explains, an Ethiopian mother would prefer her son to be employed rather than self-employed. Salomon, who does not like to be addressed as a representative of the Ethiopian community, maintains that "the Ethiopian mother as my mother wants stability for her child. You studied, have a degree, work in the field you studied. You go to work in the morning and come back in the afternoon and have a decent life." Salomon wants to succeed as a tech entrepreneurs and impact the retail industry. But he is the exception. He dreams to integrate as many members of the community in higher-management positions in the high-tech industry, "not only as programmers or developers but as managers." He has a social mission based on ethnic solidarity. Whether or not he will succeed remains to be seen.

Concluding Thoughts

"For us it's not a glass ceiling but a steel ceiling." David Abata is an Ethiopian lawyer and a social entrepreneur. He was interviewed for a newspaper article about the protests of the Ethiopian community in 2019 and expressed strong opinions about how the state abandoned their integration (Frankel, 2019).

The interviews with Salomon Mangiest, the only Ethiopian tech entrepreneur to be found, and Tekela Mekonen, CEO of Tech-Career, revealed many of the reasons for the lack of integration of members of the Ethiopian community in the Israeli high-tech ecosystem. Tracking and segregation in the education system lead to relatively low levels of relevant human capital influencing army and higher education participation. In addition, relative segregated housing prevent contact. The Ethiopians are a visible minority, which makes them vulnerable for discrimination on racist grounds, and majority of the community members still live in the margins of Israeli society. Since race—for a number of reasons that cannot be discussed in the framework of this book—receives a growing significance in the Israeli social realities, there is concern as to the spatial and social isolation of Ethiopian Israelis. Already in 2007, Offer (2007) warned that over time, members of the Ethiopian community in Israel will feel increasingly alienated from the mainstream society and "develop into a racially marginalized community, thus contributing to the formation of a racial cleavage in Israeli society" (Offer, 2007, p. 446).

The stories presented previously exemplify how hard Ethiopians have to work even when they get the chance to be part of Tech-Career. The students share bunk beds in dorms in Lod and do their own maintenance and cleaning. And although Mekonen explains a rationale of taking responsibility and learning to learn, it also attests to the limited resources the NGO actually has.

Tech-Career and Salomon Mangiest are promising and optimistic examples of attempts to be part of the Israeli high-tech ecosystem. Above and beyond these examples, the Ethiopian community is suffering from differential opportunity structures such as low status in education; occupation; income; spatial segregation; low cultural, social and material capital; low rates of intermarriage; and racism (Fanta-Vagenshtein & Anteby-Yemini, 2016). Like other visible minorities such as African Americans, Hispanic Americans and Asian Americans, Ethiopian Israelis also exemplify that racial minorities will demonstrate varying degrees of discouragement toward certain entrepreneurial activities compared to the dominant group (Neville et al., 2018). In the comparative analysis presented in Chapter 13 of this book, I will relate to the question whether and to which extent Ethiopians with a high-tech education should aim at becoming entrepreneurs or perhaps prefer employment in the entrepreneurial technological industry.

References

Ben-Eliezer, U. (2004). Becoming a black Jew: Cultural racism and anti-racism in contemporary Israel. *Social Identities, 10*(2), 245–266. https://doi.org/10.1080/1350463042000227371

Ben-Eliezer, U. (2008). Multicultural society and everyday cultural racism: Second generation of Ethiopian Jews in Israel's 'crisis of modernization. *Ethnic and Racial Studies, 31*(5), 935–961.

CBS. (2020). *The Ethiopian population in Israel.* Central Bureau of Statistics.

Ethiopian National Project. (2022, April 6). *Ethiopian national project.* Jewish Foundationla. www.jewishfoundationla.org/grant/ethiopian-national-project/

Fanta-Vagenshtein, Y., & Anteby-Yemini, L. (2016). Migration, gender, and mobility: Ethiopian—Israeli women's narratives of career trajectories. *African and Black Diaspora: An International Journal, 9*(2), 257–273. https://doi.org/10.1080/17528631.2015.1083185

Frankel, B. (2019, July 3). Ethiopian community protest: This is how the state abandoned the integration of community members in the Israeli economy (Hebrew). *Ynet.* Retrieved April 6, 2022, from www.ynet.co.il/articles/0,7340,L-5542534,00.html

Grotlüschen, A., Chachashvili-Bolotin, S., Heilmann, L., & Dutz, G. (2021). Beyond literacy and language provision: Socio-political participation of migrants and large language minorities in five countries from PIAAC R1/R2. *Journal of Adult and Continuing Education, 27*(1), 42–62. https://doi.org/10.1177/1477971419898491

Heilbrunn, S. (2019). Why do migrant women entrepreneurs enter the informal economy? Evidence from Israel. In R. Veland, D. Léo-Paul, R. Vanessa, & B. Abdylmenaf (Eds.), *Informal ethnic entrepreneurship* (pp. 211–223). Springer. https://doi.org/10.1007/978-3-319-99064-4_14

Heilbrunn, S., & Kushnirovich, N. (2015). Entrepreneurial finance of minority and migrant groups in Israel. In J. G. Hussain & J. M. Scott (Eds.), *Research handbook on entrepreneurial finance* (pp. 166–184). Edward Elgar Publishing. https://doi.org/10.4337/9781783478798.00016

Heilbrunn, S., & Rodriguez, I. D. (2016). Wrong-headed assumptions, unintended outcomes: The case of a migrant business support scheme in Israel. In M. Elo & L. Riddle (Eds.), *Diaspora business* (pp. 151–163). Brill. https://doi.org/10.1163/9781848884038_012

Ilan, S. (2019, February 25). CBS: The dropout rate of members of the Ethiopian community from academia—Double the average in the entire Jewish sector (Hebrew). *Calcalist*. Retrieved April 7, 2022, from www.calcalist.co.il/local/articles/0,7340,L-3757073,00.html

The Jewish Agency for Israel. (2022, April 6). *The law of return*. https://archive.jewishagency.org/first-steps/program/5131

Kaplan, S. (2010). Ethiopians immigrants in the United States and Israel: A preliminary comparison. *International Journal of Ethiopian Studies*, 71–92.

Kaplan, S., & Salamon, H. (2004). Ethiopian Jews in Israel: A part of the people. *Jews in Israel: Contemporary Social and Cultural Patterns*, 118.

Kashti, O. (2021, May 10). About 5% of 12th grade students of Ethiopian descent studied 5 units of mathematics, compared with 21% in Hebrew education (Hebrew). *Haaretz*. Retrieved April 7, 2022, from www.haaretz.co.il/news/education/.premium-1.9788374

Kimmerling, B. (2001). *The invention and decline of Israeliness*. University of California Press. https://doi.org/10.1525/9780520939301

Knesset. (2015). *Assistance to students of Ethiopian descent (Hebrew)*. Research and Information Center of the Knesset.

Knesset. (2017). *Integration of Ethiopian students in the education system (Hebrew)*. Research and Information Center of the Knesset.

Kotler, T. (2017, December 30). No banks and fees: Get to know "Cove," the alternative saving mechanism (Hebrew). *Globes*. Retrieved April 7, 2022, from www.globes.co.il/news/article.aspx?did=1001217184

Kushnirovich, N. (2015). Economic integration of immigrant entrepreneurs. *Entrepreneurial Business and Economics Review, 3*(3), 9–27. https://doi.org/10.15678/eber.2015.030302

Ministry of Aliyah and Integration. (2020, May 19). *Absorption of immigrants from Ethiopia*. www.gov.il/en/departments/general/etheopians_immigrants

Ministry of Economy and Industry. (2021). *Diversity index* (5th ed.). Ministry of Economy and Industry.

Neville, F., Forrester, J. K., O'Toole, J., & Riding, A. (2018). 'Why even bother trying?' Examining discouragement among racial-minority entrepreneurs. *Journal of Management Studies, 55*(3), 424–456. https://doi.org/10.1111/joms.12319

Offer, S. (2007). The Ethiopian community in Israel: Segregation and the creation of a racial cleavage. *Ethnic and Racial Studies, 30*(3), 461–480. https://doi.org/10.1080/01419870701217514

Saabneh, A., & Tesfai, R. (2019). Does immigrant selection policy matter? Labor market integration of Ethiopian immigrants in Israel and the United States. *Population Research and Policy Review, 40*(5), 955–985. https://doi.org/10.1007/s11113-021-09653-8

Salamon, H., Kaplan, S., & Goldberg, H. (2009). What goes around, comes around: Rotating credit associations among Ethiopian women in Israel. *African Identities*, 7(3), 399–415. https://doi.org/10.1080/14725840903031882

Semyonov, M., Raijman, R., & Maskileyson, D. (2015). Ethnicity and labor market incorporation of post-1990 immigrants in Israel. *Population Research and Policy Review, 34*(3), 331–359. https://doi.org/10.1007/s11113-014-9345-6

Shishon, U. (2015, January 20). Most Ethiopian immigrants have their own apartment—Most in neglected and poor neighborhoods (Hebrew). *Globes*. Retrieved April 6, 2022, from www.globes.co.il/news/article.aspx?did=1001001578

Shouach, A., & Ben-Eliezer, U. (2021). Intergenerational dialogue and positioning change in dealing with racism: Ethiopian Jews in Israel, thirty years after the immigration. *Identities*, 1–18. https://doi.org/10.1080/1070289x.2021.1903219

State Comptroller. (2013). *Aspects in promoting the integration of Ethiopians—Material flaws in the management of a national program (Hebrew)*. State Comptroller.

State Comptroller. (2021). *The conduct of law enforcement agencies vis-à-vis Ethiopians (Hebrew)*. State Comptroller.

Svirsky, S., Liberman, A., & Konor-Atias, E. (2019). *Proximity to poverty: Risk of poverty, chance of joining the middle class (Hebrew)*. Adva Center.

Swirski, B., & Yosef, K. (2005). *The employment situation of Ethiopian Israelis*. Adva Center.

Tech-Career. (2022, April 6). *Tech-Career*. www.tech-career.org/english

Trujillo-Pagán, N. (2019). A tale of four cities: The boundaries of blackness for Ethiopian immigrants in Washington, DC, Tel Aviv, Rome, and Melbourne. *Social Identities, 25*(1), 58–75.

Walsh, S. D., Kolobov, T., & Simanovskaya, O. (2019). What is it about perceived discrimination that can lead immigrant adolescents to alcohol use and delinquency? The mediating role of feelings of alienation. *Substance Use & Misuse, 54*(1), 65–77. https://doi.org/10.1080/10826084.2018.1495738

Yakhnich, L., Getahune, S., & Walsh, S. D. (2021). 'This identity is part of you, you cannot run away from it': Identity experiences among young Israelis of Ethiopian origin. *Journal of Ethnic and Migration Studies*, 1–19. https://doi.org/10.1080/1369183x.2020.1866514

Yaron, L. (2018, April 10). Ethiopian Israelis twice as likely to be arrested, police stats show. *Haaretz*. Retrieved April 6, 2022, from www.haaretz.com/israel-news/.premium-ethiopian-israelis-twice-as-likely-to-be-arrested-1.5431931

Yonah, Y. (2005). Israel as a multicultural democracy: Challenges and obstacles. *Israel Affairs, 11*(1), 95–116. https://doi.org/10.1080/1353712042000324472

7 Former Elites Moving Away from the Center?

Introduction

In an article published in 2016 in the daily newspaper *Haaretz*, Ofir Libstein, then vice president of the Kibbutz Industry Association, was interviewed and asked about the future of Kibbutzim. Here is what he answered: "The Kibbutz movement is moving from survival to growth, we want to contribute to the State of Israel again, we want to lead again. The Kibbutz Movement is reawakening and regaining the pride of the leadership position" (Schuster, 2016). This quote reflects the title of the chapter—Kibbutzim (plural of Kibbutz), once perceived as elite in Israeli society but then slowly drifting away from the center of power. Today, Kibbutzim, as communities and as organizations, engage in innovative entrepreneurship as do Kibbutz members as individuals. Whether these engagements will reposition Kibbutzim in the dominant center of the Israeli space remains to be seen.

Kibbutzim in Israel represent a particular type of collective community, with the first Kibbutz already established in 1910. Traditional Kibbutz communities were characterized by four main principles: voluntariness, public ownership of means of production, direct democracy and rotation of office holders in society and economy, and last but not least, the Marxian principle of equality '"rom each according to his ability to each according to his needs." These Kibbutzim exemplified the community organization as an extended household characterized by symbiosis of family and firm, or alternatively as a firm-cum-family organization (Barkai, 1977). Maintenance of members, rather than cash surplus, was their primary objective, and economic success was not a value in itself but a means to realize social goals and values (Heilbrunn, 2005).

Kibbutzim were perceived and perceived themselves as pioneers, fulfilling a vital role in settling and working the land, outlining the country's borders, absorbing immigration and fostering industrial development (Halamish, 2010). Therefore, Kibbutzim were supported by the Labor Party–led political leadership as perfect organizational and social forms of communities for settling the land and establishing a just society. The government invested substantial financial resources and thereby enabled their fast growth

DOI: 10.4324/9781003091042-8

and development. Consequently, Kibbutz leadership accumulated extensive political influence and monopoly power within the agricultural market (Rosenthal & Eiges, 2014). Along with political changes occurring in Israel, from a government led for years by the socialist-collectivistic-oriented Labor Party to a liberal-national Likud Party in 1977, Kibbutz privileges were challenged by socially and economically deprived groups demanding equal opportunities and the capitalization of perceptions of deprivation by the Likud government. Therefore, Kibbutzim lost the government's ideological and financial support, the latter of which caused massive debt accumulation of many Kibbutzim, pushing them into deep economic and financial crisis and even threat of bankruptcy. Following Manos and Gidron (2021), economic and political pressures, in addition to demographic social challenges, were the cause for massive reforms of the Kibbutz movement and the emergence of structural and cultural arrangements aimed at sustaining economic stability first and foremost.

Indeed, Kibbutzim have undergone fundamental changes in the last twenty years, and eventually, two organizational cultures ensued, the traditional egalitarian Kibbutzim and the changing Kibbutz, moving toward wage differentiation and a more individualistic organizational culture (Dar, 2002; Ben-Rafael, 2011; Palgi & Reinharz, 2014; Leviatan, 2013; Russell et al., 2010). Once defined as agricultural communities, farming is no longer the main economic branch, but it is still an important part of Kibbutz economy, especially as technological innovations of farming were developed in many Kibbutzim. Today, the 277 Kibbutzim account for around 50% of Israeli's agriculture sector and for about 10% of the traditional industry. In fact, some Kibbutzim have come up with such successful technologies and products that their members—once socialist farmers—have become quite wealthy. In the remaining part of this chapter, I will briefly discuss the relevant elements of the move from collectivism to individualism. I will then review briefly some literature on Kibbutz entrepreneurship and then move to high-tech entrepreneurship in Kibbutzim today.

From Collectivism to Individualism

The changes that underwent the Kibbutz movement relevant in the framework of this book concern the domains of work and livelihood.[1] Therefore, I will briefly describe the developments that took place in these domains during the last decades.

The traditional classical Kibbutz model was based on the ideology of self-labor. Kibbutz members were the major workforce, and wage labor from outside the Kibbutz was minimized as much as possible.[2] Work was looked upon as an integral element of the very existence and community building of the Kibbutz, and members would work according to the needs of the Kibbutz. They would work in regular jobs in one of the branches over a certain period of time, sometimes replace each other and sporadically work in a different job if there was shortage or any requirement for another reason. Nonskilled work in Kibbutz service branches such as laundry, dining hall, night watches, etc. was assigned to all members based on a rotation system. Following Palgi and her colleagues (2020), this transition between a variety of jobs reinforced not only the mutual evaluation of all types of work but also the skill set of Kibbutz members.

Structure-wise, Kibbutzim appointed a work coordinator (also a rotating job to be conducted for a year or two) who synchronized and matched the needs of the branches and specific tasks with members' availability, taking into consideration also individual wishes, well-being and conveniences. Overall, though, decisions concerning work were the responsibility of the Kibbutz work committee and not of the individual. In accordance with the branches existing in each Kibbutz, supplementary work needed to uphold the smooth functioning of the economic and service branches of the Kibbutz were also regulated and coordinated by the person in charge, and overall Kibbutz members had a rather high workload in terms of weekly hours.

Alongside the gradual development and expansion of industrial plants in the Kibbutzim during the 1960s and 1970s (Don, 2020; Bar-El et al., 2019; Cohen, 2020), members started to specialize professionally, some of them being sent to universities in order to receive necessary higher education, for example, in the field if engineering. This professionalization introduced a new perspective to the rotation-based former principle, and members started to demand the right to make independent decisions about their work assignments. A division of labor emerged, differentiating between members due to their employment status, influenced by stratifying factors such as professionalism and knowledge qualification and accreditation. Notions of rank, prestige and desirability emerged in the discourse of the work realm of the Kibbutz and indicated changes as to the basic assumptions of the traditional Kibbutz.

As a result of these developments, vertical rotation in work positions almost stopped, and any rotation that remained was mainly horizontal (Palgi, 1998; Topel & Ben-Rafael, 2006; Topel, 2017). Parallel to these internal developments also, the arrangement as to Kibbutz members working outside the Kibbutz changed over the years. In the past, the amount and period of members who were "allowed" to work outside the Kibbutz was rigorously limited and subordinated to the rotation principle. Those working outside the Kibbutz (often for the Kibbutz movement or in other Kibbutzim) were demanded to "give" a year of work to the Kibbutz every three years. Nonetheless, the number of members working outside the Kibbutz increased progressively throughout the years, reinforcing the normative changes in the realm of work.

At the beginning of the twenty-first century, the transition of many Kibbutz communities to the so-called "renewed Kibbutz" model occurred, which has been extensively discussed in the academic literature (Russell et al., 2013; Dar & Getz, 2020; Palgi et al., 2020; Ben-Rafael & Topel,

2020). Unquestionable is the impact of the mid-1980s financial crisis, which met many Kibbutzim in an extremely difficult economic situation. Following Abramitzky (2018), the crisis led to an internal deligitimization of the Kibbutz model in and for itself, and only rich Kibbutzim could retain egalitarian sharing without losing their most skilled members, thanks to high levels of redistribution.

I will not discuss the overall reasons, forms and consequences of these structural changes in the framework of this chapter but rather relate only to the relevant aspects for explaining the emergence of entrepreneurship in the Kibbutz. The main transformation—from a profoundly egalitarian society into a market society—impacted the realm of work since it diminished the principle of equal reward for all types of work and introduced a linkage between members' contribution and the monetary compensation received in return. It is this change that divides the Kibbutzim into two types of organizations: those retaining the more traditional egalitarian culture and those moving toward a new differential and more individualistic culture and privatization (Abramitzky, 2018; Russell et al., 2010; Ben-Rafael & Topel, 2020). Notwithstanding community taxes that exist to different degrees in all Kibbutzim today, an unequal salary system was adopted by most as a result of the previously explained developments. Accordingly, today, in about 80% of the Kibbutzim, members receive salaries according to their work's market value, therefore generating inequality and reorganization of the structure and administration of work in the Kibbutz (Palgi et al., 2020).

Summing up this part, whereas in the traditional Kibbutz, the normative orientation was collectivistic and work was valued in itself and for itself, in the new Kibbutz, the orientation is more individualistic, and work is perceived primarily in terms of livelihood and income, as a means of making a living and promoting individual and familial economic well-being inside or outside the Kibbutz. Accordingly, the responsibility for livelihood moved from the collective to the individual and family (Abramitzky, 2018).

Kibbutz Entrepreneurship

Independent individual entrepreneurship was originally antithetical to the collective ideology of the early Kibbutz, and the earliest examples of Kibbutz entrepreneurship appear in the 1980s as documented in my doctoral thesis (Heilbrunn, 1999). Once the phenomenon of Kibbutz entrepreneurship began, it has spread relatively quickly among Kibbutz households, and there has been a significant increase in the intensity of entrepreneurial activities (Heilbrunn et al., 2017). Having a closer look at the academic literature reveals that in the 1990s, entrepreneurship in Kibbutz communities implied personal, not community, activities aimed at initiation and the implementation of new business ventures within a Kibbutz (Samuel & Heilbrunn, 2001). These semi-autonomous ventures were aimed at increasing the income of the Kibbutz and, at the same time, allow for the realization of personal desires and preferences among members, who were often unsatisfied with their places of work (Dar, 2002). Heilbrunn (2010a) found an overall increase in the number of entrepreneurial ventures per Kibbutz from 1997 to 2004. These ventures were predominately in service sectors and based upon existing infrastructure, thus utilizing local resources. Thus, Kibbutz entrepreneurship originally emerged from the bottom up, utilizing the availability of economic and communal resources in terms of the organizational platforms and facilities of the existing within the Kibbutzim. Against this background, entrepreneurship of varying types and scopes emerged, initiated by Kibbutz members, newcomers with entrepreneurial abilities, or external entrepreneurs who rented premises in the Kibbutz (Schnell et al., 2017).

Since most of the Kibbutzim are located in the geographic periphery of Israel, the spatial context is of importance in order to understand the development of entrepreneurship. Vitman-Schorr (2012) examined the scope and character of nonagricultural Kibbutz businesses and found that geographic location is a crucial factor in the Kibbutz economy, affecting the scope and nature of nonagricultural businesses. She found that Kibbutzim geographically close to Tel Aviv had more and different business ventures than those in peripheral areas. In other words, her research revealed that geographic location impacts business opportunities, and the characteristics of the regional contexts shape the scope and types of Kibbutz entrepreneurship (Vitman-Schorr, 2012). Empirical data of Sofer and Saada (2017) revealed that women are overrepresented in Kibbutz entrepreneurship, mainly due to the increase in demand for personal and business services, which are more often provided by women than men. In addition, because of the changing structure of the Kibbutz, women entered the general labor market at an older age and with limited experience. Therefore, they had fewer employment alternatives within and outside the Kibbutz, and the establishment of a small business presented an opportunity for generating income (Doron, 2011).

A number of studies conducted by myself and colleagues investigated the impact of the institutional environment. The fact that Israeli Kibbutz cooperative communities have undergone fundamental changes in the last twenty years provides a fascinating research arena not generally afforded in the social sciences. As explained previously, within this arena, two types of organizational cultures have emerged: the traditional egalitarian Kibbutzim and the changing Kibbutz, moving toward wage differentiation and a more individualistic organizational culture. This structural and cultural dichotomy has provided laboratory-like conditions that enabled the investigating of the impact of different institutional environments as antecedents of entrepreneurial intentions (Heilbrunn et al., 2017), opportunity recognition (Heilbrunn, 2010b), motivations to set up a business (Heilbrunn, 2010b), entrepreneurial intensity (Heilbrunn, 2008) and entrepreneurial risk-taking (Davidovitch et al., 2009).

Over the years, Kibbutz institutions acknowledge the need for economic change, also in order to foster entrepreneurial activities in the Kibbutz movement in general and in individual Kibbutzim in particular. A number of programs were established to train potential entrepreneurs, initiated and supported by the Union of Kibbutz Industries. Also, local municipalities established programs and assigned office holders to foster entrepreneurial development in rural areas in general and in Kibbutzim in particular. Summing up and following Sofer and Saada (2017), the development of small entrepreneurship in Kibbutz communities has increased over the years, with businesses initiated by Kibbutz members, those who live in the expansion neighborhoods,[3] in collective and "new" Kibbutzim and by men and women alike.

High-Tech Entrepreneurship in Kibbutzim Today

In line with developments of technological advancement in Israel as presented in former chapters of this book, some Kibbutzim also founded very successful companies in the fields of technology and manufacturing (Paz-Frankel, 2016). Nowadays, there are 270 Kibbutzim, which together account for more than half of Israel's agricultural sector and about 9% of the traditional industry.

Maybe the most outstanding example is Neftafim of Kibbutz Magal. In the 1960s, the Israeli engineer and inventor Simcha Blass invented the drip irrigation, till today manufactured by Kibbutz Netafim. Drip irrigation is an important invention since it supplies plants with the optimal amount of water and therefore is applied globally, also and especially in regions with water shortage. Netafim opened production sites also in Kibbutz Magal and Kibbutz Yiftah and gradually expanded to additional manufacturing plants in 11 countries all over the world, with representative offices in over a hundred countries. The company has around 5,000 employees and is today ranked 59 among the 100 highest-ranking Israeli companies, as evaluated by Duns Premium Israel's 100 Leading Enterprises (Duns 100, 2022). Another example is Caesarstone of Kibbutz Sdot Yam. The economy of Kibbutz Sdot Yam located at the shores of the Mediterranean was originally based on fishery until the factory Caesarstone was established in 1987. It designs, engineers and manufactures stone surfaces, with highly functional quartz products of modern designs. Recently, the products have become popular among fashionable interior designers on the USA luxury residential market, making Sdot Yam one of the richest Kibbutzim in Israel. Caesarstone is evaluated at more than $1 billion. Like most Kibbutzim, Kibbutz Shamir, located in the Galilee, also traditionally relied exclusively on agriculture until in 1972, Shamir Optical, a company manufacturing lenses for eyeglasses, was established. Today the company is a major player in the multibillion-dollar industry due to the innovative technology. The Maytronics company produces robots that clean swimming pools and belongs to Kibbutz Yisreel.

The company is worth more than $1 billion. There are many more examples of successful plants, some of them still in sole ownership of the Kibbutz and others sharing ownership with national and/or international partners. Accordingly and naturally, also in the field of high tech, there was much development in the Kibbutz movement during the last years.

The tech incubator Hamadgera is an interesting example of a Kibbutz initiative. It is accommodated in a building that used to be the poultry hatchery of Kibbutz Revivim located in the Negev Desert in the south of Israel (Goldenberg, 2015). In an interview they gave to a national newspaper in 2016, the founders and first managers of Hamagdera, Lion David from Kibbutz Revivim and Elad Yeori from Kibbutz Erez, explain that they named the incubator Hamadgera, which is Hebrew for "incubator" and connotes poultry. This was one of the first incubators to be set up by a Kibbutz. Kibbutz Revivim has been manufacturing plastic components for the automobile industry for years and therefore ample business experience. The accelerator, which was established in 2016, is unique in a couple of ways. First, it is located within a Kibbutz; second, it is relatively far away from Tel Aviv, the high-tech center of Israel; third and partly because of its distance, it offers the innovative idea of an incubator hotel. Incubator participants are offered three months' free residential accommodation on the Kibbutz, including all services needed such as dining room, laundry, etc. Capitalizing on the fact that there is nothing to do in the middle of the desert, the incubator-hotel idea was aimed at providing an environment of talking innovation. The concept aimed at startups in the early stage of development in the field of internet and mobile data, with entrepreneurs receiving assistance and supervision in design and user-experience services, help in building business models and marketing strategy by mentors and experts. Microsoft and WIX partner with the Kibbutz, providing service packages and professional support to entrepreneurs. For the Kibbutz management, opening the accelerator was a natural step, and the manager maintained that

> the contribution of traditional Kibbutz industry to the Israeli economy is well known and it is one of the engines of growth of the country's economy. From our point of view this is a synergistic step for the Kibbutz's operations that are intrinsically entrepreneurial.
>
> (Goldenberg, 2015)

Also at the level of the Kibbutz movement, efforts have been made to foster the high-tech sector by supporting NGOs promoting technical skills and attract technological companies to open up branches in Kibbutzim. Indeed, in 2016 SouthUp was established in order to advance innovation in the so-called Gaza envelope area hosting many Kibbutzim (SouthUp, 2022). The incubator has so far recruited over $5 million and investment from private investors, from some Kibbutzim located in the area and from the Jewish Federation of San Diego. The incubator provides mentors and advisers to the startups with a variety of expertise. Startups taking part in the incubator include: Youtiligent, a big data solution the IoT field; MindTension, psychologic technology to measure ADHD; Bright AGTECH, a precision treatment platform for fields crops; Growee, a fully automated hydroponic system that allows to grow any plant using sensing and AI technologies; Kasko2go, in the insurance industry, offers an accurate price solution based on the personal needs and profile of the costumers.

SouthUp partners with an accelerator affiliated with the Kamea Fund, an Industries Association movement of the Kibbutzim,[4] and proposes a unique program for startups that is relevant to Kibbutz industries and has the potential to grow on Kibbutzim. This accelerator aims at entrepreneurs who are in advanced stages of their businesses and provides funding, professional and business knowledge, network connections with relevant industry representatives and more. Finally, SouthUp was involved in the establishment of an investment fund under the auspices of the Kibbutz Industries Association, which assists Kibbutzim in investing in cutting-edge startup companies. Other than "regular" incubators in Israel, SouthUp requires participating startups to operate from the incubator for two years and remain in the Sha'ar Hanegev region for five years. Since the geographical area is defined as periphery, the Innovation Authority provides startups with larger grants than in the center. SouthUp maintains close ties with local educational institutes at the high school and academic level, in accordance with its mission to provide opportunities to the youth of its environment. Kibbutzim are increasingly investing in the development of the technology and innovation sector, and SouthUp and Hamadgera are definitely excellent examples for this trend.

Another somehow different trend can be observed similarly in the southern periphery of Israel and also within the Kibbutz movement—but with a very different outlook. Entrepreneurship in Kibbutz Lotan, Ketura and Samar is all about sustainability. In these Kibbutzi, innovative community patterns emerged along with the implementation of a sustainable lifestyle, reminders to a certain extent of the traditional Kibbutz. For these Kibbutzim, entrepreneurship and innovation is not aimed at making profit but at spreading an ecological mission of preserving the environment. They align with the fact that Israel has signed the international Paris accord but have nationally not done enough to meet the aims at reducing emissions. Therefore, the mission-oriented entrepreneurship of these Kibbutzim focuses on environmental and economic sustainability.

Kibbutz Ketura, which is located in the Arava region just north of Eilat, exemplifies the way of life of traditional Kibbutzim. Ketura has about 400 members, many of whom are immigrants from Australia and New Zealand, North America, Europe and Latin America. The Kibbutz was established in 1973, and in 2007, some of its members founded a company that develops and manufactures photovoltaic fields (Arava Power). The company launched the first commercial solar field in 2011 and in 2013 started to plan and develop a national infrastructure project in order to ensure the supply 20MW of power from solar energy. In parallel, in 1998 the Kibbutz set up a partnership with a company from the UK and jointly established Algatechnologies, a biotechnology company that commercially cultivates microalgae. Already in 2003, the company set up a first plant in Ketora, employing Kibbutz members and people from the environment. The latter is extremely valuable since employment opportunities in the area are scarce.

Lastly, the Arava Institute for Environmental Studies, which is a leading environmental studies and research institute in the Middle East, is located in Kibbutz Ketora. The institute offers accredited academic programs, research centers and international cooperation initiatives focusing on a range of environmental concerns and challenges. The institute also reflects a political mission in line with the Kibbutz, hosting students from Jordan, the Westbank, Israel and around the world. The idea of the institute is to combine high-quality academic and professional environmental education provided by leading professionals and getting acquainted with fellow students. The institute's mission maintains that nature knows no political borders.

Not far away from Ketora is Kibbutz Samar, which is populated by about 60 families. The Kibbutz was created in 1976 and, like Ketora, is maintaining the traditional collective structure and culture. The Kibbutz's economy is largely based on agriculture, with 250 cows producing milk and the largest organic date groves in Israel. Additionally, the agricultural branch of Samar produces Paspalum grass in an ecological manner, avoiding the use of pesticides. Bryan Medwed was probably the most famous Kibbutz member of Samar, a musician and environmental entrepreneur who created the Sunergy project in order to provide energy autarchy to the Kibbutz. The prototype that was developed by Medwed is still in use in the field of renewable energy.

Further up north from Ketora and Samar is Kibbutz Lotan, which was established in 1983. The Kibbutz specializes in environmental education and developed the Center for Creative Ecology, which offers various programs based on sustainability values. Importantly, the center initiated sustainability certifications for branches such as construction, organic farming and sustainable community development. This entrepreneurial undertaking is aimed at promoting sustainable regulation, and courses offered at the center cumulate in certificates for its participants. Kibbutz members developed a biodiverse market-garden model that is environment friendly and sells its products in the immediate environment. Like Samar and Ketora, Lotan also holds on to the idea of a collectivist lifestyle, with members receiving rewards for their work on an equal basis.

Innovative entrepreneurship in agrotechnology or agriculture though does not happen only in traditional, collectivistic Kibbutzim but also in the "new Kibbutzim." A good example is Kibbutz Ramot Menashe, where entrepreneurial technologically innovative development occurred in the dairy farm during Covid-19 pandemic. In order to increase the efficiency of production and reduce labor costs, the manager of the dairy farm is experimenting with new technologies. In an interview to the dairyglobal.net, he explains,

> Right now we are using automatic manure scrapers in the barns, convertible roofs, ventilation and fogging systems to control the wheatear, and a milk taxi for feeding calves. The farm is covered with cameras and most of the systems can be controlled from afar online. The main technological support is given by Allflex as we use their neck collars on every cow from the age of 12 months to identify them.
>
> (McCullough, 2021)

Furthermore, milk quantity and quality, daily activity and health of the cows are monitored. Ramot Menashe is expanding this concept to other Kibbutzim in the neighboring area, thereby bundling resources. This outlook and practice illustrates the particularities of the Kibbutz movement till today: in spite of the fact that each Kibbutz is nowadays economically autonomous and has adopted its own structural configuration, there is still a high degree of solidarity between them.

Over the last decades, innovative technologies have mainly been developed and applied in the southern parts of Israel, which has transformed thereby into an agricultural region with high-tech and drip-irrigated farms. Kibbutzim were the major driving force for this development. Innovation and entrepreneurship in the field of agrotechnology in Israel is largely dominated by Kibbutzim and their members or those who have grown up on a Kibbutz. In line with the historical developments presented at the beginning of this chapter, Kibbutzim are attempting to reclaim their positioning in Israeli society. Their expertise in agrotechnology is definitely acknowledged, although it takes place in the northern and southern periphery. While some individual Kibbutz members are involved in the ecosystem in Tel Aviv, many are struggling to be part of it, mostly due to the fact that they are living in the geographic periphery. In the following, I present the stories of three Kibbutz high-tech entrepreneurs illustrating what one of them named the "privileged periphery."

Nitai Klein was born in Kibbutz Gareen[5] and later moved to the Golan Heights with his wife and children. There the family set up a tourism business venture, providing mainly Israeli tourists with cottage-like accommodations primarily at weekends and during holidays. He collaborated with other owners of holiday units in the township to bundle resources, resulting finally in a group of a few friends who all served in the 8200 unit (high-profile, high-tech unit of the Israeli army) and who then decided to start a high-tech project around collaborative holiday-unit ownership and operation. Nitai did not elaborate on the future of this undertaking but eventually sold his units and left the township in the Golan Heights. At the time of the interview, the family had moved to Kibbutz Dar, located at the eastern shore of the Sea of Galilee. Nitai does not provide much information on the nature of his new startup but reveals that it is in the field of agrotechnology, has to do with robotics and is focused on cows. He targets overseas markets for future products since the Israeli market does not have the necessary volume due to its small size. Klein started working on his current startup five years ago, and it has been his full-time job for the last two years. He sees the north of Israel as particularly suitable for aggrotech, and he calls it the Silicon Valley of this domain and explains that the agricultural settlements in the periphery in general and in the northern periphery in particular have a good reputation for agrotechnology businesses. However, he maintains, "Once you switch to more advanced technology, then it's the center."

Klein explains that he had a couple of meetings with investors and funds and that he managed to establish personal contacts, mostly with Kibbutz members or "ex" Kibbutz members. Being himself a Kibbutz member was an advantage, he thinks. "Also, those contacts who are actually living in Tel Aviv feel comfortable with me because we share the same upbringing." Without this network of people, "nothing would have happened." "Everything is personal in the end." In the world of agriculture, it is pretty easy to find one another. "It's easier to associate with people like us." Klein met with investors who were either ex members of the Kibbutz movement or in contact with them. His networking was based on this domain.

> As people with no tech background, it's hard for them to approach big organizations as they feel uncomfortable with them, so they stay in their comfort zone. If you try to connect with someone you don't feel comfortable with, you have to have "a lot of charisma."

The CEO of Klein's company was also born in a Kibbutz and has a PhD in sciences; he has worked in high-tech companies. So this somehow bridges the gap, but he is still not at the heart of the corporate world and does not have enough business background.

Klein maintains that there are differences between tech startups in the periphery (social and geographical) and center in terms of access to resources and education. People who haven't been to units like 8200 and live in the periphery are disadvantaged, he believes. Still, he describes the Kibbutz environment in the North as a "privileged periphery," where it's easier to make connections. "Distance and time are difficulties," he maintains. "The closer to the center you are, the more available human resources you have." "Our tech guy lives in Tel Aviv, the natural place for him to live. He has to drive two hours of traffic to get to the office. We can't work otherwise."

As they were trying to grow their business, there was a point where Nitai needed to understand the world of finance, which was located in the center. "However, if you 'have what it takes,' you'll always find a way to turn the disadvantages into advantages." He explains that there are advantages being an entrepreneur in a peripheral city since it is much easier to stand out.

There is less competition that in Tel Aviv. Klein believes that the government's support systems and grants to foster the creation of ecosystems in the periphery are important but do not replace the necessity of the entrepreneur having the required qualities. Nevertheless, he claims, "Support systems in the periphery do make it easier for entrepreneurs."

Concerning the personal and community support system, he explains that the most difficult challenge is the family, more specifically to "get the wife on board." "If you're going to not make money for a long time and even invest some, you'll need consent." Nitai believes that the family's support is crucial in order to proceed with establishing a business. Asked about the Kibbutz environment, he explains, "People are not really interested in what you are doing, also since we do not involve the Kibbutz in our financial matters." Klein also believes that there is no prestige in what he is doing but also maintains that in general status symbols do not really exist in Kibbutzim. "Everyone rides the same bicycle, wears what's comfortable, and no one cares about the car you drive." That is one reason they went there, he continues; they wanted a place "where the material things don't matter." He perceives the Kibbutz that way. When speaking about his former startup—the nature of which is not explained—Nitai claims that he lacked a support system to pilot his initial idea. Local municipality people initially invited him and his partners to pilot the project with them but ended up withdrawing their initial investment of 1 million NIS and instead chose to invest in a safer project entailing fewer risks. He then had another idea but realized it was impossible to start "from scratch." "It was then that I realized that there is no 'co-system' to pilot the startup that I envisioned. It is not Tel Aviv or Silicon Valley." By that time, Nitai and his family were already settled in Kibbutz Dar, and he repeated, "I moved there with my wife and children for good reasons." Therefore, when having to decide whether to relocate to Tel Aviv in order to pilot that additional technological business idea he had in mind, he chose to stay in Kibbutz Dar. "I decided that money and professional success weren't worth giving it up the life we have here." With his current startup, the lack of financial support also proved to have certain advantages: "We worked for a long time for very little money but an abundance of freedom." A main lesson he learned was that when meeting investors, it is necessary to be clear about the project's aim and explain in a few minutes the problem your business idea addresses.

> We had the time to think it through as we were working it out. This opportunity to not commit, to do the necessary pivoting while advancing, to move freely in the realm of the unknown, is great . . . You understand better what you're doing and why.

Klein was always an independent. However, he explains, "Running a startup is not running a business. It is about team work, and the key is in finding the right people." Nitai mentions having preferred to be employed from a stress and risk point of view but describes entrepreneurship as not having been a "choice," meaning something he was meant to do.

> I didn't choose to become a high-tech entrepreneur. There was no choice. It's like marrying my wife. I just knew it. If I did have a choice, I would have opted to be an employee, but I can't not be an entrepreneur. Once you're "touched" by the virus, you have no choice.

In a continuous elaboration, he maintains that being an entrepreneur is by and large not something adequate for everyone since there is no stability.

> The most important thing is to be aloof (detached). If you don't become aloof to the good and the bad, you won't survive. It's a roller coaster. We don't do it for the celebrations or for the stress. We do it because we have fun. It's not for the "peaks" or for the mental torture that is stress. Keep the resilience. Nurture the aloofness.

Nitai Klein describes the impact of the Covid-19 pandemic as positive, mainly because Zoom meetings have become legitimate and save a lot of time. Meetings in the center usually took up a day's work, with long hours of driving. Because of the Zoom option, there is much improvement as to the downsides of being far away from the center. When asked about the future of his business, Nitai relates to the life cycle of agriculture in general and explains,

> We are maturing slowly, accompanied by a change of state of mind. This here is not cyber but agriculture. Things go much slower. The life cycle of the cow is long: 9-month pregnancy, 2 years growing and 4–10 years' productive activity. We take it step by step.

Jordan Grossman lives on Kibbutz Falau, is married and a father of five. He was born in Jerusalem but grew up in another Kibbutz since the age of six. Today he is 49 and his family was recently accepted as Kibbutz members in Falau. Jordan describes himself as a bored high school pupil, but once he decided to join the army to serve in an elite combat unit, he finished his high school exams, necessary to get accepted into the unit of his choice. He served nine years in that combat intelligence unit of the Israeli army and explains, "I discovered the entrepreneur in me while serving in these systems, looking for challenges, finding solutions." After his service, he travelled the world with his wife (with whom he's been married now for 29 years). He started studying philosophy and physics at the university but left after three months to focus on his business. He was already an entrepreneur at that point, developing patents and ideas. He mostly worked on technological projects, with the exception of an "attraction park for extreme sport," in which he was involved until 2001. He has been working as self-employed most of his career, and in 2011, he decided to engage in an entrepreneurial project that would bring him back to the northern region of Israel. He engaged in a social entrepreneurship project and initiated an NGO for the advancement of healthy lifestyle. The aim of the NGO was to spread health education all over Israel: "Just like there is no financial education in Israel, there's no health education here. Especially during Covid, it became clear how important that is, so we started to render and spread important information to the public." Grossman tells about his entrepreneurial career and upholds that he always had an agenda to provide solutions for national problems and to create employment and innovation to the periphery. "I am very much into biotech, food tech. I met people from a superfood company and was amazed" Currently Grossman is working on a superfood product. He believes that superfood will be much appreciated and used in the close future, especially if it is organic.

> We are now developing the freshest, high-quality product for your kitchen. It's a three-part system, relatively small, a 20- to 30-liter aquarium that grows microseaweed in a controlled environment. We don't clean up the "green." You push a button, and the system takes a percentage of the fluids, filters it, takes out a paste with almost no flavour, and you get 10–20 grams of a superfood, rich in vitamins, minerals, antioxidants.

He explains that the product is very healthy and that for a family of seven, like his own, the system can generate daily doses for everyone. Grossman initially developed this system for space travel, which was of major interest for him.

> When you send people this far, think of a unit that needs to provide for itself for a long time. With this system, you get the maximum for the minimum. It has a very low carbon footprint. It even consumes CO_2.

Grossman thus started the idea of this project for space and then took it down to our kitchens. He and his partners are now in the process of fundraising, but they are still at the seed stage where fundraising is slow. Additionally, Covid-19 caused him to invest in the social entrepreneurship project, which he felt was essential for people to "survive the crisis." That somehow slowed down the work of the superfood project. Jordan is the main operator of the superfood project but has a partner who is a chemist and some more people on board, but "in the end it's me—I am 100% into the project—and only me." Grossman clarifies that he is not yet making a living from the project and that he had initiated only a few fundraising rounds. He received an "impact fund," which he used to register patents and started to approach investors in the USA in 2019. But "things are proceeding slowly," he explains. Grossmann made clear that he never had an employment problem.

> An entrepreneur is someone who will always find something. When you're independent, you need to hunt . . . because unlike the situation of an employee, revenues are not guaranteed if you are an entrepreneur. You need to either have large oxygen tanks or know how to breath underwater. You need to be an entrepreneur in your soul.

Grossman does not miss a high-tech network—"this circle of people you know and meet in the social media and at all kinds of related events and also at the so-called 'happy hour scene' of the known bars and restaurants." Although he is involved in an innovation center close to Kibbutz Falau, he is not really using the services provided there. Jordan explains that he has his own network, friends in the USA and in Tel Aviv whom he can always call. When asked about challenges of the periphery, he maintains that he was very much aware of them when working on a former project: "Bringing someone over to estimate electricity issues took a year and a half. Getting the paperwork for the ministry of agriculture ready took another year." For the present project, he is not ready for the beta site fundraising stage and is somehow reluctant to move forward. He is still missing expertise and engaged partners.

When asked about social security and the financial future of his family, Grossman explains that his parents would feel more peace and quiet if he would have remained in the army and become a lieutenant colonel and become an entrepreneur only after his retirement since that would have secured him a solid pension. He admits that his choices are difficult to deal with for his immediate environment and that his social entrepreneurship project took a lot of time away from work and home and implied heavy spending. His parents would prefer him to take more care of himself and his family and his two brothers, and three sisters look at him with critique. "My wife is putting up with me, and since she is an educational instructor, she kind of shares my sense of mission regarding social entrepreneurship." Concerning the Kibbutz, Grossman maintains that he receives ample recognition. People know that he came to the Kibbutz and started his company there out of Zionist ideology—he was offered to start the company abroad but refused and explains,

> If an investor came tomorrow and offered me to do a startup in Tel-Aviv, I'd offer him to do it here first, close to the Kibbutz. If the investor would insist that it has to be in a skyscraper in Tel-Aviv, today I won't veto it.

He has a lot of interaction with the Kibbutz and believes that it is important to involve and employ people from the Kibbutz. He is also very involved in the municipality and in other business circles of the area. He implies that it is not always easy. "For one of my former projects, I hired someone with a PhD, and she even moved to Kibbutz Falau." But eventually she left the Kibbutz because she felt she had no social life; she could not get used to the Kibbutz life in the periphery. Grossman claims that the lack of efficient public transport is a major issue. "In the end it comes down to logistics, doesn't it?" But then he says, "The people I meet in this area want to live in the periphery. They are more mature. Some of them have experienced 'high-tech' like me but are willing to make compromises for the style of life they have here." Grossman was involved in setting up an innovation center in a nearby development town, trying to develop a high-tech network. But it was difficult and challenging and demanded much time and work.

Grossman admits that he lacks business knowledge and therefore often chose partners who could complement that. For one of his projects, he asked his father-in-law to serve as CEO in order to boost the business angle, financial management and prestige for the investors. Basically, he set up a team to compensate for his lack of knowledge and took charge of the logistics. He admits that this is not an easy way to work and promote an innovative technological idea.

Personally, he describes himself as a serial entrepreneur:

> When fundraising for one of the projects, I kept telling my wife, "Just a little while longer, believe me, believe me," and when you have a company and a salary is coming in, all is fine. But when the company doesn't happen, all is not fine. I continue climbing even when there are falls. I don't look for the parachute before jumping. I jump and know there will be parachutes to hold on to along the way.

The pandemic affected the startup since he did not advance with it. Jordan said he took more responsibilities at home and was very engaged in the social enterprise and neglected the startup for some time. He can't see the future without success—he sees his product on Mars 12 years from now. He doesn't let himself think otherwise:

> Like an Olympic athlete that competes for gold, no matter the statistics, gold is his goal, and this is my goal, and this is what I see. Every time I lose sight of this, I need to calibrate myself and remind myself that this can provide sustainable nutrition to settlers on Mars, for example. This might sound far-fetched to you, but just as they need rockets, they need food. So this needs constant work.

Ziv Barkan lives on Kibbutz Ela. He is married and has three children. He has lived most of his life in peripheral areas. Since the year 2002, Ziv has been engaged in entrepreneurship. He studied physics at the Technion and got an MA in financial mathematics at Bar-Ilan University. Until recently, he was a PhD candidate in medicine, specializing in artificial intelligence at the Technion. He was involved in a number of entrepreneurial projects such as smart homes (before the concept even existed), smart supermarket carts and Bluetooth navigation, for example. He managed to raise money via the Chief Scientist Office along with his brother and another friend to work on smart nametags that cannot be forged and whose authenticity can be verified easily. Part of that project included helping students find employment by being trained by expert engineers while employed at their startup. He invested some money of his own in the startup, but after six months, they ran out of funds since they did not manage to move beyond the first stage and go to market. After a few more projects, he embarked on a venture combining AI and medicine. This project has been running for four years, beginning just before he joined the faculty of medicine. At the same time, he was employed for almost seven years in a startup specializing in identifying fake medication by using infrared light and controlling for packaging processes in pharma. He also worked in large security companies, which he defines as half startups since he dealt with innovative products that he accompanied through production. Ziv was always employed parallel to be engaging in entrepreneurship. In the present startup, Ziv is the technological expert and he is working next to a marketing specialist and two medical doctors. Their idea has been "well channelled," and today the product is before the fundraising stage. The team is in the last stages of preparing a presentation for investors and are about to start meeting potential ones for the seed stage. Ziv Barkan explains that for him the combination of being employed and work on his own startup is most suitable. "I love identifying and solving problems. I learned that in the army where I was a technician in charge of identifying problems and finding a solution." He continues and explains, "Actually, if that is your issue—to always find solutions—it doesn't matter if you're an employee or an entrepreneur." He maintains that he pursued this attitude while being employed and as an entrepreneur and is content as long as he can solve problems.

Barkan maintains further that the network in the Kibbutz and the ecosystem in the northern region of Israel is less developed and that there are barely any meetings and events. He has some connections with an "innovation center" in his area but does not really utilize the opportunities proposed by the center. He knows about state funds that support entrepreneurship for minorities but about state funds targeting the periphery. There are some accelerators, but

> to say the least, that's not an investment you would want to get into if you have the choice. Equity compared to utility is perceived as not being the best investment. The amount they invest is mostly insufficient, especially compared to what it takes today.

In other words, Barkan does not want to share the equity with an accelerator even more so since the accelerators do not raise enough money, according to his opinion. He explains further that the recruitment of high-quality employees is an issue in the periphery.

> Even taking into consideration Covid and the possibility it brought about to work from home, it is difficult to grow from a seven-person company to one which employs forty people in the periphery, especially in the field of software and algorithms, where competition to find high-quality employers is so high.

Ziv explains that there is an inherent conflict of interest—a need to pay good salaries since employees have to travel up north at least part of the week and the fact that salaries are generally lower in the North in comparison to the center. He explains why it is much easier to join the ecosystem in Tel Aviv:

> The facilities for entrepreneurship in the periphery are problematic since patent editors, business plan consultants, marketing people, etc. are difficult to find. All these kind of things sound simple but are essential in a less startup-oriented environment.

Barkan and his wife decided to live in the northern periphery of Israel. Therefore, recently they applied for Kibbutz membership. They decided to live on the Kibbutz since they like the lifestyle. His family is financially independent, and the Kibbutz has no influence on his work as an entrepreneur. Kibbutz Ela is a "renewed Kibbutz"; therefore, employment and income is the solely family's responsibility. Because Ziv was employed for many years, social security, pension and health insurance issues of the family are well taken care of. He explains that he always had his family's support when launching entrepreneurial ideas, especially from his wife, but then, "Let's put it in context, though. That was as long income was relatively guaranteed. Except for those six months when I didn't work, I do entrepreneurship on my own time while being employed full-time." He does imply that otherwise, his wife might have been less understanding.

Barkan continually develops his business knowledge and explains that the fundraising process with the head of the Scientist Office provided him with the majority of business knowledge. In addition, working with big companies provided him with important experience and expertise in the world of technological startups such as marketing himself and his ideas. "Ultimately, these are just people you need to convince."

The choice of living in a Kibbutz in the periphery and set up his company here is motivated by two interests—he upholds

> a selfish one and a 'zionist' one." "I think the periphery is important. I like the Kibbutz and I want to be part of developing the North, and

> I also hope that it will bring about tax benefits and make it worth the choice.

His partners are from Tel-Aviv and Haifa, which requires thinking where to locate the office. They still did not resolve the question and are considering opening two offices.

Since the sector of the startup is located in the field of medicine and hospitals continue to work throughout the pandemic, Covid-19 did not really impact their development. They postponed a meeting or two due to quarantines. Finally he maintains that

> as an entrepreneur, you're always optimistic, aren't you? The business will make a breakthrough, revolutionize the health domain, generate unicorns. On a certain level, the concept we bring onto the market—if it does work out—will generate a huge change in the health system. But the burden of the proof is on us. We have an agreement with a medical institution to start working even before fundraising. We already did a lot of surveying work to understand what's needed and where the important blind spots are.

Conclusion

In this chapter, I discussed technological entrepreneurship and its development in the Kibbutz movement in Israel. At the beginning of the chapter, I outlined the historical development of the Kibbutzim and elaborated on their attempt and to "move back toward the center," reclaiming their position as a major player in the Israeli society and economy. The proclamation of Udi Orenstein, director general of the Kibbutz Industries Association and a member of Kibbutz Revivim, quoted in a newspaper article in 2016, exemplifies this tendency: "The statement we're making isn't that high-tech is better than low-tech industry which is better than farming. It is that Israel is a technology nation and it isn't reasonable for Kibbutzim not to have high-tech" (Schuster, 2016). In fact, it might seem rather surprising that communities originally based off the foundations of socialism are seeking to be involved in an industry that is very much based on neoliberal capitalist principles, as has been explained in former chapters of this book. However, at the same time, Kibbutzim, once themselves perceived as an entrepreneurial innovative undertakings, adapted to changes in their political and economic environment and succeeded in utilizing resources to engage in innovative technologies. The engagement of Kibbutzim in sustainable agricultural products and ecological education and research, as described in the first part of this chapter, exemplify an attempt to combine ideological outlook with community patterns and economic success. The fact that the Kibbutz industry successfully integrated in Israeli economy provides a basis for technological entrepreneurship to flourish within the Kibbutz movement.

Nonetheless, a main takeaway from the interviews conducted with the high-tech entrepreneurs can probably be summed up in the concept "privileged periphery," coined by one the interview partners. For historical reasons, many Kibbutzim are located in the periphery and are suffering from lack of professional networks and the availability of a sufficient amount of qualified employees. Most certainly, there is a problem with investors, and one of the interview partners explained,

> I certainly experienced investors raising eyebrows about being located in the North, and even investors who have openly objected to it. . .. Some of them also objected to my age and the fact that I am a Kibbutz member.

Following Klein, especially in the field of agrotechnology, Kibbutzim can compensate for the backdrops of the geographical periphery, demanding increased travel time to connect with the ecosystem at the center of Israel with the presence of a unique pool of highly skilled individuals (in terms of education and high-tech military background) suitable specifically for agrotechnology. Here Kibbutz upbringing serves as an advantage in forming financial and human connections amongst ex-Kibbutz members, even when they have left the Kibbutz, as Nitai explained.

The material analyzed in this chapter suggests differences between the northern and southern periphery as to the involvement of the Kibbutzim in attempts to establish ecosystems, with SouthUp exemplifying the advantage of community cooperation and solidarity, attempting to compensate for the distance to and lack of services provided by the technological ecosystem of Tel Aviv. SouthUp is a project example that demonstrates to a large extent the adaptability of the collective principles, which were at the root of the Kibbutz movement. SouthUp is actively in search of organizations and individuals to support high tech in the southern periphery, with a focus on Kibbutzim.

Overall, the story of high-tech innovation and development in the Kibbutz movement is one of success and marks the entry of Kibbutz industry into the world of entrepreneurship and venture capital.

In November 2021, Israeli climate-tech companies teamed up with neighbors in the Arab world, working together to meet the threat that climate change will render much of the region uninhabitable. The meeting took place in Kibbutz Hatzerim (Rubin & Hendrix, 2021). It could mark an additional new development with Kibbutz innovations in the fields of solar, energy and food tech in combination with their political outlook, promoting peace and normalization with neighboring countries, always characteristic for the Kibbutz movement. It may create a path for Kibbutzim to reshape and reclaim their place at the center.

Notes

1. This part of the chapter leans on Palgi et al. (2020).
2. Often it was only a medical doctor and sometimes nurses who were hired from outside the Kibbutz to work in the clinic, and mostly they would then live on the Kibbutz.

3. "Expansion neighborhoods," called "harjava" in Hebrew, are new neighborhoods built in the surroundings of the original neighborhoods of Kibbutzim and villages ("Moshavim") in order to allow new members, mainly young families, to join and expand the community.
4. The Industries Association of the Kibbutzim coordinates the overall procurement activities and financing of raw materials for the kibbutz industries. In addition, the group coordinates designated independent corporations that provide strategic advantages in many different areas: energy, infrastructure and construction, equipment and vehicles, communications, import and export, insurance and financial services, financing and management of foreign exchange transactions, tourism, trade and consumerism.
5. The names of the Kibbutzim were changed for the part of the interviews in order to guarantee the anonymity of the interview partners.

References

Abramitzky, R. (2018). *The mystery of the Kibbutz*. Princeton University Press. https://doi.org/10.1515/9781400888153

Bar-El, R., Nesher, A., Schwartz, M., & Finkel, R. (2019). *Rural industrialization in Israel*. Routledge. https://doi.org/10.4324/9780429305092

Barkai, H. (1977). *Growth patterns of the Kibbutz economy*. North-Holland.

Ben-Rafael, E. (2011). André Gerrits, the myth of Jewish communism: A historical interpretation. *International Sociology Review of Books*, *26*(2), 260–263. https://doi.org/10.1177/02685809110260021302

Ben-Rafael, E., & Topel, M. (2020). The new Kibbutz economy. In E. Ben-Rafael & O. Shemer (Eds.), *The metamorphosis of the Kibbutz* (Vol. 49, pp. 27–42). Brill. https://doi.org/10.1163/9789004439955_004

Cohen, E. (2020). The structural transformation of the Kibbutz 1. In E. Krausz & D. David Glanz (Eds.), *The sociology of the Kibbutz* (pp. 75–114). Routledge. https://doi.org/10.4324/9781003070283-7

Dar, Y. (2002). Communality, rationalization and distributive justice: Changing evaluation of work in the Israeli kibbutz. *International Sociology*, *17*(1), 91–111. https://doi.org/10.1177/0268580902017001005

Dar, Y., & Getz, S. (2020). Changes in organizational behaviour—From traditional to renewed Kibbutzim. In E. Ben-Rafael & O. Shemer (Eds.), *In the metamorphosis of the Kibbutz* (Vol. 49, pp. 43–65). Brill. https://doi.org/10.1163/9789004439955_005

Davidovitch, L., Heilbrunn, S., & Polovin, A. (2009). Impact of change in the Kibbutz on risk taking of entrepreneurs. *Journal of Rural Cooperation*, *37*(2), 242–260.

Don, Y. (2020). Industrialization in advanced rural communities: The Israeli Kibbutz. In E. Krausz & D. Glanz (Eds.), *The sociology of the Kibbutz* (pp. 371–384). Routledge. https://doi.org/10.4324/9781003070283

Doron, H. (2011). Varying spousal relations in the Kibbutz and the Moshav. In M. Palgi & S Reinharz (Eds.), *One hundred years of kibbutz life: A century of crises and reinvention* (pp. 101–121). Transactions. https://doi.org/10.4324/9781315125749-9

Duns 100. (2022, March 28). *Israels 100 leading enterprises: 2021*. www.duns100.co.il/rating/Duns_Premium/Israels_100_Leading_Enterprises/2021

Goldenberg, R. (2015, July 26). Revivim opens first Kibbutz startup accelerator. *Globes*. Retrieved March 28, 2022, from https://en.globes.co.il/en/article-revivim-opens-first-kibbutz-startup-accelerator-1001055858

Halamish, A. (2010). *The Kibbutz at one hundred*. University of Marryland.

Heilbrunn, S. (1999). *Corporate entrepreneurship in the Kibbutz movement. 250* (Unpublished doctoral dissertation). University of Haifa.

Heilbrunn, S. (2005). The impact of organizational change on entrepreneurship in community settings. *Journal of Small Business and Enterprise Development, 12*(3), 422–436. https://doi.org/10.1108/14626000510612321

Heilbrunn, S. (2008). Factors influencing entrepreneurial intensity in communities. *Enterprising Communities: People and Places in the Global Economy, 2*(1), 37–51. https://doi.org/10.1108/17506200810861249

Heilbrunn, S. (2010a). Entrepreneurial opportunities in changing communities. *Journal of Small Business and Enterprise Development, 17*(2), 247–259. https://doi.org/10.1108/14626001011041247

Heilbrunn, S. (2010b). Communities in processes of change: Comparative differences in entrepreneurial motivation. *International Journal of Innovation and Regional Development, 2*(2), 36–49. https://doi.org/10.1504/ijird.2010.029853

Heilbrunn, S., Itzkovitch, Y., & Weinberg, C. (2017). Perceived feasibility and desirability of entrepreneurship in institutional contexts in transition. *Entrepreneurship Research Journal,* 7(4), 1–10. https://doi.org/10.1515/erj-2016-0046

Leviatan, U. (2013). Overcoming drawbacks of hierarchy: Examples from Kibbutz communities. *Jurnalul Practicilor Comunitare Pozitive, 13*(1), 147–164.

Manos, R., & Gidron, B. (2021). The new social economy in Israel: From the Kibbutz ideal to social-tech entrepreneurship. In B. Gidron & A. Domaradzka (Eds.), *The new social and impact economy* (pp. 95–118). Springer. https://doi.org/10.1007/978-3-030-68295-8_5

McCullough, C. (2021, March 18). Israel: Even Covid-19 won't deter this dairy farm's plans. *Dairy Global.* Retrieved March 28, 2022, from www.dairyglobal.net/world-of-dairy/farm-visits/israel-even-covid-19-wont-deter-this-dairy-farms-plans/

Palgi, M. (1998). Organization in Kibbutz industry. In U. Leviatan, U. Leviatan, H. Oliver, & J. Quarter (Eds.), *Crisis in the Israeli Kibbutz: Meeting the challenge of changing times* (pp. 41–56). Praeger Publishers.

Palgi, M., & Reinharz, S. (2014). *One hundred years of Kibbutz life: A century of crises and reinvention.* Transaction Publishers. https://doi.org/10.4324/9781315125749

Palgi, M., Sofer, M., & Heilbrunn, S. (2020). From work to income: Employment and entrepreneurship. In E. Ben-Rafael & O. Shemer (Eds.), *The metamorphosis of the Kibbutz* (Vol. 49, pp. 66–84). Brill. https://doi.org/10.1163/9789004439955_006

Paz-Frankel, E. (2016, March 28). From agricultural to high-tech: Meet five Kibbutzim that became global powerhouses. *Nocamels—Israeli Innovation News.* Retrieved March 28, 2022, from https://nocamels.com/2016/03/successful-israeli-kibbutzim-industry-technology/

Rosenthal, G., & Eiges, H. (2014). Agricultural cooperatives in Israel. *Journal of Rural Cooperation, 42*(1), 1–29. 10.22004/ag.econ.249704

Rubin, S., & Hendrix, S. (2021, November 15). Israeli climete-tech firms team up with former foes to face the threat of rapid worming. *The Jerusalm Post.* Retrieved March 28, 2022, from www.washingtonpost.com/world/middle_east/israel-uae-climate-technology/2021/11/13/49ce774c-4000-11ec-9404-50a28a88b9cd_story.html

Russell, R., Hanneman, R., & Getz, S. (2010). Antecedents and consequences of the adoption of market-based compensation by Israeli Kibbutzim. In T. Eriksson (Ed.), *Advances in the economic analysis of participatory & labor-managed firms* (Vol. 11, pp. 225–246). Doi:10.1108/S0885-3339(2010)11

Russell, R., Hanneman, R., & Getz, S. (2013). *The renewal of the Kibbutz: From reform to transformation.* Rutgers University Press.

Samuel, Y., & Heilbrunn, S. (2001). Entrepreneurship in the Kibbutz setting: Towards a classification of new business ventures. *Journal of Rural Corporation, 29*(1), 47–62.

Schnell, I., Greenberg, Z., Arnon, S., & Shamai, S. (2017). Entrepreneurship in the periphery and local growth: The case of northern Israel. *GeoJournal, 82*(2), 217–229. https://doi.org/10.1007/s10708-015-9676-9

Schuster, R. (2016, March 3). Kibbutzim in the new millennium: Cultivating high-tech. *Haaretz*. Retrieved March 28, 2022, from www.haaretz.com/israel-news/kibbutz-joins-startup-nation-with-tech-incubator-1.5412185

Sofer, M., & Saada, M. T. (2017). Entrepreneurship of women in the rural space in Israel: Catalysts and obstacles to enterprise development. *Sociologia Ruralis, 57*, 769–790. https://doi.org/10.1111/soru.12125

SouthUp. (2022, March 28). *SouthUp*. https://southup.org/

Topel, M. (2017). Kibbutz: Transformation, technocracy, and gender. In S. Fogiel-Bijaoui & R. Sharaby (Eds.), *Dynamics of gender borders: Women in Israel's cooperative settlements* (pp. 295–314). De Gruyter Oldenbourg: Magnes. https://doi.org/10.1515/9783110466218-013

Topel, M., & Ben-Rafael, E. (2006). Technocratic leadership in the Kibbutz. *Horizons in Geography, 66*, 28–43.

Vitman-Schorr, A. (2012). From equality to diversity—Non-agricultural businesses in Kibbutzim (Hebrew). *Horizons in Geography*, 75–90.

8 Where You Come from Is Important

Migrant Entrepreneurship Between the Center and the Periphery

Introduction

Since 2014 the European Commission and OECD issues yearly the Missing Entrepreneurs report. These reports examine how targeted public policies can help to overcome obstacles to startups, entrepreneurship and self-employment. Groups included in the reports are youth, women, seniors, unemployed and, always, also immigrants. The reports assume that these groups are underrepresented among the self-employed and entrepreneurs because of a number of factors, including institutional barriers, discrimination related to difficulties to access resources, skill gaps, etc.

This chapter is about the technological entrepreneurship of people who immigrated from the Former Soviet Union to Israel or who are second-generation immigrants from the Former Soviet Union. Israel has always received Jewish immigrants since the country applies an ethnonational, repatriate, government-led, assimilationist policy toward Jewish immigrants—the Law of Return (Ram, 1995; Shafir & Peled, 2019). Israel's immigration policy is selective and characterized by a guest-worker approach toward non-Jewish foreigners working in the country (many of them in agriculture, construction and healthcare) and exclusive toward asylum seekers and refugees (Elias & Kemp, 2010), meaning that no naturalization track exists for these people. Over the years, Israel's immigration scenery is getting more similar to other post-industrial countries, and the waves of immigrants from the former Soviet Union and Ethiopia have raised questions of race and religion not formerly addressed (Yonah, 2005). Desille (2019, 2020) states that Israel's immigration policy increasingly follows a neoliberal logic.

Since 1990, approximately 1.241 million immigrants came to Israel. Eighty percent arrived from the countries of the Former Soviet Union (hereafter FSU); 8% came from Europe and the Americas, mostly from the USA, France, United Kingdom and Argentina; and 6% from Africa, mostly from Ethiopia (Youngmann & Kushnirovich, 2020). The wave of former Soviet Union immigrants account for about 13.5% of the Israeli population today, and they have established a large group with widespread presence in all sectors of the Israeli society. Former research has revealed that this group

DOI: 10.4324/9781003091042-9

of immigrants had a stronger motivation to leave the Soviet Union than to settle in Israel and an even stronger desire to preserve their Russian cultural uniqueness while integrating into Israeli society (Cohen & Haberfeld, 2007). The overwhelming majority of FSU migrants are secular, and a large number of them are well-educated professionals. Some researchers maintain that FSU immigrants to Israel formed a separate ethnic subgroup, inclined to hold on to their culture and identity of origin (Kushnirovich, 2015; Heilbrunn et al., 2016).

In the following parts of this chapter, I will discuss the particularities of the immigrants from the Former Soviet Union and present some data on their engagement in entrepreneurship in general and in high-tech entrepreneurship in particular. The last part of the chapter contains two case studies of high-tech entrepreneurs from the Former Soviet Union in the northern periphery of Israel and the findings of desk research on the presence of successful high-tech entrepreneurs who are immigrants from the Former Soviet Union.

Immigration from the Former Soviet Union (FSU)

The immigration to Israel from countries of the Former Soviet Union has been widely studied in the academic literature. It is beyond the scope of this chapter to relate to the academic discourse on the subject; therefore, I will only explain briefly the major important trends relevant for understanding the patterns of involvement of the group in the high-tech industry.

Since the early 1990s, over 1 million of the 1.5 million Jews who lived in the former Soviet Union have immigrated to Israel. During the first decades, a number of difficulties challenged social and labor market integration, such as Israel's neoliberal path to reduce the public sector, high costs of housing and increasing privatization and outsourcing. Many FSU immigrants were not able to translate their educational achievements into adequate positions on the labor market and could not afford to acquire flats. The integration of immigrant children into the Israeli educational framework was challenging, and the older population experienced health and welfare problems for rather a long time after arrival in Israel. Those who were not Jewish according to Jewish Law of Return experienced additional difficulties of their own (Konstantinov, 2015). The majority of immigrants from the Former Soviet Union came from urban environments (Remennick, 2002) with an academic background. Apparently, and mainly due to their numbers, they culturally influenced Israeli society (Konstantinov, 2015). Research shows that the so-called 1.5 generation FSU immigrants are inclined to hold on to a Russian identity, concerning language, communication and cultural consumption (Raijman & Geffen, 2018). In a recent study, Remennick and Prashizky (2019) found that many underwent a process of transformation into a multicultural identity while, at the same time, developing high levels of Hebrew proficiency, a defined Israeli identity and strong Israeli social networks (Amit, 2018). Raijman and Geffen (2018, p. 152) applied the acculturation approach and explained the integration process of FSU immigrants to Israel as segmented.

> In some lifestyle domains (such as work and study), they are well adjusted and play by local rules, while in more private domains, they mostly stay firmly plugged into their co-ethnic circle, which serves as the key provider of social support and a safety net. Intimate relationships, both romantic and friendly, arise mostly within immigrant social networks.

This finding is highly consistent with previous studies on FSU immigrants in Israel, stressing that they are inclined to maintain and even cherish the culture and identity of their origin (Horowitz, 2005; Remennick, 2004; Remennick & Prashizky, 2019; Kushnirovich, 2007). In fact, it is obvious that three decades after the arrival of this wave of immigrants, there is still a distinct Russian-speaking community, culturally and politically, and, unlike other groups, not aimed at "absorption" into the Israeli mainstream (Galili, 2020).

Their rather low sense of belonging to Israeli society in combination with a comparatively low degree of life satisfaction (in comparison to other immigrants) can be explained by challenges to translate their relatively high human capital into assets in the Israeli labor market (Amit, 2010). In addition, they maintain rather exclusive co-ethnic circles and treasure feelings of superiority over Israeli culture (Remennick, 2003).

In sum, immigrants from the Former Soviet Union to Israel establish a large and distinct group characterized by high levels of human capital. Since they arrived under the Law of Return, they were eligible to state scheme aims and social and labor market integration. A large amount of empirical research exists as to the processes of integration of these immigrants into Israeli society, their impact on Israeli society and the particularities of the second generation of Israel's Russian-speaking community. Empirical research shows that the first generation of immigrants who arrived during the 1990s managed to integrate into the labor market but often far beyond their academic credentials and experience. Members of this group often suffered from professional-status loss. Those who arrived in Israel as children and those who are Israeli-born are well integrated into the labor market. Overall, their integration process has been called "segmented" due to a discrepancy between labor market integration and social integration, as explained previously.

Entrepreneurship of Immigrants from the Former Soviet Union in Israel

Unfortunately, the OECD 2019 Missing Entrepreneurs report (OECD & European Union, 2019) does not depict any updated data about immigrant entrepreneurship in Israel. Nonetheless, there are a number of empirical studies on the subject, although they are mostly based on data prior to 2010.[1] Overall, the studies show that much of the entrepreneurship of immigrants from the Former Soviet Union in Israel was very much located with a co-ethnic enclave, meaning that more than 50% of clients, suppliers and business contacts of these businesses were from the Former Soviet Union. Consequently, unlike for other immigrant groups in Israel, Hebrew proficiency contributed significantly less to the income of the business since it remains within a Russian-speaking realm. The study of Heilbrunn and Kushnirovich (2015) further revealed that for businesses initiated by entrepreneurs from the Former Soviet Union, the number of years of living in Israel contributes significantly more to income than for other groups of immigrants. Following Kushnirovich (2015), this goes along with the theory of co-ethnic dealing, according to which immigrant entrepreneurs tend to engage in co-ethnic business activity. Since the group of immigrants from the Former Soviet Union in Israel is extremely large, dealing within the co-ethnic community and utilizing co-ethnic networks and resources contributed to the entrepreneurs' income, whereas co-ethnic dealing in small communities constitutes a problem for scaling up a business. A study focusing on the challenge of financing business establishments revealed that in Israel, problems accessing bank loans are affected by the affiliation of entrepreneurs to ethnic and immigrant groups, and minority entrepreneurs are disadvantaged when seeking bank loans. The data revealed that FSU immigrants, in spite of their relatively high human capital, nevertheless received significantly less bank loans than the majority of entrepreneurs (Heilbrunn & Kushnirovich, 2015). Finally, in a study based on data collected in 2007, Kushnirovich and colleagues investigated the question of risk aversion among immigrant entrepreneurs and found that FSU immigrants were no less entrepreneurial than native-born individuals but were influenced by a high level of apparent immigration-related risks that they had experienced in the past (Kushnirovich, 2007). The authors found that the high level of risks that immigrants from the former Soviet Union had experienced in the past, particularly the risks of immigration, directed them to be less likely to take more risks, thus decreasing their risk-taking propensity and, therefore, their perceived feasibility of establishing businesses. Risk aversion can also depend on the immigrant experience when a successful experience would make immigrants less risk-averse. Overall, the academic literature shows a high labor market integration of FSU immigrants in Israel, with self-employment very much concentrated around small businesses within the ethnic enclave.

Policies to Foster Entrepreneurship Among Immigrants

In a study on Israeli governmental policy to foster entrepreneurship conducted in 2008, Kushnirovich and Heilbrunn found a variety of policies offered through a widespread and developed system of public agencies (Kushnirovich & Heilbrunn, 2008). The core characteristic of the Israeli support system was the close cooperation between government institutions and associations. One of the first initiatives to foster immigrant entrepreneurship was opening the Centers for the Advancement of Entrepreneurship (MATI in Hebrew), established in the 1990s by the Innovation Authority. Some of these centers were dedicated to potential immigrant entrepreneurs, and the initiative was realized by a cooperation of the Ministry of Immigrant Absorption. Immigrant entrepreneurs in Israel could receive training and advice, financial support, and support for creating and maintaining business links. Financial support consists of designated loan on favorable terms. Non-financial support includes businesses courses, workshops and panels, courses on language proficiency, guidelines and brochures, guidance, business mentoring, assistance with the development of business plans, business clubs, the establishment of business networks and support in market analyses. The available existing support for immigrant entrepreneurs in Israel was diverse and extensive. However, most of the policy mechanisms reflected mainly the supply side of immigrant entrepreneurship: focusing upon the increase of availability of resources. There was less concern with the demand side—actively enhancing opportunities for entrepreneurship—by creating new markets or reducing rules regulating business startup and activities (Heilbrunn & Kushnirovich, 2008a).

Additionally, the Office of the Chief Scientist initiated an incubator program targeting engineers and scientists from the Former Soviet Union. The idea was to assist immigrants with innovative ideas of export potential through the first-round investments in product development, detect strategic partners and raise venture capital on the market. The government set up 24 technological incubators throughout the country with an investment of more than $30 million. The main idea was to provide funding at the very early stage of technological innovation, at Which risk and uncertainty are high and private funding is difficult to achieve. Immigrants with adequate technological education and experience were the target population of these incubators, especially since it was rightly assumed that they did not have the social capital to raise funding. Each of the 24 incubators hosted about ten projects at the same time, providing incubator conditions for the first two or three years of the project development. The average budget of the projects was around $450,000 per year, with 85% provided by the Israeli government. In addition to government funds, the incubator management provided grants financed by venture capital firms or the incubator in exchange for equity shares (Lopez-Carlos & Mia, 2006).

Technological incubators still exist in Israel but no longer target immigrant entrepreneurs in particular. Today, the Innovation Authority (Dyduch & Olszewska, 2018) is the main institutional player, which was established by merging the Office of the Chief Scientist of the Ministry of Economy and MATIMOP—the Israeli Industry Center for R & D. Also, the Ministry of

Science, Technology and Space; the Ministry of Finance; and finally, the Planning and Budgeting Committee of the Council for Higher Education, which promotes and allocates funding for scientific research in the academic sector, are involved in the development and implementation of innovation policy (Dyduch & Olszewska, 2018).[2]

Israel's policy to support the absorption of Jewish immigrants in general is based on Zionist ideology. In the case of the big wave of immigrants from the Former Soviet Union in the early 1990s, it also leaned on the assumption that the influx of highly educated people would pay off economically, an expectation that was largely met considering the high-tech boom of the late 1990s (Remennick, 2013). The incubator program was one of these policies, aimed at promoting scientific innovation and patents by immigrant scientists and engineers.

High-Tech Entrepreneurs from the FSU Community in Israel

High-tech immigrant entrepreneurs—like all immigrant entrepreneurs—have to deal with what Gurău et al. (2020) call liability of foreignness. The authors review the existing models of immigrant entrepreneurship and identify three key elements that conceptually structure these models: individual resources, socioeconomic embeddedness in various social and/or professional networks and specific entrepreneurial behavior/attitude (Gurău et al., 2020, p. 705). Analyzing case studies with a narrative approach, the authors suggest that different types of immigrant entrepreneurs utilize different strategies to overcome the liability of foreignness. Thus, following Gurău et al. (2020), the hazards and manifestations of liability of foreignness for knowledge-based entrepreneurs are unfamiliarity and relation due to lack of status, nonacceptance of academic and professional certifications, and lack of knowledge of professional networks and markets. Knowledge-based entrepreneurs can overcome the liability of foreignness by employing cultural and symbolic capital in terms of education related achievements to develop economic and social capital and achieve self-employment (individual resources). They can surpass foreignness by promoting embeddedness into global, knowledge-based, educational and professional networks (socioeconomic embeddedness). Finally, knowledge-based entrepreneurs can deal with foreignness due to a habitus grounded in personal abilities and skills, hard work and strategic pragmatism. After presenting two case studies of immigrant high-tech entrepreneurship in the northern periphery of Israel and the findings of a desk research on successful immigrant high-tech entrepreneurs, I will evaluate the acquired data in light of the previously presented model of liability of foreignness.

Alexander Solcin was born in the former Soviet Union in 1983, and his parents immigrated in 1991 to Israel. He did his four-year army service in the 8200 intelligence unit and received a BSc in biomedical engineering and an MSc in machine engineering, both at the Technion. Together with his wife and children, Solcin lives in the city of Haifa. Since 2009, he has worked as a development engineer in biomed and biotech projects. In 2017, he initiated a startup on an advanced solution for obesity and diabetes. He is the CEO of the startup until today. In 2018, he signed a contract with an Israeli-based company that specializes in the production of extracts for flavor and fragrance. In 2019, he started to work within the framework of an accelerator, which was established following a tender procedure with the Israeli Innovation Authority. Solcin explains that this accelerator is not an ordinary one but rather an "innovation lab." "It allows for more flexibility," he explains, "especially during the first stages of development." The accelerator is located in a rural vicinity in the north of Israel.

Alexander explains that before being engaged in the startup, he held a very convenient and lucrative job. He never had problems finding employment due to his technological background, which also helped him in the process of initiating and promoting the product idea. "It's very hard to start a tech startup without having experience and knowledge," he maintains.

Asked about the high-tech network in his environment, Alexander maintained that the ecosystem in the North is not ripe enough; the investors focus very much on Tel Aviv and its surroundings, and he perceives this as a problem. "There are many good, smart and talented people up North, but the lack of a professional and financial network is definitely a problem." Interestingly, he tried to activate his personal 8200 army unit network to recruit capital for the seed stage but did not succeed. "It may be because this [the 8200] unit is less focused on biotech." Recruiting resources is definitely a major problem—according to Solcin—since hedge funds have usually no branches in the northern periphery of Israel. "One meeting in Tel Aviv may consume an entire day of work, and that is a problem."

When asked about the support he receives from his immediate environment, he explains, "The salary I make as an entrepreneur is the bare minimum for my wife to not kick me out." Entrepreneurs in Israel work really hard. "It's sometimes insane, constantly juggling lack of budget." His parents and friends support his idea, but following his evaluation, in their eyes, it is not a glorious status symbol. "It's not like my parents say to their friends, 'One of my sons is a doctor, and the other founded a startup.'" Solcin clarified that he had very little business knowledge prior to setting up the startup and perceived this as a major problem. He remembered a situation in which the team of the innovation lab asked him to present a forecast of losses and gains and future net sales. "And you nod while not understanding a damn thing." So I talked to people with the right knowledge who were willing to help him. He maintains that he still does not have the ability to speak in front of an audience in English: "Ninety percent of investors don't care about results and business models. They care about the story you tell them, whether it connects to a unicorn or not." He continues, "They don't teach public speaking at the Technion."

He reported that he invested much time and effort to learn these skills. Solcin states very clearly that he would discourage anyone from undertaking entrepreneurship.

> If you're not addicted, don't do it. It has an impact on your health, social life, on your relationship. I don't have anything else in my life than the startup. My friends are tired of me talking about it. I don't work out. I sleep five hours a night. It sounds rosy, but it's very, very hard. As an entrepreneur, you do the most annoying things no one else wants to do. The paperwork, accounting, the downsides, especially during the first years, are very significant.

He addresses people from the former Soviet Union by postulating, "Don't be afraid to break the glass ceiling. That's what I'm doing right now, and I hope I can keep doing it for those that come after me." And he continues somewhat angrily:

> Of course there is an impact of being an immigrant from the former Soviet Union, most definitely, no question about it. There is a glass ceiling, annoying and low, faced by immigrants from the Soviet Union who came during the 1990s. I can't understand why. I've been here for over 30 years. The home I live in right now is traditional Jewish. I'm Israeli and Zionist. How many ministers do we have that came from the former Soviet Union? Liberman [the politician] doesn't exactly count because he came in the 1970s, even though he still has the accent.

Here, Solcin is referring to the fact that the highest-ranking Israeli politician—Avigdor Liberman—belonged to a much-smaller wave of Former Soviet Union immigrants who arrived in Israel during the seventies. This wave contained about 150,000 people and was catalyzed by a surge of Zionism and facilitated by strong political pressure from Western countries on the USSR government (Remennick, 2015). Solcin stresses the fact that even after many years in Israel, Liberman still has a Russian accent, identifying him as an immigrant. Alexander Solcin continues and explains what he perceives as obstacles of an immigrant entrepreneur: "I see this in the attitudes of investors. They categorize you through a stereotype: you need to be an engineer, sit in the lab and make us rich. That's the 'rubric' many people put me in."

Alexander Solcin describes his family situation as rather complex and personal. He mentions that he is afraid of the future since he does not have pension savings like other people his age; security is low and precarity high. However, he continues, "I am like an addict. I'm hooked and can't stop. I wish I could work for intel, make three times the salary I make today, have a nine-to-five workday. I just simply can't."

In his life, there is no balance, although he makes sure to spend at least three afternoons a week with his children, after that working late into the night. "An entrepreneur always juggles at least 15 balls, and this is a ball I won't drop." During the pandemic, Solcin had problems to keep up the fundraising, and this he evaluates as a major threat to his startup. Since they have only proceeded to the stage of animal research, it is still a long way ahead for the startup. Solcin is carefully optimistic that his idea will make it.

Nora Weinberg, born in Ukraine, immigrated to Israel at the age of 32 in 1990 together with her husband and two daughters, then 13 and 11 years old. At the time of the interview, Nora was 62. She describes her family as a rather "atypical," with both her and her husband having good professions.

> My husband is a math and physics professor, and I'm a chemist. We had work experience, no young children, and no handicapped elderly parents. Therefore, we were pretty free to choose where to live and what to do. It went smoothly.

When arriving in Israel, they lived in Netanya for the first six months and then resettled to Barkai Yaacob, where they were able to access state-owned housing. Nora maintains that the lack of information was the biggest problem during the absorption process in Israel. "We could have joined a Kibbutz program, but we didn't know about it. We could have had Amidar[3] apartment six months earlier, but we did not know how." After moving to Barkai, Yaacob Weinberg took a teacher's course at a nearby college and started to work at a camping facility in the environment. She was in charge of the toilets and showers, and in parallel, she and her husband were washing dishes at the only event venue in town. She then started teaching chemistry and biochemistry at a nursing school in Netanya:

> That was pretty coincidental. I helped someone there study, and eventually the girls I helped study passed all the exams, and the rest of the group failed. So I was invited there and asked to teach biochemistry to groups of Russian speakers.

She took the teaching job and traveled to Netanya once a week. In parallel, she started to work at an innovation and technological hub (Lagim) near Barkai Yaacob. Nora explains that also this time, she was exposed by coincidence to this opportunity. "There was an entrepreneur in the city that wanted to set up a shop with Russian entrepreneurs. I was asked to do translation at the city hall since I had already achieved a good level of Hebrew." She was heard by someone sitting there looking for pharma people for his team. "I made it clear that I was not exactly pharma but a chemist who previously worked for pharma for many years, with a specialization in developing medications." Eventually, she became the lab manager for chemistry and plant extracts but maintains, "I was always different. Everywhere I was different." Nora Weinberg describes what she calls her first entrepreneurial action.

> It was entrepreneurial to run the lab first of all since I did not hold a PhD like all the other lab managers in the center. Secondly, I am a woman, and there was not a single woman that was a lab manager. Thirdly, I was an "Ola Hadasha" [recent immigrant]. I'd only been in Israel for a couple of years.

One of the managers of the center came up with exactly these three reasons for not appointing her as head of the laboratory. She continued and explains,

> I told him that on the contrary, it would really help him—a woman, you have to have a woman. A new immigrant, "Ole Hadash"—every time you need government support, you can state that you are supporting the immigration policy. And indeed, we went to the Israeli parliament on this issue a couple of times.

Finally, she explained to him that the industry prefers to work with people who "can go down to the factory and drive a forklift, which I do."

Nora Weinberg is a classical serial entrepreneur. She engaged in business ideas from the very beginning of her managing the laboratory at Lagim, the technological hub. She started a business in the field of microcapsulation in 1997 together with a partner, and the center of her activity then became a new company, which today employs 50 people and sells to 30 countries, with a factory located in the Tel-Hai industry area. She worked there as founder and CTO until 2008. During the interview, Nora Weinberg describes in length her experience with the company growing, becoming a leader in its field, recruiting clients such as Estée Lauder. Eventually she was fired and explains, "That happens often when companies grow. They let go of their founders." In 2011, she set up a consulting and management firm focusing on strategy and management of developing new products and startup companies in the food industry. Once she generated profit, she set up her own small lab under Emma Consulting and Management Inc., within which she launched two main projects, promoting them with the revenues of the consulting firm. In 2019, she launched one of the projects as an independent company. In March 2020, the laboratory started developing N pearls, a nutritional-food enrichment product. Today, the company employs ten people. It is located in the Tel-Hai industrial area, and Nora managed to raise $4 million from private and public investment funds. An additional project idea is still in its seed stage.

Nora perceives herself as an entrepreneur but stresses that for her entrepreneurship is about creating value, more than about being innovative or making money.

> I do care about how much money I earn, but in every place, I worked I cared about entrepreneurship generating value. I prefer the term "value" to "innovation." Entrepreneurship needs to create more workplaces. I created 75 workplaces here in the industry area, and now 10 more and in Misgav [an additional northern district] too. I think that is entrepreneurship. Entrepreneurship needs to generate stability, income, profit, welfare. It can be innovative or not.

She sees entrepreneurship as a social mission aimed at creating prosperity for the immediate and larger environment.

Weinberg believes that being an immigrant woman from the Former Soviet Union is definitely an issue in the world of entrepreneurship. She explains that she was never harassed sexually or openly addressed as an immigrant but believes that the successful businessmen have a hard time accepting anything from her. "No one ever told me openly about these stereotypes, except for a manager at Lagim, but that was a long time ago. As an immigrant from the former Soviet Union, I am always a 'foreigner,'" she maintains,

> no matter where, Israel, the US or back in Ukraine. Sometimes I use it in my favor, as a marketing tool. With my accent, in the US, it helps them feel progressive, being their "ex-enemy." In Germany it helps me being an ex-Soviet chemist—we did the same studies, went to the same places. In Israel, however, it's a hurdle. If I could, I would not raise money in Israel. It's the hardest place to raise money. After having worked with around 30 countries, I can say Israel is the most ruthless place to raise money, compared to Europe or the United States.

Nora relates to the peripheriality of Barkai Yaacob and explains that on a personal level, she enjoys living there:

> It's a small town, everyone knows everyone, we are very pleased to have raised our children here and "saved" them in a sense from things that have happened to my friends' children who stayed in Netanya. Barkai Yaacob is a small city. Everyone knows everyone. You can live a city life on the one hand but also be very social and tied to your community and other people on the other hand.

At the same time, she complains about the lack of professional network in the area, which makes it difficult for her to find high-quality employees. "The distance makes it difficult—especially for the workforce, a little less for networking since Israel is a small country." Nora communicates that she used to fly two to three times a month abroad and drive to Tel-Aviv, Beer-Sheva and Haifa twice a week. "This route takes at least two hours, often more, and I had very high transportation expenses at that time." After Covid-19, Weinberg barely travels and maintains, "For the networking part, it does not really matter where you live, but for the laboratory work, physical presence is demanded. The employees need to be willing to mover their families to the North." She continues and complains that in Israel, access to laboratory equipment is very challenging. "The state of these things in Israel is hard as it is. There is no shared lab culture. There is no 'pilot' culture of development, even at universities. Prices are horribly high." She describes the process of acquiring raw material as extremely long and costly, shipping it around from Germany and back. "In this sense, periphery or not, it doesn't matter—we don't know how to provide service here, and everything is expensive, whether you live in Tel-Aviv or Barkai Yaacob." During Covid-19 lockdowns, she explains that there were problems releasing shipments of supplies and moving them to the laboratory. Eventually, good connections and acquaintances between the people in her network enabled the smooth functioning of her companies. Importantly, Weinberg stresses that those employees who decided to move to the North in order to join her company usually stay for many years. She described this as positive employment stability, typically to be found in peripheral areas. Regarding support from friends and family, Nora said that she definitely would not have succeeded without it. She believes in a somewhat Soviet relationship to work: "My husband will work until his last moment because children need to know physics and mathematics." Weinberg believes that she paid a price since she was so invested in her work: "Often throwing in 16 hours daily, spending two weeks a month abroad, there is a lot I have not done for my children and grandchildren, and they forgave me." Asked about business knowledge, Weinberg clarifies,

> What I didn't have is information and support in contract management, understanding business development, what it means to be a member of the directory board, what director insurance means, what different types of contracts mean and what's written in the small letters, raising money, patents, financial strategy and decision-making, accounting. Entrepreneurs don't know these things, and that has nothing to do with me being a woman or coming from the Former Soviet Union. This is the knowledge gap, and today I obviously know some of these things, but I am equipped with loads of lawyers.

She continues and maintains that there are critical differences between the life sciences and high-tech projects. Life-science projects are long-term and often not only risky but also dangerous in operation. Although she herself and her family are financially well situated and have no issues with insurance or retirement funds, Nora tells a different story for many entrepreneurs in the life sciences who would live in precarious conditions if they did not succeed with their business idea or alternatively were "kicked out."

> The story I told you [of her being fired from the company she founded] is very typical. It is the story of professors, of people more expert and sophisticated than I am. I do not know one project where the entrepreneur stayed and very few where the entrepreneur made any sort of "exit." Entrepreneurship definitely has a cost of financial and social security.

For Weinberg, Covid-19 had a positive impact on her business:

> Our achievements in terms of our company's advancement were excellent. However, now there is a great uncertainty regarding the budget for next year. But all of that has nothing to do with being in the periphery. That was the case for the entire country.

Nora elaborates on the lack of support from the local authorities. She upholds that the area needs more industry so that people will stay and settle down with their families. The municipality is—according to her opinion—not actively involved in a strategic plan of how to recruit more resources and implement policies. Although a nearby academic college is constantly growing and attracting more students, "this is not enough if people can't find work in the area once they finished their academic education. They will simply leave." She repeats that she has created 75 workplaces from scratch, but when there was a panel in the framework of a food-tech festival, she was not invited. "There's a panel of small companies, and they know we exist but didn't invite us to speak for even five minutes. I asked them why, and they said they forgot." Obviously, Nora Weinberg is disappointed for not getting public acknowledgement for her work and contribution to the community.

Successful Foreigners

Immigrants from the Former Soviet Union in Israel established a number of highly successful startups. Some examples include the Israeli security firm Demisto Inc., cofounded by Slavik Markovich (Palo Alto Networks Inc. bought it for $560 million); Twistlock Ltd., a cloud security company cofounded by Dima Stopel (Palo Alto Networks Inc. bought it for $410 million); the security company Luminate Security Ltd., founded by Leonid Belkind; the cybersecurity startup GuardiCore Ltd., cofounded and headed by Pavel Gurvich, which managed to raise a $60 million series C funding round; the official unicorn stamped Lightricks Ltd., cofounded and headed by Zeev Farbman, raised $135 million at a $1 billion valuation; Pic-a-Cake, a digital editing system for creating edible images, cofounded by Katia Tzalmayar; prooV, a service platform that helps enterprises to accelerate technology adoption, cofounded by Alexey Sapozhnikov.

Some of the founders of these companies have been interviewed and presented in the media. The following presents some important and relevant insights from media items. Yevgeny Dibrov, for example, is CEO and cofounder of the cyber company Armis Security. He was born in the Ukraine but spent most of his life in Israel, and he represents the "new Russian voice, the one that does not conform to any stereotype. In his own words, he and his generation are the new face of the Russian-Israeli tech ecosystem" (Shulman, 2020). Lightricks cofounder and CEO Zeev Farbman was born in Zaporizhia, a city in southeastern Ukraine, and his family immigrated to Netanya in 1992, when he was 13. Lightricks has an annual turnover of over $100 million. "I have a fixation on financial indices and consider it important to not burn money and not rely on external elements," Farbman explained in an interview to Shulman (2019). Unlike most startups today, he did not approach investors at the beginning stage but worked with the revenues of the company.

> It is true that there are countless examples of companies that started bringing in revenue years after being founded and succeeded above and beyond, such as Facebook. But I thought about things in a way that is influenced by my Russian upbringing—you want to see that things work rather than believing in stories.
>
> (Shulman, 2020)

Igor Rabinovich is the chief technical officer at early-stage venture firm AltaIR Capital, which he cofounded. He is a Soviet-born Israeli and a well-established investor. Rabinovich immigrated from Moldova to Israel in 1991 and served in the Israeli military's central computing system unit Mamram (Center of Computing and Information Systems). After he finished his army service, he worked as an employee and eventually as a freelance consultant. Michael Marash is cofounder and CEO of medtech company P-Cure Ltd. In 1990, when he was 20 years old and a medical student in Grodno, Belarus, his parents decided to immigrate to Israel. He holds a PhD in sciences and led P-cure from the initial concept to the stage of product commercialization. Dima Broslavsky also immigrated to Israel from the Ukraine, where his parents were both civil engineers. In 2013 he cofounded Fundbox, a financial platform for small businesses, employing more than 200 people today with offices in the USA and Tel Aviv. Fundbox has received numerous awards, including the prestigious Forbes Best Startup Employers and AI 50, Red Herring Top North American 250, CB Insights Fintech 250, and Fintech Breakthrough Awards.

Expressions of Liability of Foreignness

As explained previously, the idea of liability of foreignness implies that knowledge-based entrepreneurs can overcome it by employing cultural and symbolic capital in terms of education-related achievements, to develop economic and social capital, and achieve self-employment (individual resources). They can surpass foreignness by promoting embeddedness into global, knowledge-based, educational and professional networks (socioeconomic embeddedness). Finally, knowledge-based entrepreneurs can deal with foreignness due to a habitus grounded in personal abilities and skills, hard work and strategic pragmatism.

Undoubtedly, all tech entrepreneurs presented in this chapter have high levels of human capital in terms of formal educational achievements, either from their country of origin (Weinberg) or mainly in Israel (all the rest). In other words, their individual resources were many, and they managed to translate these resources in occupational assets. Most of the male entrepreneurs served in a military unit, which provided them with the background for developing high-tech ideas. Alexander Solcin is the only one who said that he could not translate his army service into an asset. Those entrepreneurs operating mainly from Tel Aviv are obviously well embedded with the high-tech scene, whereas both Solcin and Weinberg reported that they have to invest a lot of effort to overcome liabilities of the geographic periphery: Solcin stressed that the network in the periphery is rather weak. Weinberg maintained that it is difficult to recruit qualified employees in the periphery, but she herself is well connected with the network in the center. All the previous details are not astonishing since the desk research targeted successful cases only and the case studies were purposefully chosen in the periphery of the country. However, the data provide interesting insights concerning the feeling of foreignness. Alexander Solcin talks about the annoying and low glass ceiling to be met by all immigrants from the former Soviet Union, even after 30 years. He also maintains that investors in the high-tech scene still categorize and apply stereotypes. "You need to be an engineer, sit in a lab and make us rich." Nora Weinberg experienced foreignness—especially at the beginning of her professional career in Israel—but rather translated this into an asset. "I am always a foreigner. . .. Sometimes I use it in my favor." Dibrov is still a "Russian in the tech industry" and tells about sometimes ugly incidents questioning his Jewishness. Marash brings forward the use of Alex as a generic Russian name. Neither Dibrov nor Marsh seem to be very concerned with the stereotyping. They do make a point, though, mentioning the issue. Marash explains that after many years, he finally feels comfortable with his ethnic identity.

Importantly, a notion of a "Russian work ethic" was brought up by Dibrov, Farbman and Broslavsky, in combination with a need "to be on the safe side," as expressed by Rabinovitch. The "Russian work ethic" implies also the idea of spending only the money you have, as Farbman puts it very nicely: "You bake a bun, you sell it, you receive money—that's the basic concept of a business." He explains that he was skeptical of investors at the beginning of his high-tech career. Rabinovich explains that he has many friends who have a consulting firm since that keeps them on the safer, less risky side of the industry.

Dibrov elaborates the historical development of a generation of immigrants from the Former Soviet Union in the Israeli high-tech industry. He explains that the first generation (his parents) arrived in Israel; they did not know Hebrew, but those with a technological background integrated into the Israeli industry relatively easily. He continues and maintains that the next generation—educated in Israel—have a high level of technological knowledge and integrated into the industry as employees. Along the same line, Rabinovitch states that those belonging to the second generation receive a relevant degree and do find a good, secure job at a tech company. "It used to be that out of 10–20 startups I saw each week, all had someone Russian in a prominent role but almost never at the front of the company or in a leading position."

Based on the examples presented previously, it seems that during the last years, more high-tech entrepreneurs with an immigration background can be found in the Israeli high-tech scene.

Concluding Thoughts

In this chapter, I discussed technological entrepreneurship among immigrants from the former Soviet Union in Israel. At the beginning of the chapter, I briefly outlined the historical roots of Israel's migration policy and presented a short overview about immigration from the Former Soviet Union and their group characteristics. Although no updated data about the entrepreneurship of this group are available, I briefly summed up the main academic articles that have been published during the last years. Israel has implemented a number of policies that targeted immigrant entrepreneurs and provided tools and mechanisms that aimed at fostering the establishment of businesses by immigrants. Technological incubators—already initiated by the Office of Chief Scientist in the early 1990s—reflected Israel's expectation that the wave of highly and often technologically educated immigrants from the Former Soviet Union would translate their human capital into innovative projects benefitting the Israeli society and economy as a whole. The main takeaways from the case studies and the desk research[4] can be divided into two categories. The first concerns the fact that overall, immigrants from the Former Soviet Union in Israel established a number of highly successful startups. They are well integrated into the Israeli high-tech scene and hold positions at all levels of organizational structures of smaller and larger companies. Additionally, it seems, that over the years, more have made the transition from being employed in high tech or being a consultant for high-tech firms to being the founder of cofounder. So why do they still feel foreignness? The case studies, both on high-tech entrepreneurs in the periphery of the country, exemplify this transformation in the occupational history of Solcin and Weinberg. Despite the overall positive state of affairs of this immigrant group in the Israeli high-tech, there is still a liability of foreignness present. Whereas at the center of the country, this liability is often translated into assets, it seems that in the periphery, it weighs more heavily. Furthermore, based on the insights of the stories of Solcin and Weinberg, their location in the geographical periphery of the country, relatively far away from the high-tech center in Tel Aviv, probably presented an obstacle with more impact than the liability of foreignness.

Notes

1. For further information, see the extensive research of Heilbrunn and Kushnirovich (Heilbrunn & Kushnirovich, 2008a, 2008b; Kushnirovich & Heilbrunn, 2008; Kushnirovich, 2009; Kushnirovich, 2007; Heilbrunn & Kushnirovich, 2015; Kushnirovich, 2015; Kushnirovich et al., 2018).
2. For a detailed discussion on the Innovation Authority, see Chapter 4 of this book.
3. It is a government-owned company for public housing, founded in 1949. The company has built affordable housing for millions of immigrants.
4. For more details and examples, see Len (2020); Liphshiz (2020); Rowley (1997); and Goldstein (2010).

References

Amit, K. (2010). Determinants of life satisfaction among immigrants from Western countries and from the FSU in Israel. *Social Indicators Research*, *96*(3), 515–534. https://doi.org/10.1007/s11205-009-9490-1

Amit, K. (2018). Identity, belonging and intentions to leave of first and 1.5 generation FSU immigrants in Israel. *Social Indicators Research*, *139*(3), 1219–1235. https://doi.org/10.1007/s11205-017-1758-2

Cohen, Y., & Haberfeld, Y. (2007). Self-selection and earnings assimilation: Immigrants from the former Soviet Union in Israel and the United States. *Demography*, *44*(3), 649–668. https://doi.org/10.1353/dem.2007.0023

Desille, A. (2019). Revisiting the diversity-urban development nexus: Perspectives from Israeli immigrant towns. *Political Geography*, *73*, 1–16. https://doi.org/10.1016/j.polgeo.2019.05.001

Desille, A. (2020). Jewish immigrants in Israel: Disintegration within integration? In S. Hinger & R. Schweitzer (Eds.), *Politics of (dis) integration* (pp. 141–159). Springer. https://doi.org/10.1007/978-3-030-25089-8

Dyduch, J., & Olszewska, K. (2018). Israeli innovation policy: An important instrument of perusing political interest at the global stage. *Polish Political Science Yearbook*, 265–283. https://doi.org/10.15804/ppsy2018208

Elias, N., & Kemp, A. (2010). The new second generation: Non-Jewish Olim, Black Jews and children of migrant workers in Israel. *Israel Studies*, *15*(1), 73–94.

Galili, L. (2020). *The other tribe: Israel's Russian-speaking community and how it is changing the country*. Foreign Policy at Brookings: Governance.

Goldstein, T. (2010, July 2). Did Russians save Israel? *Ynet*. Retrieved March 28, 2022, from www.ynetnews.com/articles/0,7340,L-3845104,00.html

Gurău, C., Dana, L. P., & Light, I. (2020). Overcoming the liability of foreignness: A typology and model of immigrant entrepreneurs. *European Management Review*, *17*(3), 701–717. https://doi.org/10.1111/emre.12392

Heilbrunn, S., Gorodzeisky, A., & Glikman, A. (2016). Identity of immigrants—between majority perceptions and self-definition. *Israel Affairs*, *22*(1), 236–247. https://doi.org/10.1080/13537121.2015.1111635

Heilbrunn, S., & Kushnirovich, N. (2008a). The impact of policy on immigrant entrepreneurship and businesses practice in Israel. *International Journal of Public Sector Management*, *21*, 693–703. https://doi.org/10.1108/09513550810904514

Heilbrunn, S., & Kushnirovich, N. (2008b). Impact of ethnicity on financing of immigrant businesses. *International Journal of Business and Globalisation*, *2*(2), 146–159. https://doi.org/10.1504/ijbg.2008.016623

Heilbrunn, S., & Kushnirovich, N. (2015). Entrepreneurial finance of minority and migrant groups in Israel. In J. G. Hussain & J. M. Scott (Eds.), *Research handbook on entrepreneurial finance* (pp. 166–184). Edward Elgar Publishing. https://doi.org/10.4337/9781783478798.00016

Horowitz, T. (2005). The integration of immigrants from the former Soviet Union. *Israel Affairs*, *11*(1), 117–136. https://doi.org/10.1080/1353712042000324481

Konstantinov, V. (2015). *Patterns of integration into Israeli society among immigrants from the former Soviet Union over the past two decades*. Myers–JDC–Brookdale.

Kushnirovich, N. (2007). Immigrant women's entrepreneurship. *Institute for Community Studies at Bar Ilan University*, *12*, 103–118.

Kushnirovich, N. (2009). Policy for supporting business minorities: A study of women and immigrant entrepreneurs. *International Journal of Management and Enterprise Development*, 7(4), 394–408. https://doi.org/10.1504/ijmed.2009.026306

Kushnirovich, N. (2015). Economic integration of immigrant entrepreneurs. *Entrepreneurial Business and Economics Review*, *3*(3), 9–27. https://doi.org/10.15678/eber.2015.030302

Kushnirovich, N., & Heilbrunn, S. (2008). Financial funding of immigrant businesses. *Journal of Developmental Entrepreneurship*, *13*(02), 167–184. https://doi.org/10.1142/s1084946708000910

Kushnirovich, N., Heilbrunn, S., & Davidovich, L. (2018). Diversity of entrepreneurial perceptions: Immigrants vs. native population. *European Management Review*, *15*(3), 341–355. https://doi.org/10.1111/emre.12105

Len, S. (2020, January 24). Thirty years have passed since the great wave of immigration from Russia: This is how Israel has changed beyond recognition (Hebrew). *Globes*. Retrieved March 28, 2022, from www.globes.co.il/news/article.aspx?did=1001315925

Liphshiz, C. (2020, November 7). Israel funds Jewish community-focused high-tech projects in former Soviet Union. *The Times of Israel*. Retrieved March 28, 2022, from www.timesofisrael.com/israel-funds-jewish-community-focused-high-tech-projects-in-former-soviet-union/

Lopez-Carlos, A., & Mia, I. (2006). *Israel: Factors in the emergence of an ICT powerhouse*. World Economic Forum, INSEAD and Palgrave Macmillan.

OECD & European Union. (2019). *The missing entrepreneurs 2019: Policies for inclusive entrepreneurship*. OECD Publishing. https://doi.org/10.1787/3ed84801-en

Raijman, R., & Geffen, R. (2018). Sense of belonging and life satisfaction among post-1990 immigrants in Israel. *International Migration*, *56*(3), 142–157. https://doi.org/10.1111/imig.12386

Ram, U. (1995). *The changing agenda of Israeli sociology: Theory, ideology, and identity*. Suny Press.

Remennick, L. (2002). Transnational community in the making: Russian-Jewish immigrants of the 1990s in Israel. *Journal of Ethnic and Migration Studies, 28*(3), 515–530. https://doi.org/10.1080/13691830220146581

Remennick, L. (2003). The 1.5 generation of Russian immigrants in Israel: Between integration and sociocultural retention. *Diaspora: A Journal of Transnational Studies, 12*(1), 39–66. https://doi.org/10.1353/dsp.2011.0043

Remennick, L. (2004). Language acquisition, ethnicity and social integration among former Soviet immigrants of the 1990s in Israel. *Ethnic and Racial Studies, 27*(3), 431–454. https://doi.org/10.1080/01491987042000189213

Remennick, L. (2013). Professional identities in transit: Factors shaping immigrant labour market success. *International Migration, 51*(1), 152–168. https://doi.org/10.1111/j.1468-2435.2011.00733.x

Remennick, L. (2015). The two waves of Russian-Jewish migration from the USSR/FSU to Israel: Dissidents of the 1970s and pragmatics of the 1990s. *Diaspora: A Journal of Transnational Studies, 18*(1–2), 44–66. https://doi.org/10.1353/dsp.2015.0005

Remennick, L., & Prashizky, A. (2019). Subversive identity and cultural production by the Russian-Israeli generation 1.5. *European Journal of Cultural Studies, 22*(5–6), 925–941. https://doi.org/10.1177/1367549418810091

Rowley, S. H. (1997, March 3). Russia's brain drain is Israel's gain. *Chicago Tribune*. Retrieved March 28, 2022, from www.chicagotribune.com/news/ct-xpm-1997-03-03-9703030073-story.html

Shafir, G., & Peled, Y. (2019). Citizenship and stratification in an ethnic democracy. In *Stratification in Israel* (pp. 365–384). Routledge. https://doi.org/10.4324/9781351323406-17

Shulman, S. (2019, September 6). From Russia, with coding skills. *Ctec, by Calcalist*. Retrieved March 28, 2022, from www.calcalistech.com/ctech/articles/0,7340,L-3769789,00.html

Shulman, S. (2020, January 7). "Russian" entrepreneurs come to the forefront of Israeli high-tech. *Madan*. Retrieved March 28, 2022, from http://madan.org.il/en/news/russian-entrepreneurs-come-forefront-israeli-high-tech

Yonah, Y. (2005). Israel as a multicultural democracy: Challenges and obstacles. *Israel Affairs, 11*(1), 95–116. https://doi.org/10.1080/1353712042000324472

Youngmann, R., & Kushnirovich, N. (2020). Income as a resilience factor for the impact of discrimination and institutional unfairness on minorities' emotional well-being. *Social Science Research, 91*, 102462. https://doi.org/10.1016/j.ssresearch.2020.102462

9 Women Still Lagging Behind

Introduction

Underlying most entrepreneurship and innovation ecosystem frameworks is the assumption that all entrepreneurs have equal access to resources, participation and support as well as an equal chance of a successful outcome (e.g., venture startup). However, empirical data show that globally, women are chronically underrepresented in entrepreneurial ecosystems, and a persistent gender bias continues to exist in entrepreneurship discourse and practice. GENRE is a three-year research project funded by the European Union H2020 program, which addresses the underrepresentation of women in technological innovation. The project aims to investigate and cross-culturally compare the lived experiences of female technology entrepreneurs in incubation and investing ecosystems in four different countries. Israel is a partner in the project, and some ideas and data presented in this chapter are taken from the Israeli research data.

Entrepreneurial ecosystems involve several interconnected elements such as a conducive culture, the availability of financing, the acquisition and development of human capital, new markets for products and services and a range of institutional and infrastructural support, which are mutually reinforcing and facilitate innovation and the growth of entrepreneurship (Brush, 2014; Isenberg, 2010; Kantis & Federico, 2012). All these elements are, by their very nature, dynamic, and actors and institutions are interdependent in that they are influenced by and, in turn, influence their particular entrepreneurship ecosystem (Acs et al., 2017; Spigel, 2017; Stam, 2015). It is common practice to think of the diversity of ecosystems to include a variety of businesses and industries and system participants (e.g., stakeholders) as well as business models supporting organizations and the growth orientation of ventures (Roundy et al., 2017). To succeed in building sustainable entrepreneurial environments, there is a need for engagement with the entrepreneurs themselves as the entrepreneurs play a central role in creating, maintaining and developing the ecosystem (Spigel, 2017; Freiling & Baron, 2017).

DOI: 10.4324/9781003091042-10

However, the entrepreneurial ecosystem is not equally open for all (Ahl & Marlow, 2012). There is still a dominant male norm in tech entrepreneurship; dominant stereotypes still portray the entrepreneur as a white heterosexual male tech genius. In line with the meritocracy myth, it is often believed that ideally, entrepreneurial ecosystems should spur entrepreneurial activities, and the success of the venture should be based on effort, energy and creativity and be available to all regardless of race, gender or class (Broadbridge & Simpson, 2011). Obviously, this is not the case, and recent research has demonstrated that women are underrepresented in successful entrepreneurial ecosystems and that a persistent gender bias continues to exist in entrepreneurship discourse and practice (Marlow & McAdam, 2012; Kuschel et al., 2020).

In the remaining part of this chapter, I will firstly present some data from relevant international sources such as the Global Entrepreneurship Monitor (GEM) and the OECD's The Missing Entrepreneurs report. I will then present updated data on women in Israeli high tech published in 2022 by the Israeli Innovation Authority. Furthermore, the potential reasons for the gender gap in technological entrepreneurship will be discussed, followed by the presentation of four interviews with women founders.

Global Data

Already in the chapter on immigrant entrepreneurs, I related to the report titled The Missing Entrepreneurs published yearly by the Organization for Economic Cooperation and Development (OECD & European Commission, 2021). The report reveals that between 2016 and 2020, less than 5% of women in the European Union (EU) were involved in creating a business. In OECD countries, 9% of women started and managed a business as opposed to 13% of men. In addition, the results show, that women are 40% less likely than men to be self-employed. The 10% self-employment rate of women in the EU has been persistent over the last 20 years. The Global Entrepreneurship Monitor (GEM, 2021) published a comprehensive report on the state of female entrepreneurship worldwide in 2021; it highlights that globally an estimated 274 million women are involved in business startups and about 139 million are owners or managers of established businesses. Furthermore, data show that women are about 10% less likely than men to report on perceiving new business opportunities and have lower confidence in their capabilities and feasibilities to start a business (54.7% of women versus 66.2% of men). Furthermore, the rate of necessity entrepreneurship is considerably higher among women, and there are a number of academic studies highlighting that the necessity-driven focus often leads to business closure. Importantly, women-owned businesses have been more affected by the outbreak of the coronavirus

(Covid-19) pandemic than firms owned by men; thus, globally, female-owned businesses experienced higher closure rates in 2020 (Statista, 2022). In both reports quoted prior, no data about the technological entrepreneurship of women are provided, but based on the OECD report from 2019 (OECD & European Union, 2019), women entrepreneurship in digital and technology industries is almost completely absent, "thereby depriving women access to one of the fastest-growing markets worldwide" (Strawser et al., 2021, p. 53).

Israeli Data

The yearly reports published by the Israeli Innovation Authority usually include a part relating specifically to women. The 2021 report revealed that women's underrepresentation in the Israeli high-tech industry persevered throughout 2020. As of 2020, only 34% of high-tech employees were women; importantly, this percentage has not changed significantly during the last 20 years. The report shows that while the number of men employed in high tech increased by 10,000 over the past year, the number of women working in the industry rose by only 3,000. In addition, the report elaborates on the long-term impact of Covid-19 on women in high tech in Israel. The fact that educational frameworks were closed during lockdowns intensified gender-role differences. Overall, the report showed that Israeli high tech is characterized by a large male majority, especially in the technology professions (Israel Innovation Authority, 2021).

In 2022, the Innovation Authority published a report dedicated to women in high-tech entrepreneurship (Israel Innovation Authority, 2022). In the following, I will present its most important findings:

In a global comparison, Israel lags behind in the ratio of women entrepreneurs (9.4%); the majority of prominent ecosystems in the USA and Europe have higher ratios (Silicon Valley 12.9%; Boston 12.8%; New York 16.8%; London 13%; Berlin 10.2%; Stockholm 12.9%), and only Amsterdam and Paris have lower ratios.

In Israel, the growth rate of employed persons in high tech was 6% for women and 9% for men in 2021, and the rate of women in core technology jobs is between 26%–28% of the last years. Women are underrepresented in senior executive roles in high tech, and if they do hold senior roles, they are mostly in less paid positions such as human resource, legal counseling and finance. Women setup and manage startups in sectors such as content and media (27.6%), life sciences (21.7%), and organizational software and infrastructure (17.7%). Primarily during early funding stages, women raise less money than men, and the data show that only about 4% of the total capital raised was invested in startups led by women. Nonetheless, the amount of the average size of funding rounds conducted by startups led by women increased significantly between 2018 and 2021. Significantly fewer women than men request grants, but according to the report, the rate of approval is similar. More than half of the large venture capital funds active in Israel have no female partner (57%), and of the partners in Israeli venture capital funds, only 16% are women.

According to the Central Bureau of Statistics (CBS), female students are underrepresented in academic STEM degrees (30% female versus 48% of male students), 35.5% of high school students taking the highest course in computer sciences are girls, and still, female students comprise only 7.3% of all undergraduate degrees in high-tech related courses. Finally, there is a lack of female role models in STEM-related academic disciplines. The report further shows that the ratio of female soldiers in the core technology roles of the army is lower than the ratio in high tech in general, and the share of women in military cyber roles was only 13% in 2019.

Reasons for the Ongoing Gender Gap in Technological Entrepreneurship

Much academic work has been done internationally in an attempt to better understand the reasons leading to the gender gap and formulating analytical frameworks contributing to unpack processes by which women are underrepresented in technological entrepreneurship. Special issues have been published in a variety of high-quality academic journals such as *Entrepreneurship Theory and Practice* (Wright et al., 2007); *International Journal of Gender, Science and Technology* (Webster et al., 2011)*; Venture Capital* (Leitch et al., 2018); and *Small Business Economics* (Brush et al., 2019), and academic conferences have been dedicated to the phenomenon such as the Diana International Research Conference in Dublin (ISBE, 2022), calling for papers on women's digital entrepreneurship.

In the following, I will briefly outline theoretical approaches relevant for the present chapter. It is beyond the scope of this chapter to present a literature review on female tech entrepreneurship. Strawser et al. (2021) overview research frameworks for female entrepreneurship in general and maintain that gender can be employed as a variable explaining differences and similarities among men and women, as constructed via processes or the practice of how it is done (Strawser et al., 2021, p. 58). The levels of analysis in order to understand gender in entrepreneurial ecosystems are presented by Brush et al. (2019) as intuitional, organizational and individual in levels. Gender is embedded and "done" at all three levels. At the institutional level, gender is embedded in regulatory, normative and cultural cognitive institutions, reflecting societal values. At the organizational level, gender is embedded in hierarchical divisions of social structures and symbols and images, reflecting organizational values, and at the individual level, gender is expressed and "done" in perceptions of gender identity and roles. Mickey and Smith-Doerr (2022), applying an intersectional lens, exemplify the previous topic in their discussion on gender inequality in innovation. Based on a solid literature review, they maintain that cultural institutions associating men and masculinity with science, math and engineering constrain women's career choices. Furthermore, structures of power in the ecosystems generate gendered (and racialized) perceptions of the ideal entrepreneur and often exclude the "others" who then are confronted with the "chilly climate" of excluding networks and hierarchical structures. The authors quote a number of academic articles showing that even if women have the necessary skills and experiences to initiate technological startups, they are very often excluded from relevant networks (Etzkowitz et al., 2000; Rosser, 2009; Meng, 2016; Whittington, 2018). Finally, accounting for the intersectionality approach utilized in this book, it is important to stress that the multiple identity layers of an individual—in terms of gender, race and socioeconomic status—impact opportunities and barriers according to or depending upon contextual settings (Wheadon & Duval-Couetil, 2019).

This chapter discusses female technological entrepreneurship in Israel. It thereby targets relatively highly educated women, mainly from a middle- or upper-class socioeconomic background, with most of them belonging to the dominant Jewish majority. Additionally, it is important to mention that policy makers for quite some time now have recognized the fact that women are potentially an extremely important asset for the Israeli high tech, which is suffering from a chronic lack of adequate employees and potential entrepreneurs. In spite of this understanding, the data provided previously show that women are severely underrepresented in the Israeli high-tech industry. This gender gap is reflected in wage gaps, gaps in capital raising and what has been called the "leaky pipe" (Branson, 2018). The "leaky pipe" phenomenon addresses the complexity of promoting women in many fields such as academia, politics, economy and also technological entrepreneurship. In the framework of the latter, the concept implies that with progress in the entrepreneurial managerial chain of command, less and less women are present.

Figure 9.1 was adopted from the 2022 Women in High-tech report published by the Israeli Innovation Authority and reflects the path of women in the Israeli high-tech industry from high school to becoming CEOs (Israel Innovation Authority, 2022).

The data presented in Figure 9.1 reveal the typical leaky pipeline, leading to a mere 9.4% of women among CEOs who founded startups.

Reasons for the Underrepresentation of Women in the Israeli High-Tech Industry

In 2019 Getz et al. (2019) prepared a report on women in technological and scientific entrepreneurship in Israel, which was based on desk research

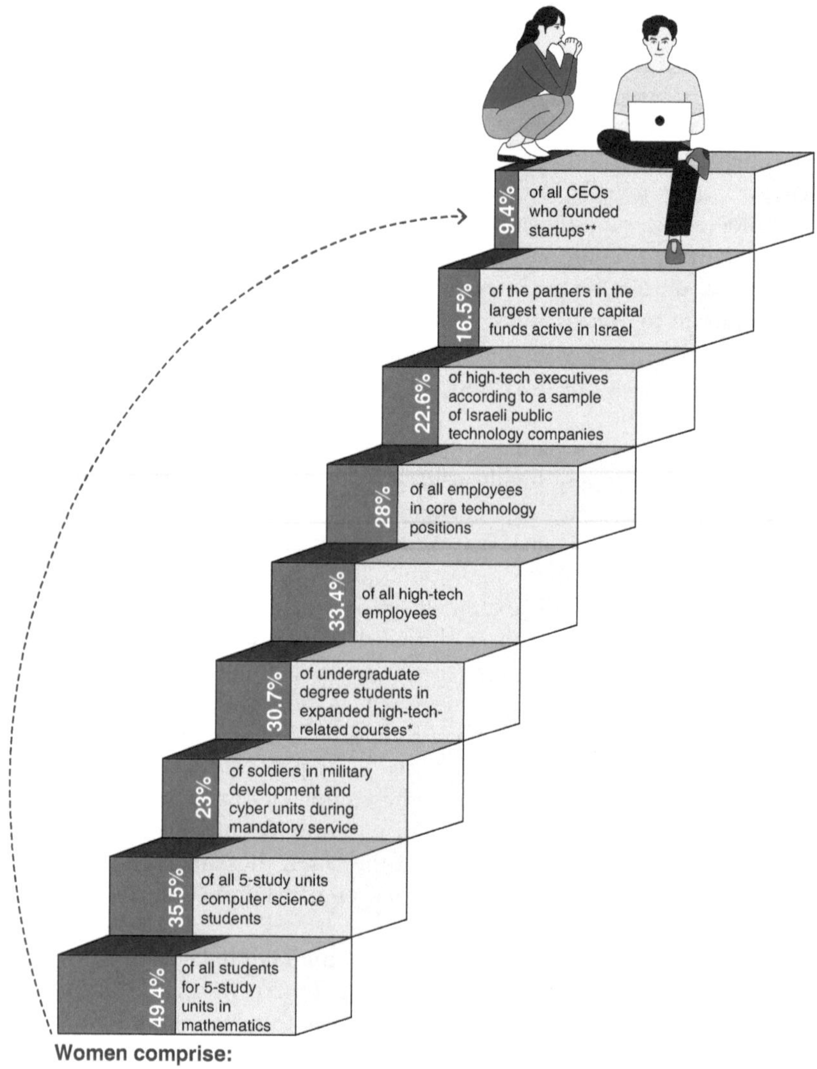

Figure 9.1 This figure was adopted from the 2022 Women in High-Tech report published by the Israeli Innovation Authority and reflects the path of women in the Israeli high-tech industry from high school to becoming CEOs.

Source: Israel Innovation Authority's Women in High-Tech 2022 Status Report, p. 4 (Innovation Authority adaptation of CBS, IDF, and IVC data, as well as websites of the companies and VC funds).

and forty-four interviews with expert stakeholders from across the Israeli technological ecosystem. Notably, the authors summarized the obstacles to female scientific and technological entrepreneurship in Israel, which I present in the following table:

Table 9.1 Obstacles to women's (high-tech) entrepreneurship.

Work–private life balance	Challenges to becoming and entrepreneurs at age 25 to 40 and balancing long work hours and long absence from home without family support.
	Men who take on household chores to enable their wives' personal advancement (including entrepreneurship) are not supported by society.
	Women obey the dictates of society and are not willing to pay a social price.
Personality differences	Lack of self-confidence (mainly the ability to confidently talk about a subject without fully understanding it), self-marketing, assertiveness and competitiveness.
	Traits that women do have, such as ability to work in teams or risk aversion, are considered not suitable for entrepreneurship.
Motivation differences	Men want to make money. Women want to solve problems.
	Investors in Israel prefer to invest in deep technology while women tend to focus their technological and scientific ventures on different fields.
	Investors don't tend to invest in technological solutions for female problems.
Lack of women in the entrepreneurial ecosystem	Lack of women in sciences and technology.
	Lack of women in top management positions (e.g., of companies, boards of directors and venture capital funds).
	Feelings of loneliness and discomfort being the only women in the room.
Funding	It is harder for women to raise funds due to bias and prejudice against them.
	Investors perceive women-founded ventures as more risky.
	Women are challenged to procure initial funding from family and friends.
Nature and scope of networking	Women have few opportunities to develop networks.
	Women don't maintain contacts that can be leveraged for professional purpose (low-intensity contacts).
Lack of role models	Lack of female role models and mentors.
Lack of practical knowledge and tools	Lack of business knowledge and soft skills.
Military service	Lack of women in technological-development roles in the IDF technological units (mostly intelligence units).

Source: Getz et al. (2019, pp. 4–5)

Four High-Tech Women

In this part of the chapter, I will present the findings from interviews with four female entrepreneurs in the high-tech industry. The interviews were conducted in the framework of the GENRE Project in 2019 and 2020.

Maya Ram is in her fifties and married and had three children aged 4, 7 and 9 at the time of the interview. In the army, she served in the 8200 technological intelligence unit, and she holds an MSc in engineering. She is the founder of a company in the field of life sciences. The company develops and promotes a medical device based on a noninvasive platform technology that enables pain assessment. Ram explains, "I discovered that advanced algorithms are used frequently in many different industries like semiconductors, communication, but not in medicine." Maya joined a technological incubator operated via the incubator program of the Israeli Innovation Authority. The incubator is located in the southern periphery of the country, and Maya decided to apply, joining it at the very beginning of developing the business idea, and reported that she received funding and mentorship from the incubator.

Hagar Manosevitch is 45 years old and married and has two children aged 8 and 6 at the time of the interview. She lives with her family in a town close to Tel Aviv, and she holds a PhD in biomedical engineering. Her startup is in the realm of higher education and psychometric testing. Hagar is cofounder of the company. The product is still in the development stage, and therefore, the company itself is still very small. In the past, Hagar was involved in a startup in the sector of digital health based on her professional background, biomedical engineering. She has many years of experience in the medical-device industry, where she held positions in senior development and strategic and business development.

Tal Ardi is a dentist. She has three children aged 16, 18 and 20 at the time of the interview, a dog and a husband. She has a PhD in biotechnology and an MBA. "I am the CEO of the company; the founders are actually two American surgeons that are also serial entrepreneurs." The company started out in an incubator at a time when Tal was responsible for the idea evaluation there. "So I basically did the due diligence on the idea of the surgeons, and then we started the company." Soon after that, she became the CEO of the company.

Jonit Keter is an entrepreneur and investor. She is in her late 30s. She lives in the northern center of Israel, is married and has three children; the youngest was two years old at the time of the interview. Together with two other women, she created a venture fund that invests in deep-tech innovation applied to sectors such as health, education and agribusiness. The venture capital fund targets Israeli–Mexican relations. Jonit immigrated to Israel from South America at the age of 31. "Therefore, I did not serve in the army, and that makes a big difference," she explains. "A big difference, a big difference when looking for a job in key positions." She continues and complains, "I've heard VCs telling me, 'We've hired this guy. You know, he's a great pilot.' And I think to myself, 'What does that have to do with the position he wants?'"

In the following, I will present the insights from the interviews with the four women along the lines of the obstacles to female high-tech entrepreneurship as presented by Getz et al. (2019). It is important to remember that the interviews were purposefully conducted with women who actually succeeded in joining the high-tech industry; thus, individually, they obviously succeeded to overcome many of the barriers.

Work–Private Life Balance: "You Have to Have a Mindset to Do a Lot of Juggling—All the Time"

Maya Ram reported that she received support from her husband and extended family when starting her business and stressed that her situation was essentially ideal since her parents could help with the children and her husband holds a very good job. Also, Hagar Manosevitch received support from her family but still maintained that she had daily issues with "juggling the family and work calendar." Tal described the situation of coming back to the technological incubator after maternity leave as a bit challenging.

> It is not only that there are no adequate facilities—like a place for breast pumping and, you know, a place in the fridge where to put the milk—but also, it is very difficult to combine work, motherhood and the startup. You know you come to the incubator to work, but then still, the startup is much more than work.

Tal maintains that it is always very demanding. "You have to have a mindset to do a lot of juggling—all the time." Jonit Keter agrees and maintains that in technological entrepreneurship, "you can't take your kids to school every day." For her a real challenge is the fact that her husband is also an entrepreneur. "So entrepreneurship is our life."

Personality Differences: "I Just Pretend That I Know It All"

Concerning personality differences between men and women, Tal Ardi maintains,

> I think they are not daring. I think they don't have a lot of the drive. They have a lot of the abilities, and I know a lot of woman that are very ambitious and are really doing, and maybe they just need someone to push them.

But on the other hand, she also describes herself as really strong, as having a mindset of struggling all the time to deal with failure and negative responses. Jonit Keter explains that she became more assertive after having her children. "It's like I understood that time is so precious that I needed to be much more focused, decide what will work and not, and go for it." None of the four women interviewed reported on lack of self-confidence, but then they all have an excellent academic and occupational record. Hagar mentioned that she would sometimes like to be able to act like men, "just pretend that I know it all."

Keter provides an example from her perspective of an investor:

> You know, men are very self-confident. I give you an example. I'm consulting two companies in fundraising. One is founded by a man, another is founded by a woman. Both companies are great and have a lot of potential, but he's much more self-assured and confident most of time. She's less assertive. He looks for investment, he's really straight to the point in every single email, he answers really fast and tries again, and I think that that's a little bit different for women.

Motivation Differences—Women Want to Solve Problems

The choice of businesses of the four women goes along with the statement in Getz's et al.'s (2019) list of obstacles: Men want to make money, and women want to solve problems. Accordingly, two of the present startups of the women are in the field of medical devices, one is in the field of learning and Jonit set up a fund for women entrepreneurs in the fields of education, medicine and agribusiness. One of the entrepreneurs was involved in a former startup targeting explicitly female medical problems. All the interviews reinforce the statement that women want to solve problems.

In addition, when asked about the preference of being self-employed or employed, Hagar definitely voted for self-employment. "I really love being independent, and I really believe in the business. I think it is important since it improves the quality of medical treatment of people. I am proud of that."

Lack of Women in Entrepreneurial Ecosystem and Lack of Role Models—"They [the Men] Just Don't Pay Attention"

The main issue coming up in all the four interviews concerns the fact that due to the male dominance in the industry, often the needs of the women—as mothers—are not taken into consideration. Maya explained that she constantly had to negotiate meeting schedules so that she could handle her family issues. Hagar explained that in the incubator, she got an agreement to leave early in order pick up her children from kindergarten but was expected that she fill in the hours later. "It was horrible." She continues and explains, "The administrative secretary of the incubator was very nice and also a mother. I always asked her not to have group meetings in the evenings, to have me first in personal meetings with the incubator manager." Hagar mentioned that only the women understood this constant juggling of calculating driving hours, the babysitter and the meetings, and since there were few women around, it was always a challenge. Tal also experiences this problem and mentioned that "the men just don't consider it an issue, you know, having meetings in the evening, doing whatever they want and when. There is nothing intentional about it. They just don't pay attention." Overall, the interviews reinforced the finding of Getz et al. (2019) that the underrepresentation of women in the ecosystem causes a climate that does not necessarily consider the needs of women as tech entrepreneurs and mothers.

Funding—"There Is Still a Barrier to Cross. But I Don't Know Why"

Hagar Manosevitch applied for a dedicated grant from the Israeli Innovation Authority and is in the phase of negotiating with some private investors too. She maintains, "These negotiations are challenging, and I never do them by myself. I always have one of the male partners with me. I just have this feeling that the investors, especially if they are men only, don't really trust me." She also maintains that this is a frustrating experience, "as if I did not prove my qualities."

Tal Ardi upholds that they are in the stage of the first human clinical study and hope to acquire the FDA clearance within the next 12 months. They have already raised about $3 million, mostly acquired via the Israeli Innovation Authority. They also did some crowdfunding. She continues and explains that they are in contact with one of the bigger players in their field and are optimistic. Also, Tal mentions that she "has to prove that she is excellent, always excellent so for the investors to accept her on an equal basis."

Jonit Keter brings it nicely to the point: "Eventually I think you need to prove more. I see the reaction you know when you go to an investor. First of all, you're a woman. Second, you develop a company for women's health." And she continues and explains that the investors are often not used to dealing with women, but in the medical-device field, there are female engineers and doctors, and still, they may be reluctant to deal with a woman CEO. "When you go to raise funds, you need to convince, the investor needs to relate to what you do, so how many men would relate to the female condition?" And she further maintains, "I don't think they [women-led startups] are less successful then other companies, probably the other way around. But still, I think there is still a barrier to cross. But I don't know why." Keter further maintains that she thinks over time the situation is improving and there are less gender prejudices, and investors resistant to women-led companies are decreasing. She does believe that "a lot of it depends on chemistry between the management and the investors, but yes, it's more challenging, it's more challenging."

Nature and Scope of Network—"Traveling Is not Always Easy to Arrange with the Family in the Background"

Maya Ram maintained that the incubator introduced her to the high-tech network of entrepreneurs and investors in the field of her business.

> You know, that was one of the reasons I applied to enter the incubator, next to the funding issue. In spite of my technological background, I did not know many people who could have assisted with the startup. The incubator gave me great opportunities in this aspect.

She maintains that there were four or five companies at the same time in the incubator, so "we created our own ecosystem in combination with the facilities provided by the incubator management." She continues and says that she met colleagues and made friends "You know, having lunch together with an additional 10–15 people was great. We started out with two employees only, and we found a social professional network in the incubator."

Hagar Manosevitch has a professional network that goes back to the Technion (the prestigious technological university in Haifa where she studied). When asked whether she has a network of people to turn to for advice, she maintains, "Yes, mainly my personal network, people from my previous company and from the Technion." She did not need the incubator for networking. She does have a preference for female contacts and maintains that she is working with a lawyer's office concerning the regulatory issues. "It's only women and it's really great. I really like them and they're more expensive than others, but I have confidence working with them, and if I need advice, I call them." She is in the process of building an international network too. "I attended conferences in the USA and Europe in order to build a pool of potential clients for our startup, but then, you know, traveling is not always easy to arrange with the family in the background." There were no indicators in the interviews pointing at the character of the network ties of the women.

Lack of Practical Knowledge and Tools

All four interviews presented in this chapter concern highly educated women with employment experience before starting their own business. Nonetheless, two of them mentioned that they were lacking explicit business knowledge, and Hagar Manosevitch had previous experience with setting up a startup. Maya Ram was employed in soft and hardware R & D management. Nonetheless, she explained that she had little knowledge of "doing business," and "that was one reasons why I decided to go for an incubator. I knew that I would be able to get assistance with these issues there." Tal Ardi served as VP of new ventures in a technological incubator and was responsible for screening new technologies and initiating the startup designs of those ideas chosen to be promoted. "I know the Israeli market well. I learned a lot, and then after three years doing that job in the incubator, I became the CEO of our startup." Tal is the exception and has ample knowledge of business development.

Military Service—"the 8200 Gig"

Maya Ram herself has served in the 8200 technological intelligence unit, known as a breeding house for technological entrepreneurs in Israel. She mentioned that her CV was very much that of a typical high-tech entrepreneur—"you know, with the 8200 gig and an academic degree in engineering." So for her, the army service was definitely an asset. There is no mention of the army service of Hagar Manosevitch and Tal Ardi, but Jonit Keter, being an immigrant, did not serve in the army and did mention that "the Israeli way works for men and for women" and explicitly mentioned that she was not part of it.

Some Concluding Insights from the Interviews

Considering the themes addressed in the other chapters of this book dealing with groups of technological entrepreneurs in the social and geographic periphery of Israel, a number of key issues are worth mentioning. For the genre project, we interviewed ten female technological entrepreneurs in Israel. Due to their personal educational and socioeconomic background, all of them had employment experience and employment alternatives to entrepreneurship. Thus, they were all opportunity entrepreneurs, developing business ideas to set up startups to solve problems they identified in their professional environment. These women made careers in the high-tech industry but are pioneers of the fact that they decided to start a business. As such, they do encounter gender-related obstacles. Maya Ram explained that she dealt well with the obstacles of juggling a family and a startup but did pay some social price. "You know, the ecosystem is not very accepting, not ready to deal with the particularities of us women. I hope that will change in the future." Hagar perceives herself as working much harder than the men in an attempt to juggle family and business, and Jonit Ardi compares the startup to having a baby:

> To start a company is like having a child. You really have to be there at the beginning, at least at the beginning of the life of the company. You really have to give 100%, like you give to a baby.

She maintains that she has seen many women struggle with this—and their companies failed.

> Because they don't get the support, even if their husbands are supportive, we're talking about a lot of time and effort to put into the company, and I think that's one reason for the lack of female entrepreneurs in the high-tech industry.

Concluding Thoughts

Globally, women are underrepresented in high-tech ecosystems, as has been discussed in the beginning part of this chapter. Concerning Israel, there is consensus among academics, policy makers and all stakeholders of the high-tech industry that women are underrepresented. There is also consensus that there is a chronic shortage of high-tech employees in general and potential high-tech entrepreneurs in particular. Israeli reports such as the *Women in Technological and Scientific Entrepreneurship* by Getz and colleagues, published in 2019 (Getz et al., 2019); the *Women in High-tech 2022 report* of the Israel Innovation Authority (Israel Innovation Authority, 2022); and the *Power in Diversity Women in Startups Report* published in January 2022 (Power In Diversity, 2022) reveal the ongoing gender gap of the Israeli high-tech industry.

Women still have to explain how they intend to combine the work hours expected in high tech with raising children as men are usually not asked about parenthood at all. Orpaz, in an article published in 2019 in the Israeli newspaper TheMarker (Orpaz, 2019), claims that the women she interviewed told her that they think very carefully about the timing of conception since it will definitely have an impact on their ability to raise funds for their startup. She cites a few female entrepreneurs warning women against going on a fundraising round when pregnant. In addition, she maintains that women have to deal with questions that men are not required to answer. This goes along with the fact that men are usually not expected to explain how they will juggle parenthood with business. "Women are expected to talk about this, and then they are constricted into a biological space. How many men have been interviewed and said, 'It's very hard to be a father and raise money at the same time'?" (Degani, 2022). In addition, as evidenced in an international research project including Israel, the narratives of the Israeli women tech entrepreneurs revealed that expectations were perceived to be higher for women than for men. In particular, the women felt they needed to be better qualified and to work harder than their male counterparts to stand out (McAdan et al., 2022).

According to the Missing Entrepreneurs 2020/2021 Report,

> Governments can do more to cultivate entrepreneurial aspirations among women, address market failures in the areas of skills and finance,

> and support for growth-oriented female entrepreneurs. In addition to addressing institutional conditions that influence entrepreneurship decisions (e.g. access to childcare, taxation), governments need to increase funding for dedicated initiatives and increase gender sensitivity in general entrepreneurship programs by setting gender objectives and tracking progress.
>
> (OECD & European Commission, 2021, p. 22)

However, several studies have highlighted that often the underlying assumption of policy schemes is that entrepreneurship is fundamentally male and that women have to "adjust" (Heilbrunn et al., 2020).

In Israel, much effort is made to realize some of these recommendations, although not very successfully. It seems that cultural and traditional gender roles and norms are still strongly embedded within the Israeli society, preventing equal gender participation in the high-tech industry. Israel is a very religious and traditional society, as reflected in its fertility rates, which is atypical for developed economies. Thus, society does not support men who take on household responsibilities to facilitate their wives' professional careers, and women are rather conform to society's expectations, not willing to "pay a social price" (Getz et al., 2019). The underrepresentation of women in high-tech is a global phenomenon, and explanations on the individual level often concern the risk-taking adversity of women and a perceived lack of self-efficacy and confidence. In addition, Israeli religious, cultural and societal norms and values place female technological entrepreneurs in a challenging position with contradictory expectations hardly to be consolidated.

The integration of underrepresented populations into the high-tech industry is important for the Israeli economy in general—the high-tech industry in order to potentially deal with the shortage of suitable employees and the underrepresented populations themselves. In Israel, most women who are integrated into the high-tech industry are of privileged background, allowing them to overcome—at least partly—obstacles and barriers. In order to overcome gender gaps and increase gender equality, much and genuine efforts from all stakeholders involved in the high-tech industry are needed.

References

Acs, Z. J., Stam, E., Audretsch, D. B., & O'Connor, A. (2017). The lineages of the entrepreneurial ecosystem approach. *Small Business Economics*, 1–10. https://doi.org/10.1007/s11187-017-9864-8

Ahl, H., & Marlow, S. (2012). Exploring the dynamics of gender, feminism and entrepreneurship: Advancing debate to escape a dead end? *Organization*, *19*(5), 543–562. https://doi.org/10.1177/1350508412448695

Branson, D. M. (2018). *The future of tech is female*. New York University Press.

Broadbridge, A., & Simpson, R. (2011). 25 years on: Reflecting on the past and looking to the future in gender and management research. *British Journal of Management, 22*(3), 470–483. https://doi.org/10.1111/j.1467-8551.2011.00758.x

Brush, C. G. (2014). Exploring the concept of an entrepreneurship education ecosystem. In S. Hoskinson & D. F. Kuratko (Eds.), *Innovative pathways for university entrepreneurship in the 21st century* (Vol. 24, pp. 25–39). Emerald Logo. https://doi.org/10.1108/s1048-473620140000024000

Brush, C. G., Edelman, L. F., Manolova, T., & Welter, F. (2019). A gendered look at entrepreneurship ecosystems. *Small Business Economics, 53*(2), 393–408. https://doi.org/10.1007/s11187-018-9992-9

Degani, C. (2022, January 13). This story can help solve one of Israeli tech's biggest problems. *Haaretz*. Retrieved January 13, 2022, from www.haaretz.com/israel-news/tech-news/.premium-this-story-can-help-solve-one-of-israeli-tech-s-biggest-problems-1.10535876

Etzkowitz, H., Kemelgor, C., & Uzzi, B. (2000). *Athena unbound*. Cambridge University Press. https://doi.org/10.1017/cbo9780511541414

Freiling, J., & Baron, T. (2017). A resource-based view of entrepreneurial ecosystems. In W. Burr & M. Stephan (Eds.), *Technologie, strategie und organisation* (pp. 65–84). Springer Gabler, https://doi.org/10.1007/978-3-658-16042-5_4

GEM. (2021). *GEM 2020/21 women's entrepreneurship report: Thriving through crisis*. Global Entrepreneurship Monitor (GEM).

Getz, D., Shacham, O. K., & Klein, R. (2019). *Women in technological and scientific entrepreneurship*. Samuel Neaman Institute for National Policy Research.

Heilbrunn, S., Alsos, G., Arntzen-Nordqvist, M., Balkmar, D., Callerstig, A., Delaney, D., . . . Weinberg, C. (2020). *Cross-cultural variations in technological ecosystems, a gender perspective*. Kinneret College on the Sea of Galilee.

ISBE. (2022, April 8). *Call for papers: Women's digital entrepreneurship*. Institute for Small Business and Entrepreneurship. https://isbe.org.uk/call-for-papers-womens-digital-entrepreneurship/

Isenberg, D. J. (2010). The big idea: How to start an entrepreneurial revolution. *Harvard Business Review, 88*(6), 40–50. Retrieved March 30, 2022, from https://hbr.org/2010/06/the-big-idea-how-to-start-an-entrepreneurial-revolution

Israel Innovation Authority. (2021). *Israel innovation authority's 2021 innovation report*. Israel Innovation Authority—Economics and Research Division.

Israel Innovation Authority. (2022). *Women in high-tech 2022 — status report*. Israel Innovation Authority.

Kantis, H. D., & Federico, J. S. (2012). *Entrepreneurial ecosystems in Latin America: The role of policies*. International Research and Policy Roundtable.

Kuschel, K., Ettl, K., Díaz-García, C., & Alsos, G. A. (2020). Stemming the gender gap in STEM entrepreneurship—Insights into women's entrepreneurship in science, technology, engineering and mathematics. *International Entrepreneurship and Management Journal, 16*(1), 1–15. https://doi.org/10.1007/s11365-020-00642-5

Leitch, C., Welter, F., & Henry, C. (2018). Women entrepreneurs' financing revisited: Taking stock and looking forward. *Venture Capital, 20*(2), 103–114. https://doi.org/10.1080/13691066.2018.1418624

Marlow, S., & McAdam, M. (2012). Analyzing the influence of gender upon high—Technology venturing within the context of business incubation. *Entrepreneurship Theory and Practice, 36*(4), 655–676. https://doi.org/10.1111/j.1540-6520.2010.00431.x

McAdan, M., Delaney, D., Bedenik, T., Heilbrunn, S., Callerstig, A.-C., Balkmar, D., . . . Weinberg, C. (2022). *Cross-cultural variations in technology incubation provision: An examination of representation and gender dynamics*. Dublin City University.

Meng, Y. (2016). Collaboration patterns and patenting: Exploring gender distinctions. *Research Policy, 45*(1), 56–67. https://doi.org/10.1016/j.respol.2015.07.004

Mickey, E. L., & Smith-Doerr, L. (2022). Gender and innovation through an intersectional lens: Re-imagining academic entrepreneurship in the United States. *Sociology Compass, 16*(3). https://doi.org/10.1111/soc4.12964

OECD & European Commission. (2021). *The missing entrepreneurs 2021: Policies for inclusive entrepreneurship and self-employment*. OECD Publishing. https://doi.org/10.1787/71b7a9bb-en

OECD & European Union. (2019). *The missing entrepreneurs 2019: Policies for inclusive entrepreneurship*. OECD Publishing. https://doi.org/10.1787/3ed84801-en

Orpaz, I. (2019, December 13). High-tech entrepreneur in pregnancy—What do you do with it? (Hebrew). *Women in High-Tech*. Retrieved April 9, 2022, from www.womanintech.net/post/women-entrepreneurs-pregnancy

Power In Diversity. (2022). *Women in startups report 2021*. Power In Diversity.

Rosser, S. V. (2009). The gender gap in patenting: Is technology transfer a feminist issue? *NWSA Journal*, 65–84.

Roundy, P. T., Brockman, B. K., & Bradshaw, M. (2017). The resilience of entrepreneurial ecosystems. *Journal of Business Venturing Insights, 8*, 99–104. https://doi.org/10.1016/j.jbvi.2017.08.002

Spigel, B. (2017). The relational organization of entrepreneurial ecosystems. *Entrepreneurship Theory and Practice, 41*(1), 49–72. https://doi.org/10.1111/etap.12167

Stam, E. (2015). Entrepreneurial ecosystems and regional policy: A sympathetic critique. *European Planning Studies, 23*(9), 1759–1769. https://doi.org/10.1080/09654313.2015.1061484

Statista. (2022, April 8). Closure rates of female-owned businesses worldwide in 2020, by region. *Statista*. www.statista.com/statistics/1207894/closure-rates-of-female-owned-businesses-worldwide-by-region/

Strawser, J. A., Hechavarría, D. M., & Passerini, K. (2021). Gender and entrepreneurship: Research frameworks, barriers and opportunities for women entrepreneurship worldwide. *Journal of Small Business Management, 59*(Sup 1), s1–s15. https://doi.org/10.1080/00472778.2021.1965615

Webster, J., Castaño, C., & Palmén, R. (2011). Special issue editorial. *International Journal of Gender, Science and Technology, 3*(2), 358–363.

Wheadon, M., & Duval-Couetil, N. (2019). Token entrepreneurs: A review of gender, capital, and context in technology entrepreneurship. *Entrepreneurship & Regional Development, 31*(3–4), 308–336. https://doi.org/10.1080/08985626.2018.1551795

Whittington, K. B. (2018). "A tie is a tie? Gender and network positioning in life science inventor collaboration." *Esearch Policy, 47*(2), 511–526. https://doi.org/10.1016/j.respol.2017.12.006

Wright, M., Hmieleski, K. M., Siegel, D. S., & Ensley, M. D. (2007). The role of human capital in technological entrepreneurship. *Entrepreneurship Theory and Practice, 31*(6), 791–806. https://doi.org/10.1111/j.1540-6520.2007.00202.x

10 From the Periphery to the Center? Ultraorthodox Jews in High Tech

Introduction

This chapter deals with the ultra-Orthodox population of Israel and their involvement in the high-tech industry. Within the kaleidoscope of Israeli populations, the ultra-Orthodox community stands out for a high level of segregation and poverty.

In 2020, the ultra-Orthodox community numbered 1,175,088 people, 13% of the Israeli population (Tableau Public, 2022). Following the projections of the National Economic Council, they will make up 24% of the population by the end of 2050. With an average of 7.2 children per women, the community is the fastest-growing population sector in Israel, which is the top OECD country in terms of birth rate, 3.1 children per women (OECD, 2022). Jerusalem and Bnei Brak are the two major cities housing over 40% of the ultra-Orthodox population. In 2019, 44% of the families lived in poverty, about twice the rate of the total population (The Israel Democracy Institute, 2022).

The ultra-Orthodox community is largely separated from the rest of the Israeli society, and rabbinical leaders of the community encourage men to biblical studies at dedicated seminars instead of entering the labor market. These seminars continue to exist and are based on the deal that whoever studies in these seminars is released from military service and receives state funds in accordance with the size of the family. Therefore, the majority of ultra-Orthodox young men and women are not serving in the Israeli army, with recent years even showing a decline in numbers; 1,906 ultra-Orthodox enlisted in the army in 2016 compared to 1,222 in 2019 (Ram, 2021). The burden of supporting the family falls on the women, who are expected to work, run the household, give birth and raise children. Also, women are not permitted to be active in the political arena. The ultra-Orthodox community expects gender segregation in public spaces, such as in public transport, universities and cultural and public events, a fact that causes much tension with the non-ultra-Orthodox population and reinforces social and geographical separation. The upholding of segregation, promoting religious restrictions on the public life for all Israel and securing state funding is the

DOI: 10.4324/9781003091042-11

agenda of the ultra-Orthodox political parties. These parties have been continuously part of almost all Israeli governments since 1977 (Malah, 2021). It was only in the last election in 2021 that they moved out of the government and gave way to the opposition. During these decades, the ultra-Orthodox parties' influence on governments has exceeded their relative size since they have been a balance between the left-wing bloc and the right-wing bloc (Shalev, 2019). Since they have been in almost every government, they managed to exploit their power and influenced legislation in subjects relevant to religion, state and budgets.[1]

Employment Rates

In fact, about 60% of all ultra-Orthodox high-school pupils attend schools where no core curriculum such as mathematics, sciences and English is taught (reference needed) and that in spite of state funding for these schools.

Employment rates of the ultra-Orthodox community are relatively low, especially for men. As of 2020, the employment rate among ultra-Orthodox men of primary working age (64–25) was 52%—in comparison to 87% among non-ultra-Orthodox Jewish men (Lifshits et al., 2021). Importantly, this employment rate for men has remained the same since 2015 (Cahaner & Malach, 2021).

In parallel, the rate of ultra-Orthodox women employed has been constantly on the rise and stands at 78%. However, the income of ultra-Orthodox employees is significantly lower than that of the Jewish population (59%), which is following the Israeli Democracy Institute due to less working hours and concentration in lower-paying occupations. Ultra-Orthodox women change their occupational profile, which becomes more similar to that of non-ultra-Orthodox working women (Cahaner & Malach, 2021). More specifically, if in the past Orthodox women were mainly working in education and other services within the ultra-Orthodox community, during the last years, they also increasingly participate in the labor market outside their community and in a variety of fields.

In short, the data show that the ultra-Orthodox population will become an ever-increasing part of the Israeli population, but their contribution to the economy remains extremely limited. Although recently there is an increase in labor market participation especially among women, the overall tax payments are extremely low. Moreover, they are highly dependent on state funds, their overall unemployment is high and workforce productivity per capita is actually on the decline (The Israel Democracy Institute, 2022). The ultra-Orthodox education system is separated and does not include the teaching of core curricular such as English, mathematics and sciences. The combination of the projected demographic growth with the community's low productivity and overly dependence on state funds has led to a public discourse perceiving the ultra-Orthodox community as a major threat to Israeli society.

Policies to Encourage Labor Market Participation

Over the years, government initiatives have been targeting the employment increase of the ultra-Orthodox population in Israel. Following a report from the Institute for National Security Studies at Tel Aviv University (Black et al., 2021), the Unit for the Promotion of Haredi Employment in the Ministry of Labor & Welfare promoted training programs and instruction courses in core curriculum studies (English, sciences and mathematics) and some dedicated schemes aiming toward employers. The overall percentage of employed ultra-Orthodox increased as a result of these initiatives, primarily among women. The major setback remained the employment of ultra-Orthodox men, whose employment rate remains extremely low in comparison to the general Israeli population and in comparison to ultra-Orthodox women. An additional policy matter concerned the attempt to integrate the ultra-Orthodox into vocational and higher education. At the beginning of these initiatives, the number of ultra-Orthodox students increased, but eventually, the dropout rate especially for men was extremely high. According to the State Comptroller's Report, whereas about 47% of ultra-Orthodox women who registered for higher education were likely to achieve a degree, for men the percentage was as slow as 24% (Black et al., 2021). Black et al. (2021) explain that based on the research conducted in the framework of his PhD, from a sociocultural perspective, the integration of the ultra-Orthodox in non-ultra-Orthodox environments has failed, probably due to the fear of the assimilation of the ultra-Orthodox and their rabbinic community leaders alike. Therefore, policies aimed at increasing labor market participation have largely failed. Similarly, measures to increase vocational and higher education rates failed largely because institutional frameworks proposing higher education or vocational education were not ultra-Orthodox, therefore perceived as a threat to the Jewish lifestyle by potential students and the rabbinic establishment alike (Black et al. 2021).

Tragically, the feeling of threat to lifestyle exists also among the non-ultra-Orthodox population (Peter, 2020). Following a poll conducted in 2017, 90% of the non-ultra-Orthodox population perceived the ultra-Orthodox as an economic burden to society (Rosner & Ruskay, 2017). Bystrov and Sofer (2012) cautioned that Israel might become a religious state. In parallel, the ultra-Orthodox population fears for their religious identity and perceives the state as a coercive secular regime threatening their existence (Rosner & Fuchs, 2019).

Reasons for Underrepresentation in High Tech

Since this book concerns the Israeli high-tech industry and the representation or underrepresentation of a variety of groups in this industry, I will attempt in the following to further discuss the reasons for the underrepresentation of the ultra-Orthodox. According to the 2020 High-Tech Human

Capital report (Israel Innovation Authority, 2020), the share of ultra-Orthodox employees out of all high-tech employees remained stable in 2020 and stands at 3.3%. Of all ultra-Orthodox high-tech employees in 2020, 73.5% were women, reflecting a pattern similar to that of the general employment in terms of gender. The reasons for this underrepresentation are various and in the following. I will discuss the most prominent ones.

Firstly, and as has been explained previously, the daily routine of ultra-Orthodox persons demands for an adequate environment to enable religious routines, such as times of prayer, kosher food, observing holidays and Shabbat rules, appropriate dress codes and restrictions as to gender contact (Rosenberg, 2018). In addition, normative expectations of the community are interwoven with control structures that ensure the adherence of most ultra-Orthodox to the religious rules and regulations. The latter can hardly be combined with companies operating in the high-tech industry.

Furthermore, as has been mentioned previously, the majority of ultra-Orthodox children attend schools where no core curriculum is taught; therefore, they are lacking both basic knowledge and skills that are necessary preconditions for any involvement in the high-tech sector.

In addition, following Cahaner and Malach (2021), the internet use of the ultra-Orthodox increased from 28% in 2008 to 64% in 2020. However, when comparing daily internet use between population groups, data provided by Dorot (2021) reveal gaps, precisely 77% of the of Arab-Palestinians, 82% of the non-ultra-Orthodox Jews and 37% of the ultra-Orthodox Jews.

Finally, the Israeli army is a major path to enter the high tech via the experience soldiers gained in technological units in particular. The majority of ultra-Orthodox men and women do not serve in the army; therefore, they are not exposed to this path at all (Peretz, 2018).

Indeed, in recent years, government policies invested hundreds of millions of shekels in an attempt to integrate ultra-Orthodox men into high-tech. However, following the results of a research published in a report prepared by the Haredi Institute for Public Affairs (Lifshits et al., 2021), an average of only 150 ultra-Orthodox men could be added to the high-tech industry per year, indicating a failure of the policies in spite of substantial financial investment. These results are verified by a report of KamaTech, an association established by ultra-Orthodox entrepreneurs to facilitate the integration of young Haredi men and women in the forefront of the Israeli professional high-tech workforce, and the IATI (The Israel's Advanced Technology Industries). The results of the report points to the same 3% of ultra-Orthodox employees in high tech in 2021 (Menomadin, 2022).

The authors of the report maintain that short-term courses designed to prepare people with no background at all for the high-tech industry within three months is inadequate. The research showed that before technological subjects, the students have to gain knowledge in English and mathematics and an internship including professional training. The authors of the report believe that a meaningful preparation enabling the integration of the ultra-Orthodox into the high-tech industry needs at least three years, which demands a substantial investment and commitment of the candidates.

Most of the ultra-Orthodox in high tech (71%) are women, but it is important to mention that in 2018, only 6,900 ultra-Orthodox women were employed in the high-tech industry, making up only 5% of all working ultra-Orthodox women (IATI; KamaTech, 2020). Ultra-Orthodox women are predominantly employed in segregated "women only" hubs in or near the community, where female programmers who work in such hubs earn much less than their female secular counterparts. Raz and Tzruya (2018) conducted a research on ultra-Orthodox women who are recently entering the high-tech labor market in what they call segregated (ultra-Orthodox only) and assimilate (mixed) organizations while expected to be mothers and earners to enable their husbands to engage in religious studies only. Following Raz and Tzruya (2018), in spite of the lower income, ultra-Orthodox women prefer to stay in the segregated hubs since they are more appropriate and free of challenges to be met in non-ultra-Orthodox organizations. The latter potentially burden religious family and community expectations.

High-Tech Entrepreneurship of Ultra-Orthodox

To the best of my knowledge, there is little academic literature on high-tech entrepreneurship of ultra-Orthodox in Israel yet. Monnickendam-Givon et al. (2018) investigated non-high-tech micro-entrepreneurship among ultra-Orthodox women. They found a separate social group that has a wide general social network, engaged in everyday life. However, the women did not utilize the network to promote their business. The authors maintain that business networking among ultra-Orthodox women was extremely limited. Levy's (2019) article is about an educational program to promote technological education in a college, and there are few articles as to ultra-Orthodox women's integration into the high-tech labor market (Wasserman & Frenkel, 2020a, 2020b). However, academic literature addressing high-tech entrepreneurship of the ultra-Orthodox is still missing. However, the Israel Advanced Technological Industries and KamaTech, an NGO, published a report (IATI; KamaTech, 2020) that reflects the development of the sector and its present situation. Following the report, the branch of Haredi startups in high tech is showing significant growth in recent years.

The NGO Promoting High Tech in the Ultra-Orthodox Community: KamaTech

In 2012 KamaTech was established, targeting the promotion of ultra-Orthodox in the high-tech industry. Ultra-Orthodox women and men manage the NGO, which is working under the observation of the rabbinic authorities. The NGO is well integrated into the high-tech industry.

Following their report (IATI; KamaTech, 2020), there is significant growth in ultra-Orthodox high-tech entrepreneurship also and maybe mainly due to the engagement of Kamatech.

KamaTech's programs include training, placement and an accelerator. The latter focuses on training the potential entrepreneurs in business development. In December 2013, the KamaTech organized the first startup competition for ultra-Orthodox entrepreneurs. The event was sponsored and supported by a number of leading people in the Israeli high-tech industry, such as Yossi Vardi, one of the first Israeli high-tech entrepreneurs, the CEO of Microsoft, investors and the CEO of the Ministery of Economy. The winners of the competition received grants to develop their business idea.

Following this event, in 2014 the accelerator for ultra-Orthodox entrepreneurship was established, which exists until today. In parallel, the government, via the Innovation Authority, initiated a program for groups underrepresented in Israeli high tech—such as Israeli Palestinians and the ultra-Orthodox. The program offered government grants of up to $735,300 in the first year and $1,470,600 in the second year. These grants could cover 75% of the budget of the startup in the first year and 70% in the second year, therefore covering for the difficulty of high-tech entrepreneurs from minority groups to recruit money.

Following the KamaTech report (IATI; KamaTech, 2020), a number of additional programs to promote high-tech entrepreneurship in the ultra-Orthodox community have been established, some by NGOs and others by government agencies. According to the Innovation Authority, since the inauguration of the Beginning Companies program, 100 startups by ultra-Orthodox entrepreneurs have approached them for grants, and 33 have received funds. According to data of the Innovation Authority presented in the report, in 2020 the accelerator released 50 ultra-Orthodox graduates to start their high-tech business among them 12 women. The report further maintains that in accordance with estimates of a number of agencies, since 2015 about 200 ultra-Orthodox set up high-tech startups and about 100 of them applied to the Innovation Authority for grants. Thus, overall the high-tech activity of ultra-Orthodox is on the rise.

Examples of Ultra-Orthodox High-Tech Entrepreneurs

KamaTech published a list of some of the most successful Haredi businessmen in the world. Most of the Israeli founders listed, with the exception of Shlomo Eisenberg, are graduates of the NGO's accelerator program. In the following are some examples based on the website of Kamatech (KamaTech, 2022):

Clark Valberg of Brooklyn is the founder of Invision, a digital product design platform that is valued at more than $1 billion. The company employs more than a thousand people, and has raised $350 million from some of the largest investment funds and banks in the world, such as Goldman Sachs and

Axel Capital. Valberg is well known in the world of Torah and is a prominent philanthropist.

Yoni Luksenberg and Ariel Klikstein are among the founders of Elementor, a company developing systems for WordPress users to create and edit site templates. The two founded the company in a warehouse in Bnei Brak in 2016. The platform, now worth hundreds of millions of dollars, is available in over 57 languages and is the fifth-most popular WordPress plugin, with over five million active installations worldwide.

Yisrael Gross is a cofounder of L7 Defense, a Beersheba-based cybersecurity company that specializes in web-application security and protection solutions. Gross founded L7 in partnership with Elbit Systems. The company raised $6.6 million since 2015, and its value is estimated at tens of millions of dollars.

Rabbi Rony Ohayon, an important member of the ultra-Orthodox community in Rehovot, was the cofounder and CTO of LiveU, a product offering simple video livestreaming for social media. LiveU was sold to private equity firm Francisco Partners Management and Tel Aviv–based Israel Growth Partners in 2019 for $200 million. Ohayon is currently the cofounder and CEO of DriveU, dealing with communications for autonomous vehicles. In addition, he is founder and CEO of the AI company DeepKeep.

Simcha Neumark and Shmuel Kalmus, both immigrants from South America, started Weel, a Jerusalem-based payment and financing solution for small businesses in Brazil, in 2014. The company has raised some $60 million, and its worth is estimated at hundreds of millions of dollars.

Shlomo Eisenberg is the owner and CEO of Malam Team, which provides software solutions to government ministries, local authorities and large corporations. Malam is one of Israel's largest tech employers and trades on the Tel Aviv Stock Exchange at a market value of NIS 2.2 billion.

Joseph Bornstein developed and owns a crowdfunding platform that enables companies to use matching grants to encourage a higher frequency of donors and larger gift sizes. He is located in Jerusalem and cooperates with Yehuda Gurwitz, who established a similar platform in Brooklyn called Charidy. The two companies assisted mainly Jewish NGOs to recruit high-volume donations.

Gilles Gade is the founder, president and CEO of Cross River Bank, a New Jersey bank employing more than 300 people and a forerunner in digital lending. During the pandemic, the bank was one of the most popular lenders, mainly for small businesses.

Yisrael Gurt cofounded the cybersecurity company Reflectiz in 2016 with a nonreligious hacker, and together they created a solution to monitoring vulnerabilities in third-party applications. Reflectiz is located in Ramat Gan and has recruited more than $5 million in funding.

Racheli Ganot is an ultra-Orthodox mother of three who founded Rachip, a semiconductor development firm in Bnei Brak. All her employees are ultra-Orthodox. Ganot has a degree in computer science. She worked in the semiconductor industry for a couple of years and then decided to set up her own company.

Nili Davidovitch is a mother of five and the founder of Daat Solutions, an outsourcing center in Tel Aviv that specializes in cellular and web development. In an interview she gave in 2013, she pointedly explains the challenges of ultra-Orthodox tech entrepreneurs in general and of women in particular:

> People in the high-tech world here just don't know us. We don't serve in 8200 [the Israel Defense Forces' prestigious military intelligence unit] and we are not graduates of the Technion. But what we do have are lots of fears.
>
> (Maltz, 2013)

She continues and maintains that challenges are even more intimidating for female entrepreneurs in the ultra-Orthodox community.

> We grow up hearing constantly how important it is for us to maintain modesty as women, and suddenly we've got to go out there and sell ourselves—well, not ourselves, but our ideas. It goes against everything we've been taught.

I interviewed two ultra-Orthodox tech entrepreneurs for the purpose of this book.

Moshe Friedman is one of the most prominent ultra-Orthodox high-tech entrepreneurs and promoter of high-tech entrepreneurship within the ultra-Orthodox community. He grew up in Jerusalem and describes himself as curious, passionate and persistent, and he believes that these are the traits needed in order to be successful.

> It is difficult to change the world, to create new things, to build companies, to be an entrepreneur. You face many challenges. You need to be very persistent to believe in what you do and keep going through all the difficulties. Most of the people who choose the path of entrepreneurship, they will be successful eventually. It may be that most of the ventures fail, but most of the people pursuing ventures, the entrepreneurs, they become successful.

Friedman explains that the ultra-Orthodox society is late in its integration into the world of employment in general—with men studying Torah and women mainly working within the community as teachers. Very few ultra-Orthodox were working outside the community a couple of years ago. "Things are changing now. Although we still do not have many doctors or lawyers, the trend is towards more employment."

Asked about his personal history, Friedman explains that when he was 30 years old and wanted to be a famous rabbi, he bought a computer.

> I had published a few books, and I needed a computer. The computer was connected to the internet, and all of a sudden, I realized a lot of very interesting stuff about the outside world. Everything was amazing. All of a sudden, when I got the computer and the internet, I realized I am living in Israel, which is a country of innovation, technology and science.

Friedman began to be involved in the startup scene and increasingly attended events and lectures. He then decided to start a business with his brother.

> "We are building a startup," I told him, and he asked me, "What is a startup?" We had no education, no connections; we grew up with a lot of religious education, zero technology, no background in technology or business. We didn't even speak English. However, we had so much passion. We started a company for online video editing. It was a good idea at the time, but we were apparently not the best entrepreneurs in town.

That was the beginning of his deep involvement in the Israeli high-tech industry.

Friedman explains the underrepresentation of ultra-Orthodox entrepreneurs in the high-tech industry; clearly, he has talked about this often. He starts out and maintains that there are large gaps in education between the ultra-Orthodox and non-ultra-Orthodox populations and between men and women within the ultra-Orthodox population. "Boys and men are supposed to study Torah, not mathematics, sciences and English. But then, without the latter, you can't succeed in high tech." The educational gap is—according to his opinion—overlapping with a cultural gap. "The ultra-Orthodox male elite," he continues, "wants to study Torah. But also the high-tech industry wants the best, but it won't get the best men." Friedman mentions an interesting and specific phenomenon here. Within the ultra-Orthodox male population, the "best and brightest" will choose Thora studies over high-tech. But high-tech targets the same group—thus there is an inherent conflict. He further explains that the ultra-Orthodox women do study core subjects, but do not get their higher education at the best universities in Israel; they will rather attend all-orthodox seminars. In addition, he maintains, "An ultra-Orthodox woman who is already going to work will not always feel comfortable in a pluralistic environment." Thus, he upholds, "The education gap and the cultural gap meant that not many and not necessarily the best went to high tech."

Second, he explains, "Many of the high-tech technologies are developed in the army, where people meet people and networks evolve. We are not part of this network since most of us do not serve in the army."

Third, he maintains that there are still role models missing. "Ultra-Orthodox do business in the field of diamonds and real estate. They are role models for others to follow." He believes that young people will more easily follow known paths—like becoming a rabbi or a real estate man. "The relative lack of visible role models was one reason for introducing the successful ultra-Orthodox entrepreneurs on the website of KamaTech."

Friedman started his career upon meeting Yossi Vardi, the chairperson of a high-tech conference he attended with a partner. Vardi was surprised to see two ultra-Orthodox people among the hundreds of entrepreneurs and said, "I [Vardi] am a 70-year-old person, and I have never seen an ultra-Orthodox start a tech venture." Friedman continues and explains that Vardi was curious and thought that "our business idea was not interesting but that the real startup is that the ultra-Orthodox want to set up a startup." Vardi became his partner, and together they founded KamaTech, promoting the entrance of ultra-Orthodox into the Israeli high-tech industry. KamaTech initiated a number of events, and over the years, the number of people from the ultra-Orthodox community attending these events raised steadily. In 2013, at the first event, they managed to recruit 20 potential entrepreneurs. One of them was Itzik Crombie, who has also been interviewed for this book. Together with non-ultra-Orthodox leaders form the Israeli high-tech scene, Friedman and his partners organized a number of events in the community, exposing the world of high-tech entrepreneurship and providing a platform for ultra-Orthodox tech entrepreneurs who are already active.

Since then, much has happened around KamaTech and additional initiatives. At the time of the interview, Friedman believed that nearly 20,000 people have attended these lectures and events, and slowly, a high-tech community is evolving, exposing talented people in the ultra-Orthodox world to stories of startups.

Friedman proudly tells that over the years, the accelerator program, which he set up with Arnon Shashua, hosted many startups. They started out with 20 registered, and two years later, the number went up to over 200. "In each cycle, ten ultra-Orthodox startups enter. To date, 60 startups have passed the program, and nearly 2,000 ultra-Orthodox entrepreneurs have signed up for the program."

Friedman believes that ultra-Orthodox women can become the game-changers concerning the participation of the ultra-Orthodox in the high-tech industry. "The higher the numbers are, the higher the chances that more will become high-tech entrepreneurs."

He explains that currently, about 1,000 ultra-Orthodox women are attending practical software engineering programs. Since the natural increase of the ultra-Orthodox population is extremely high, numbers will rise constantly and steadily. "The problem has always been that because they study at the ultra-Orthodox seminary and are relatively low level, they are not good enough for Google or Intel."

At KamaTech, Friedman initiated a program that had the potential to introduce 1,000–2,000 ultra-Orthodox women into the heart of the high-tech industry. The program includes ten courses altogether encompassing 700 hours and is all about computer science, including algorithms and coding. The course is taught in English only, and successful graduates are placed within big companies. In order to overcome the cultural challenges, they invented a traffic light system, a set of rules. First, the women are recruited to companies in groups, and second, they are physically separated. Friedman explains, "It's both good for companies and good for the women." The deal concerning employment conditions of the women is red: no go; yellow: to be discussed; and green: possible. The same accounts for the permissions the women have to receive from the rabbinic authorities. Friedman explains that this traffic light method enabled the companies to hire women and the women to become employees. He continues and explains that excellent companies employ 200 graduates every year.

As for high-tech entrepreneurs, Friedman believes that the Innovation Authority and government schemes did not reach their goals in enabling more ultra-Orthodox high-tech entrepreneurship. "I am recruiting donors, private individuals and investors for KamaTech, and the entrepreneurs, the government should have done it and did not do it." Friedman maintains that the government decided on a strategy to integrate the ultra-Orthodox into academia and invested a lot of money in that project. "Academia does not fit the ultra-Orthodox population, and the CEOs of the potential companies maintain that the degree programs are not practical." Friedman explains and maintains that the government did not see this point and invested a huge amount of money into the academic programs and not enough into vocational high-tech and entrepreneurship programs.

Friedman believes that a few entrepreneurs really can change the world. "If we will find the few ultra-Orthodox entrepreneurs, they will change the ultra-Orthodox community." He explained that when he and Vardi started the KamaTech accelerator, each entrepreneur received $5,000 and the necessary network and connections.

> Since then we have released hundreds of ultra-Orthodox high-tech entrepreneurs into the market. One of the most proud moments for me was two weeks ago, that one of our companies, called Elemental, was nominated to be the second best startup in Israel in general.

The young ultra-Orthodox people—he upholds—want to be part of Israel, part of the future, part of innovation and technology. They still want to be religious, but they want to participate. "We were maybe the right people at the right time to build those bridges between the ultra-Orthodox community and the Israeli innovation ecosystem."

However, at the end of the interview, Friedman points to the difficulties:

> I am an ultra-Orthodox man, and I am sure that an Arab man will feel like me, as well as women. You are an outsider, dressed differently, looking differently. You are not a part of it. Anyone who is different has a hard time entering this circle.

He continues and states that in the end, the high-tech industry in Israel belongs to a very specific population. "Not that it is anyone's' fault—it just happened." They are Ashkenazi men from the center of the country, secular, from high socioeconomic backgrounds and with an army record. Nevertheless, Friedman is optimistic:

> When I founded KamaTech, people told me that the idea was just a dream, that there was no way ultra-Orthodox would ever find a place in the tech world, but now, a couple of years later, I know of 1,500 ultra-Orthodox in the process of building companies.

Izik Cromby lives in Kfar Habad, is 38 years old and married and has five children. He studied information systems at the Technion and set up a company in the domain of professional services then a startup in the domain of guided selling. He sold the startup in 2016. Cromy is currently a research fellow and head of the employment sector at the ultra-Orthodox (Haredi) Institute for Policy Research. In addition, he runs an entrepreneurship and innovation center for the ultra-Orthodox population, which has two locations, Jerusalem and Bnei Brak. Each of the centers provides a big coworking space that is occupied by 80–100 companies. Companies at the center are usually small, and the we-work provides physical infrastructure like office space, coffee, internet, printers, etc. for a fixed monthly price. Prices are not particularly subsidized; however, the center is nonprofit. In addition, the centers provide business consulting, English, digitation, time management, public speaking and workshops in additional skill acquirement. They also have designated programs for graphic designers who have learned how to be designers already and work in this field but need accompanying for a year, teaching them how to make money. Cromby maintains that the centers also accompany startups in relatively advanced stages of development, meaning that they already have a team and a product and have raised $50,000. These startups receive six-month coaching as an accelerator program. Cromby is convinced that it is one of the best accelerators in Israel, regardless of the fact that it targets ultra-Orthodox entrepreneurs only. "In Jerusalem every type of startup can apply, but we decided that in Bnei-Brak we focus on medical equipment and digital health, in collaboration with Wolfson hospital." The accelerator is part of a partnership with Google, Amazon and others who fund this activity. The target audience is ultra-Orthodox men only, "because that is where the challenge is." He explains, "The story with women is different—there are less women entrepreneurs, generally speaking, and in the ultra-Orthodox society even less because they prefer to focus on their families." The managing board of the center contains two ultra-Orthodox women. In 2017–2018 Crombie and additional partners teamed up with the Innovation Authority and compared the performance of ultra-Orthodox entrepreneurs to that of non-ultra-Orthodox entrepreneurs in high tech. They revealed that the ultra-Orthodox did fine on the innovation and technology track but that they rated significantly lower on other criteria compared to others. These criteria were team building, understanding the market, business development and financing. Therefore, Cromby and partners set up the accelerator to promote the business skills of ultra-Orthodox entrepreneurs with potentially promising technological innovations. "It seems to work out well. Most companies that have graduated from the accelerator have not gone broke within a year so far. There also have not been any success stories yet." Cromby points to the main obstacles for ultra-Orthodox high-tech entrepreneurship:

> The chances of an ultra-Orthodox man to make it to high tech—at any position—stand at around 2%. Today there are about 3,500 ultra-Orthodox men in high tech. Some work in services and not in industry. Out of this small number, you take the entrepreneurs, and that leaves you with a very small pool of people.

He receives messages and questions around twice a week from ultra-Orthodox entrepreneurs who seek consulting and want to be part of the centers. "But 90% of them don't have tech training. They do not admit it and work with those without tech training." Cromby does not believe that it is possible to succeed without that training. He believes that the fact that there is no middle class of ultra-Orthodox businesspersons is a problem. "The model for work, career and success in the community is false. There is a misconception about work that it necessarily conflicts with the ultra-Orthodox religious lifestyle." He continues and explains that many in the community still believe that founding a startup will hurt them morally, and therefore, they prefer to be teachers in an ultra-Orthodox bible school. "I try to show people that you can be a high-tech entrepreneur and still remain a part of the ultra-Orthodox community and maintain the religious lifestyle. We try to create role models within the community."

However, most participants in their programs are not "hard-core" ultra-Orthodox, some of them were originally secular, some Anglo-Saxons with more liberal traditions. Cromby defines the main goals of his programs as creating role models and a critical mass of ultra-Orthodox people specialized in technologies. "You need to have a big-enough pool of potential people, a community that is constantly growing." Cromby believes that the business angles are looking for good ideas and are open to engage with and invest in ultra-Orthodox entrepreneurs. Overall, he believes that much work is needed in the future to overcome the obstacles for integrating ultra-Orthodox into the Israeli high-tech industry.

Concluding Thoughts

The ultra-Orthodox population composes currently 13% of the Israeli population and is projected to make up nearly a quarter in 2050. In light of the community's particularities, huge challenges can be expected. Today, Israel is a modern democracy with a per-capita gross domestic product similar to that of France and the UK. The country has a vibrant high-tech industry and scientific community and is rather progressive in issues such as gay rights. The ultra-Orthodox live as a separate community, with the majority of boys and men devoted to religious studies instead of working. There is an expectation that the state will pay for men's lifelong studying. Sixty percent of ultra-Orthodox high school pupils do not receive a core curriculum in math, science and English. Labor market participation of ultra-Orthodox men is extremely low (around 50%), and few work in the productive markets of the economy. Whereas ultra-Orthodox women are more involved in the labor market, they are still restricted by traditional and religious expectations. The data provided previously and the stories told about ultra-Orthodox technological entrepreneurship reveal that there is a part of the ultra-Orthodox community interested to enter the Israeli high-tech industry. For them, like for other minorities, this is not an easy task since they differ fundamentally from the mainstream Israeli high-tech entrepreneur.

The main takeaway from the interviews and material of this chapter concerns three agendas, not necessarily overlapping. One encompasses the difficulties of a very different population to integrate into the "closed circle" of the high-tech scene at the center of Israel. Challenges related to cultural differences, traditional and religious normative expectations, communal separation and lifestyle make it difficult for ultra-Orthodox to be part. As Friedman explained, to the point,

> I am an ultra-Orthodox man, and I am sure that an Arab man will feel like me, as well as women. You are an outsider, dressed differently, looking differently. You are not a part of it. Anyone who is different has a hard time entering this circle.

The second agenda concerns the willingness of the community to adjust to organizational and societal circumstances. More specifically, differently than other minorities, the data and interviews reveal that the ultra-Orthodox expect high degrees of adjustment from the high-tech industry in terms of gender separation in public spaces and other regulations. In addition, the adjustment of their educational system to requirements of the labor market in general and the high-tech industry in particular is not decided upon by the religious authorities who control the system. Therefore, there are internal community constraints preventing more integration of the ultra-Orthodox into the high-tech industry in general and as entrepreneurs in particular. Above and beyond these constraints, for those who want to "enter the circle"—as Friedman said—the "otherness" remains a barrier to consider.

The efforts and financial resources invested by the government and its agencies in order to increase the partaking of ultra-Orthodox women and men in the high-tech industry concerns the third agenda. In spite of these efforts and in spite of the very optimistic picture drawn by Friedman and Kamatech's agenda, following the 2021 report of the Innovation Authority, the share of ultra-Orthodox among high-tech employees amounts to 3% only. There are no exact data on the number of ultra-Orthodox startups, but it is safe to state that they are few. Thus, it seems that the efforts are not effective, the intentions don't translate into results and new strategies should probably be considered by policy makers within and outside the ultra-Orthodox community. In light of the demographic prognosis explained previously, the future of Israeli society might well be linked to the trend of the ultra-Orthodox population and their ability and willingness to enter the high-tech industry. As Friedman sums up this agenda,

> I'm trying to build a bridge between our community and the outside world. At the beginning, the ultra-Orthodox community counted a few hundred families in Jerusalem, and then a hundred years later, there are more than a million ultra-Orthodox people. Today, 27% of the kids in first grade are ultra-Orthodox, with numbers constantly rising. We should ask ourselves whether Israel will remain to be the startup nation if one third of the kids do not study computers, English and science. Maybe we will face a different Israel in the future.

Note

1. For a detailed description of the ultra-Orthodox community in Israel, see Elizur and Malkin (2014); Baum et al. (2014); Finkelman (2011); Kook and Harel-Shalev (2021); and Rosenberg and Blondheim (2021).

References

Baum, N., Yedidya, T., Schwartz, C., & Aran, O. (2014). Women pursuing higher education in ultra-orthodox society. *Journal of Social Work Education, 50*(1), 164–175. https://doi.org/10.1080/10437797.2014.856242

Black, S., Fadlon, T., & Elran, M. (2021). *Integrating the ultra-orthodox into the labor market.* The Institute for National Security Studies.

Bystrov, E., & Sofer, A. (2012). *Israel: Demography 2012–2030: On the way to a religious state.* University of Haifa.

Cahaner, L., & Malach, G. (2021). Standard of living—Chapter 3. In *Statistical report on ultra-orthodox society in Israel.* Israel Democracy Institute.

Dorot, R. (2021). *Media influx matrix: Israel. CEU democratic institute*. Center for Media, Data and Society.

Elizur, Y., & Malkin, L. (2014). *The war within: Israel's ultra-orthodox*. Abrams Press.

Finkelman, Y. (2011). Ultra-orthodox/Haredi education. In H. Miller, L. D. Grant, & A. Pomson (Eds.), *International handbooks of religion and education* (Bd. 5, S. 1063–1080). Springer. https://doi.org/10.1007/978-94-007-0354-4_58

IATI; KamaTech. (2020). *The Haredi high-tech report 2020*. Israel Advanced Technology Industries (IATI) and Kamatech.

The Israel Democracy Institute. (2022, April 3). *Statistical report on ultra-orthodox society in Israel*. The Israel Democracy Institute. https://en.idi.org.il/haredi/2021/?chapter=38441abgerufen

Israel Innovation Authority. (2020). *2020 High-tech human capital report*. Israel Innovation Authority. Abgerufen am March 24, 2022, von https://startupnationcentral.org/wp-content/uploads/2021/04/2020-Human-Capital-Report-Eng.pdf

KamaTech. (2022, April 8). *KamaTech*. Von KamaTech. www.kamatech.org.il/abgerufen

Kook, R. B., & Harel-Shalev, A. (2021). Patriarchal norms, practices and changing gendered power relations-narratives of ultra-orthodox women in Israel. *28*(7), 975–998. https://doi.org/10.1080/0966369X.2020.1762546

Levy, D. (2019). Bridging between Jewish ultra-orthodox and the start-up nation: A case study. *International Conference on Human-Computer Interaction*, 524–534. https://doi.org/10.1007/978-3-030-21902-4_37

Lifshits, H., Somkin, S., Exelrad, H., Krombi, I., & Zilberman, A. (2021). *Integration of ultra-orthodox men in high tech (Hebrew)*. The Institute for Economic Policy of the Haredi Society.

Malah, G. (2021, June 14). The new government and the ultra-orthodox—Is it really a change of direction? (Hebrew). *Israel Democracy Institute*. Abgerufen am April 4, 2022, von www.idi.org.il/articles/34714

Maltz, J. (2013, January 15). Haredi women closing the high-tech gender gap in Israel. *Haaretz*. Abgerufen am April 4, 2022, von www.haaretz.com/jewish/.premium-haredi-women-closing-the-high-tech-gender-gap-1.5224682

Menomadin. (2022). *Integrating the ultra-orthodox into premium hi-tech jobs*. Menomadin Foundation.

Monnickendam-Givon, Y., Schwartz, D., & Gidron, B. (2018). The surprising lack of connection between social networks and the enterprise success of ultra-religious female micro-entrepreneurs. *Journal of Enterprising Communities: People and Places in the Global Economy*, *12*(3), 395–415. https://doi.org/10.1108/jec-05-2017-0031

OECD. (2022, April 8). *Israel*. OECD. https://data.oecd.org/israel.htm abgerufen

Peretz, S. (2018, April 24). Some Israeli soldiers get tech experience that can triple their earning power. *Haaretz*. Abgerufen am April 4, 2022, von www.haaretz.com/israel-news/business/some-soldiers-gain-experience-that-can-triple-their-earning-power-1.5445030

Peter, L. (2020). The Haredim as a challenge for the Jewish state: The culture war over Israel's identity. *Stiftung Wissenschaft und Politik-SWP – Deutsches Institut für Internationale Politik und Sicherheit*. https://doi.org/10.18449/2020RP14

Ram, T. L. (2021, July 9). There is no influx on the bureaus: The numbers behind the fiction of the Haredi recruitment to the IDF (Hebrew). *Walla News*. Abgerufen am April 4, 2022, von https://news.walla.co.il/item/3447029

Raz, A. E., & Tzruya, G. (2018). Doing gender in segregated and assimilative organizations: Ultra-orthodox Jewish women in the Israeli high-tech labour market. *Gender, Work & Organization*, *25*(4), 361–378. https://doi.org/10.1111/gwao.12205

Rosenberg, D. (2018). *Israel's technology economy: Origins and impact*. Springer. https://doi.org/10.1007/978-3-319-76654-6

Rosenberg, H., & Blondheim, M. (2021). The smartphone and its punishment: Social distancing of cellular transgressors in ultra-orthodox Jewish society, from 2G to the Corona pandemic. *Technology in Society*, *66*, 101619. https://doi.org/10.1016/j.techsoc.2021.101619

Rosner, S., & Fuchs, C. (2019). *IsraeliJudaism: Portrait of a cultural revolution*. The Jewish People Policy Institute.

Rosner, S., & Ruskay, J. (2017). *Jerusalem and the Jewish people: Unity and division*. The Jewish People Policy Institute.

Shalev, S. (2019, Februar 21). Israel's ultra-orthodox parties explained. *Israel Policy Forum*. Abgerufen am April 4, 2022, von https://israelpolicyforum.org/2019/02/21/israels-ultra-orthodox-parties-explained/

Tableau Public. (2022, April 3). *Regional population scenarios for the state of Israel 2020–2050*. Tableau Public. https://public.tableau.com/app/profile/israel.national.economics.council/viz/Draft_c/2020-2050 abgerufen

Wasserman, V., & Frenkel, M. (2020a). The politics of (in) visibility displays: Ultra-orthodox women manoeuvring within and between visibility regimes. *Human Relations*, *73*(12), 1609–1631. https://doi.org/10.1177/0018726719879984

Wasserman, V., & Frenkel, M. (2020b). Manoeuvring within and between visibility regimes: Ultra-orthodox women in-between subjugation and agency. *Open Futures*, *9*(2), 30.

11 Arab-Palestinian[1] Technological Entrepreneurs in Israel—Double Periphery?

Introduction

Technological entrepreneurship is often presented as an endeavor that is easily accessible to everyone. The underlying subtexts of a huge media presentation of high-tech entrepreneurship success stories globally is that they can presumably be replicated by anyone, anywhere and anytime (Boulus-Rødje & Bjørn, 2021). However, high-tech industries reflect and often reinforce existing socioeconomic inequalities and social injustice. Consequently, entrepreneurial ecosystems are not equally open for all (Ahl & Marlow, 2012), and tech entrepreneurs are often portrayed as "generic superstars" (Brück et al., 2013), with the dominant stereotypes still white, male heterosexual tech genius. In line with the meritocracy myth discussed in previous chapters of this book, technological entrepreneurs are supposedly self-taught, self-reliant and self-employed and entirely responsible for their own faith. However, and in contradiction with the meritocracy myth, much research shows that entrepreneurs in general and technological entrepreneurs in particular are a reflection of their time and place, which shape the types of challenges and opportunities they encounter. As I have outlined in previous chapters of this book, there is increased academic and policy attention to entrepreneurship unfolding at the margins of societies, highlighting the significantly circumstances, challenges and barriers entrepreneurs have to deal with in comparison to the high-tech heroes at the centers.

In Israel, the Arab-Palestinian citizens[2] constitute about 21% of the overall Israeli population. Following the Central Bureau of Statistics (CBS) of the Arab-Palestinian citizens, 82.9% self-define as Muslims, 9.2 % as Druze, and 7.9% as Christians (Haj-Yahya et al., 2022). The identity of these minorities is multifaceted, typically encompassing conflicting features, including national (Palestinian), civic (Israeli), religious (Muslim/Christian/Druze) and local community identities (Amara & Schnell, 2004; Diamond, 2020). Almost half of the population reside in local councils (69 local Arab municipalities), and about 41% live in cities—mostly in one of the 12 Arabs Palestinian cities and 7 mixed cities. The socioeconomic status in the majority of the Arab municipalities (in 64 out of 79, which represent 81%) is in the

DOI: 10.4324/9781003091042-12

lowest three (out of ten) levels. Major socioeconomic gaps with the majority Jewish population encompass education, health, transportation, personal security and more. Following a report prepared by Tsofen, a prominent NGO active in the public space of Israel, reasons for the gap include an inequitable division of public resources, inadequate opportunity structure, discrimination and neglect, lack of proper infrastructure and inaccessibility of capital. In addition, there are internal cultural challenges such as low participation of women in the workforce, hindrances for women to work outside their communities and low-level training of the workforce. Arab-Palestinians earn significantly less than their Jewish counterparts, with an average household income of about 11,000 NIS as opposed to 23,000 NIS of the average non-orthodox Jewish household. Both populations are employed at overall similar rates, although Arab-Palestinian employees are younger and the participation of women in the labor market is still lower. As a result of the previous, the poverty rate among the Arab-Palestinians is significantly higher in comparison with the Jewish majority. Although educational achievements in general and entrance into higher education in particular have significantly increased during the years, there is still a gap with the dominant Jewish population (Holzmann & Halabi, 2017). The Arab-Palestinians constitute about a fifth of the Israeli population; however, they are continuously underrepresented in higher education and in the high-tech industry.

In sum, higher rates of minority poverty (Mahajne et al., 2022); ideological divisions regarding the Jewish nature of the country (Ghanem & Rouhana, 2001); religious differences (Tatar, 2006); separate Arabic- and Hebrew-language education systems (Khamaisi & Abu-Saad, 2015); the context of conflict (Nasie et al., 2016); and social distance that results in feelings of alienation, discrimination and racism (Al-Haj, 1995, 2002) comprise the main factors contributing to the social and cultural distance between Jews and Arab-Palestinians in Israel (Diamond, 2020).

In the remaining part of this chapter, I will first present a short overview of the literature on nontechnological and technological entrepreneurship of Arab-Palestinians in Israel. Second, I will provide data as to the current situation of the Arab-Palestinian population in the Israeli high-tech industry and discuss the reasons for their underrepresentation. A small collection of agencies promoting high-tech employment and entrepreneurship in the Arab-Palestinian population are presented, followed by interviews with high-tech entrepreneurs and additional stakeholders. Concluding remarks close this chapter.

Literature on Non-technological and Technological Entrepreneurship of Arab-Palestinians in Israel

A number of academic articles based on empirical research exists on entrepreneurship of the Arab-Palestinian citizens in Israel. Heilbrunn and Abu-Asbeh

(2010, 2011; Abu-Asbah & Heilbrunn, 2011) investigated patterns of entrepreneurship evolving under conditions of double discrimination characterizing the situation of Arab-Palestinian women entrepreneurs in Israel and found that they were "overembedded" within their minority ethnic milieu in the periphery. The women established rather traditional businesses mainly in the realm of personal services and reported on many difficulties and lack of opportunities to receive business counselling. A study conducted by the same authors in 2014 focused on difficulties faced by women entrepreneurs in Israel in general and among them Arab-Palestinian women entrepreneurs in particular. The findings revealed that at the intersection of gender, class and ethnicity, Arab-Palestinian women faced relatively more difficulties, also but not only due to their geographic and social peripheral positioning (Heilbrunn et al., 2014). Schnell and Sofer (2002, 2003) examined the unbalanced embeddedness of Arab-Palestinian entrepreneurs. They identified mechanisms perpetuating their peripheral status such as selective state policies that privilege new Jewish towns over neighboring Arab ones; the abuse of power by Jewish corporations; and low profitability generated by the presence of many small competitors. Also, in 2017, Schnell and colleagues (2017) found that Arab-Palestinian entrepreneurship represented peripheral activities with very limited potential to overcome marginality.

Abu Nasra and Oliver (2018) investigated the role of the founder's human and social capital in the success of ethnic high-tech startups and found that in life sciences, successful Arab-Palestinian technological entrepreneurs have higher human and social capital measures in comparison to Jewish entrepreneurs. The authors point out that for minority populations, academia is an important path to enter the high-tech industry.

Rosenberg (2018), in his book on Israel's technological economy, devotes a chapter called "Outsiders" to the Arab-Palestinian population in Israel. He explains their underrepresentation in the high-tech industry as resulting from institutional discrimination and cultural traditionalism, which is a barrier in modern labor markets.

Harel et al. (2021) and Shilon et al. (2021) investigated conditions to integrate socioeconomically disadvantaged minorities in ethnically mixed regions into technological entrepreneurship and high-tech activities. They found that in mixed regions where the minority population is extremely weak socioeconomically, it is necessary to implement readiness for high tech. Thus, a pre-preliminary phase aimed at legitimizing high tech in general and high-tech entrepreneurship in particular will increase acceptance as an occupational trajectory.

The Arab-Palestinian Population in the Israeli High-Tech Industry

Following data presented by 2021 Report of the Innovation Authority (Israel Innovation Authority, 2021), the share of Arab-Palestinian employees in the high-tech industry employment has been moderately rising over the years but is still extremely low, 2 % in 2021. The share of women among Arab-Palestinian employees stands at 31.8%, with a decrease from 42.4% in 2019 (Israel Innovation Authority, 2020). Most of the Arab-Palestinians integrated into the high-tech industry are employed in large multinational companies and not in local companies and startups. Following the estimation of Takwin[3] (Weeks, 2022), Palestinian Arab-led companies account for just 1.3% of Israeli startups, about 100–150, the majority in early stages of development. The share of Arab-Palestinian students enrolled in academic high-tech disciplines has increased from 7.2% to 12.7%. In 2020, the number of Arab-Palestinian male students amounted to 3,456 and 1,760 female students (Israel Innovation Authority, 2020).

Reasons for the Underrepresentation of the Arab-Palestinian Population in the Israeli High-Tech Industry

The following part of this chapter integrates and summarizes the data and insights provided in a number of reports prepared by agencies involved in the field,[4] such as the Innovation Authority, Start-Up Nation Central, Bank of Israel, Inter-Agency Task Force on Israeli Arab Issues and NGOs active in the field. The reasons for the underrepresentation of the Arab-Palestinian population in the Israeli high-tech industry are listed one by one but definitely overlap within the complex realities of the context.

Socioeconomic Gaps

The socioeconomic gap between the dominant Jewish population and the Arab-Palestinian population is still big and inherently implies resource and cultural barriers. The majority of Arab-Palestinians in Israel live in disadvantaged communities with little or no exposure to advanced industries. In addition, the share of the Arab-Palestinian population in low-quality employment is high; there are few opportunities to develop networks skills to compete in the high-tech industry.

Level of Education

The Arab-Palestinian educational system has been underbudgeted for years, and only lately has the attitude of the government changed, based on the insight that the Israeli labor market, especially the high-tech industry, is in need of a highly qualified workforce. Until lately, computers were scarce in Arab-Palestinian schools; the internet connection was extremely unstable and classes and school buildings poorly equipped. To close the gap in educational achievements is a long-term undertaking. Disciplines necessary to integrate into higher education aimed at the high-tech industry include mathematics and English- and Hebrew-language skills, all of which have been underrepresented in the Arab-Palestinian school system until now. Thus, a major reason for the low representation of Arab-Palestinian employees in the high-tech industry originates in gaps in human capital development from early childhood education through university.

Army/Military

Israel's high-tech industry has profound roots in security and military defense. The majority of the Arab-Palestinian young women and men do not serve in the Israeli army. This causes two partly interrelated issues. First, over the last years, service in one of the technologic intelligence units such as the elite 8200 intelligence unit constitutes a primary talent pipeline and training resource for the high-tech industry. Second, some high-tech companies in Israel demand security clearance of the potential employees, usually not granted to people who did not serve in the army. Thirdly, the army-related network is an asset in the high-tech industry and is not open to those who did not serve in the army in general and in the relevant units in particular.

Geographic Distance

Up to today and as has been explained in previous chapters of this book, the Israeli high-tech industry is geographically concentrated in Tel Aviv and its close vicinities. However, more than 70% of the Arab-Palestinian population reside in Israel's periphery (the Galilee and the Negev), in a distance far from the high-tech hub and its employment opportunities. Furthermore, Arab-Palestinian citizens traditionally refrain from relocation and are inclined to build their family homes in their home locations. Commuting to the center from the periphery is challenging due to low-quality public transport and frequent traffic bottlenecks.

Lack of Financial Resources

For Arab-Palestinian potential entrepreneurs, the lack of financial resources constituted a major barrier in the past, but lately there are dedicated funds provided by the Innovation Authority for underrepresented groups such as ultra-Orthodox, women and Arab-Palestinians. In addition, NGOs and a dedicated VC fund (Tawkin) target Arab-Palestinian entrepreneurs. These developments are yet to show results, overcoming the fact that Arab-Palestinian investors are more risk averse and less familiar with the high-tech industry.

Strategic Institutional Support

Strategic institutional support is crucial for integrating underrepresented groups into the high-tech industry in general and in Israel in particular.

Since the Israeli government perceives the integration of minority populations into high tech as crucial, during the last years, a number of initiatives have been established by agencies such as the Innovation Authority, Start-Up Nation Central and the Council for Higher Education to foster entrance of young Arab-Palestinian women and men into then industry. Slight improvements have been observed during the last years. Whether these initiatives will indeed be successful remains to be seen.

High-Tech Industry Insularity

The distance of the Arab-Palestinian population from the high-tech industry also results from what has been called its "insulated" nature. Jobs are often kept within small homogeneous circles, excluding "others" on a variety of grounds. In addition, when recruitment companies are engaged, they often do not have the expertise to understand and account for cultural differences and group particularities. Furthermore, few Arab-Palestinians have "friends" who can recommend them.

Employers

Employing high-tech companies are concerned with potential and assumed differences in the mentality and availability of Arab-Palestinian employees, in particular but not only women, constrained to work long hours and travel abroad. Lack of familiarity and long-lasting common experiences between Jews and Arab-Palestinians in the high-tech industry affect the readiness of employers to hire. In addition, political tensions coming up frequently in Israel due to internal or external events are challenging in coexisting spaces, and maintaining productive work environments requires extra effort.

Cultural Issues

The Arab-Palestinian community is still rather unfamiliar with the Israeli high-tech industry, and that concerns the younger generations too. Women consider it a masculine field, and especially in more traditional and religious circles, working with computers is not considered appropriate and fashionable. There is a call to rebranded high tech in the Arabic Palestinian society so that the younger generations perceive it as a viable and attractive career trajectory.

Dedicated Agencies Promoting High-Tech Employment and Entrepreneurship in the Arab-Palestinian Population

The Israeli Innovation Authority and Start-Up Nation Central as well as additional governmental agencies are engaged in promoting underrepresented populations, among them Arab-Palestinians' integration into the Israeli high-tech industry. In addition, there are a number of dedicated NGOs such as **Tsofen** (Tsofen, 2022), a nonprofit organization founded in 2008 by Jewish and Arab-Palestinian high-tech professionals and economists. The NGO operates in Nazareth and Kfar Kasem. The website of the NGO states their mission was to develop the high-tech sector in the Arab-Palestinian community in order to upgrade its economy and provide a mechanism for a sustainable shared society. More specifically, Tsofen identified the fact that there are many Arab-Palestinian engineers not employed in the high-tech labor market. Tsofen aims to overcome the barriers to integration, promoting an economic reality for all groups. Nazareth is one of the centers of Tsofen's activities, where today a couple of major high-tech companies are located.

Hasoub is a grassroots movement paving the way for the coming generation of Arab tech entrepreneurs. In January 2015, the first event of the organization took place, discussing tech entrepreneurship in our own Arab towns and villages. According to the organization's website (Hasoub, 2022), Hasoub focuses on "filling the pipeline with more potential Arab entrepreneurs by empowering university students and early-stage entrepreneurs with the knowledge, skills, network and resources they need to pursue their dreams and build their Startups." Hasan Abo-Shalley is one of the founders of Hasoub. He explained the motivation for initiating the NGO: "We were all sharing an amazing time and experience when developing our ideas. But at the same time, we also shared the pain of exclusion and the financial consequences this exclusion has on the Arab-Palestinian society."

Takwin is the Haifa-based VC firm supporting high-tech Arab-Palestinian startups in Israel and assisting them to accelerate their transition from high potential to high growth. Tawkin was founded in 2017 by a cooperation between high-profile VCs. According to the organization's website, by fostering an established Arab presence in Israel's high-tech industry, Takwin

> seeks to create a strong foundation for Arab-Israelis to contribute to "Startup Nation" and bolster Israel both socially and economically. Takwin empowers the next generation of Arab-Israeli entrepreneurs to "Dare, Dream, Compete, and Deliver" through its Takwin 1 and Takwin 2 funds.

The funds provide early startups with a pool of support mechanisms, such as office space, research assistance, financial support and connection to professional networks.

These initiatives, in combination with government policies, has led to some positive outcomes such as the city of Nazareth, where the high-tech industry has grown over the years. The city hosts incubators and accelerators for startups, an industrial park, coworking spaces and networking meetings. Furthermore, there is a growing tech center in Kfar Kasem.

Following the media, the Israel Ministry of Science, Technology and Innovation and the Israel Innovation Authority have initiated an economic program to encourage minorities to get involved in the high-tech industry. The purpose of the five-year plan is "to advance hi-tech and innovation in Arab Society in Israel is the continuation of its socio-economic development by integration into the Israeli hi-tech industry—the main 'engine' of the Israeli economy" (Tsofen, 2000). Accordingly, Tsofen founded the Public Council for the Advancement of Arabs in High-Tech and Innovation. The council presented a strategic plan encompassing the following goals: developing high-tech-oriented human capital in the Arab-Palestinian society in Israel; integrating Arab-Palestinians into the high-tech industry; advancing expansion and innovation in the Arab-Palestinian municipalities; supporting and promoting leadership and "high-tech culture" in Arab-Palestinian communities (Inter-Agency Task Force, 2022).

The Interviews

This chapter includes four interviews with Arab-Palestinian entrepreneurs. In addition, I interviewed an investor, the manager of an innovation center, and the CEO of Tsofen (his interview is also part of Chapter 13 of this book). Table 11.1 summarized the interview answers of four Arab-Palestinian tech entrepreneurs, two women and two men. The two women, Hanya Tarabi and Nuseiba Hassan, are well established in the life-science industry; both have started their businesses in an incubator and are now in the growth stage. Hussein Amer is currently employed in a multinational company (MNC) and, in parallel, develops a digital platform and content for a startup. Aiman Hazima is only at the beginning stage of his startup idea and has trouble setting up the business plan and recruiting funding.

All four entrepreneurs have academic degrees and reported that they had no problem finding employment prior to starting their entrepreneurial endeavor. Aiman Hazima can lean on a network of high-tech professionals that he acquired within his position as a developer in an MNC. He is the only one who has international experience. Both women reported that they had to work hard to establish and enter a professional network; being part of an incubator definitely helped. Except for Hussein, three of the entrepreneurs enjoy the support of their social environment. Hussein explained that his parents would prefer that he proceeded in a career as an employee in the municipality. Only Nuseiba maintained that in her environment, to be a tech entrepreneur is considered desirable. Hazima and Amer explained that their families do not really appreciate the field and are not aware of its importance and glory in Israeli society. The two women explained that one motivation for entering the incubator was their own perception of lack of business knowledge. For Hussein, the lack of business knowledge was the main reason for not proceeding with the project. The three active tech entrepreneurs are convinced that they have an impact on their community

Table 11.1 Structured summary of interviews with four Arab-Palestinian tech entrepreneurs.

	Hanya Tarabi	*Nuseiba Hassan*	*Hussein Amer*	*Aiman Hazima*
Demographics	Female, around 45, married + children.	Female, 50, married + 3 children.	Male, 34, married + 2 children.	Male, 35, married + 1 child.
Education	PhD in biomedical engineering.	MA in chemical engineering.	PhD candidate in Education.	IT engineer with international experience.
Availability of employment opportunities?	She was employed, many employment opportunities.	She was employed, many employment opportunities.	He is currently employed.	He is currently employed.
Access to high-tech networks?	Yes, she has access but she had to work hard.	She put a lot of effort into establishing a network.	Not many opportunities to establish a network.	Since he is employed in the high-tech industry and has international experience, he is part of a network.
Access to financial and material resources?	She joined the incubator in order to get access to these resources.	She joined the incubator in order to get access to these resources.	He joined the we-work innovation center in order to be exposed.	He has access to financial and material resources.
Support or lack of support of family and friends.	Family and friends support her.	Family and friends support her.	Family does not support his startup ideas. Friends do.	Family and friends support him but actually, he is supporting them all.
In your environment, is establishing a startup evaluated as something desirable? Is it a status symbol?	Not really.	Yes.	No.	Not necessarily.

(*Continued*)

Table 11.1 (Continued)

	Hanya Tarabi	*Nuseiba Hassan*	*Hussein Amer*	*Aiman Hazima*
Knowledge of "doing business"?	She joined the incubator to acquire business knowledge.	She joined the incubator to acquire business knowledge.	No, he does not have business knowledge; therefore, he could not proceed with his startup.	He has ample business knowledge and experience.
In what way does your startup affect your community?	Role model.	Role model.	Not relevant since he did not realize the idea.	Role model.
Would you rather be employed (have a secure place of work)?	No.	No.	Not relevant.	Not relevant.
How would you evaluate the financial situation of your family?	Well-off.	Well-off.	Struggling.	Well-off.

as role models. Except for Hussein Amer, the tech entrepreneurs are financially well-off.

The following summarizes the answers given by the interview partners to the question of their experience as Arab-Palestinian entrepreneurs.

Hanya Tarabi talks about the challenge of living in the periphery: "The majority of us live in the periphery, very far from Tel Aviv, far from the center of the technology and innovation, investments and adventure capitals, so we are isolated from this industry." She continues and maintains,

> For me, as an entrepreneur, it was very difficult to establish the company, and it was very difficult to raise funds for the company because I felt isolated. I felt very far from what is happening, and I wasn't in the middle of the high-tech scenario, and I was an Arab woman.

She explained that the expectation of investors was to see a Jewish man since the Jewish men are the dominant figures in the scene. She also explained that there is a lack of Arab-Palestinian investors and that they don't have enough money to invest in life-science companies, which demand high amounts and long-term commitment. She does complain,

> The ecosystem is focused only on a very small group of people. They mainly invest in the center of Israel; they are in control of everything. They control the market, they control the funding, they control everything. If you're not part of this network or ecosystem or group of people, you're not part of anything, you will be always separated. I think it needs a lot of work to convert it into a fair and equal ecosystem. That's my evaluation, so I think presently, the ecosystem failed—my vision is to see an equal opportunity for everyone despite the fact of being a woman, a man, an Arab or a Jew. It shouldn't be an issue, and the opportunity should be provided equally for each and every one, but sadly it's not what is going on today.

She explains that the companies founded by Arab-Palestinian tech entrepreneurs are trying to survive on their own, outside the Israeli (Jewish) ecosystem, but there is no separate ecosystem.

Nuseiba Hassan explains that the incubator was not the only place in her career path where she was the only woman. Throughout her higher education, she collaborated with mechanical engineers, who were men only. When trying to look for funding, she had some difficulties:

> Because I come from a different community, I have a different mindset. It is very difficult for an investor to invest in a different person—from an unknown environment. To invest in someone whom they do not know how they think and whether they can lead the company—what tools do they have, because they didn't go to the army? So all these

> things raise actual question marks from the side of the investor and make it very difficult for them to make the decision to invest in an Arab entrepreneur.

In addition, Nuseiba mentions the language issue, explaining that not all Arab-Palestinians—even if they have university degrees—are really fluent in Hebrew. Hebrew is their second language and English the third. So that is a hurdle they have to deal with. Nuseiba also points to a cultural barrier.

> And I can tell you that unfortunately, not all the men feel comfortable to look me in the eyes and talk to me. I don't know why. And I'm not talking only about Arabs. It is the same for Jewish men.

Aiman Hazima has international experience and is still employed in an MNC. He maintains that he never felt discrimination in his immediate work environment, neither in Israel nor in the countries where he worked. The main subject he communicated was his consideration of where to live. He explain,:

> I have a flat in Leimrac [a midsize Jewish town]. There is an industrial park and a college and a small high-tech infrastructure. My village has now become a city, but there are so many problems: infrastructure, education and distance from the center.

He continues and explains, "I want to own a high-tech company in the future, so I should leave Leimrac, but then my family is here and I want to help others in my community." He maintains that there are more than 100 engineers in Isaui, but there is not one high-tech company, and many of the engineers do not find jobs and then work as teachers. He definitely sees himself as driving high tech forward within the Arab-Palestinian community.

Hussein Amer wanted to combine technology with pedagogic content and change the space of schools in the Arab-Palestinian society. He maintained, "I got stuck in the investment stage. I thought I could do it all by myself. I do not have the money to continue. I am not sure I want to at this stage." He works as the IT manager and coordinator in the municipality of Isaui so he knows about the infrastructure problems. He believes that the low quality of the infrastructure in terms of traffic, public transport and internet access are hurdles for Arab-Palestinian potential tech entrepreneurs. He refers to the impact of struggling with these hurdles on the mindset and maintains, "Also, you dream lower, and I can't really explain why."

In addition to the interviews with the tech entrepreneurs, I conducted interviews with an investor from the Arab-Palestinian community, with the CEO of Tsofen, with an incubator manager and with the manager of a newly established innovation center and we-work.

Azem Fatan manages the newly established innovation center in Isaui, which is also a we-work. The center was established and funded by the municipality and the governmental office for the development of the Negev and the Galil. Then, the intention was to increase high-tech entrepreneurship in the Arab-Palestinian communities, especially those located in the geographic periphery. The center cooperates with another governmental agency, providing courses and training in a variety of employment concerned fields. "The most important thing is to create a space where people can meet and talk innovation, talk business, have affordable space for promoting business ideas or just set up their office here." Azem has many plans to develop the center and is particularly concerned with young academics who do not find adequate employment. "The engineers are the biggest problem. You know the medicine students and those who study paramedical professions do find jobs. The engineers have much more problems." Her husband, an IT engineer, is working in a city far away from Isaui and is driving about 3.5 hours in each direction every day. He is not allowed to do home office at all since the company is in the field of security.

Alon Lev is the manager of a technological incubator in Latour. He explained that Latour is still periphery, and periphery is a different story.

> There are consequences to being in the periphery. First of all, at the formal level, we get more money than what an incubator in the center would get. Our projects are higher budgeted because we are in the periphery. But then, the Innovation Authority has to make sure that the companies are really in the periphery.

Lev explains that additionally, it is not easy to recruit adequate employees, but having local employees will, in the end, make the company stay and not move to Tel Aviv. "Relocation is not an option for most Arab-Palestinian entrepreneurs—that is why they have less opportunities to find employment." The traffic infrastructure is a major obstacle for peripheral areas in general and Arab-Palestinian smaller villages in particular, maintains Lev. "You know, although Israel is a small country, traffic bottlenecks are a major issue and can cause you to be on the road for long hours."

Jamil Hajub is the owner of a successful VC company. First he explained that he is not investing in Israeli tech startups any more but only in the Gaza Strip, the West Bank and Jordan. The startups from Jordan have to have significant presence in either Gaza or the West Bank so as to contribute to the economy of these territories. Hajub explains,

> I have been involved in the Israeli ecosystem for years. I know it very well; Tel Aviv and Herzliya are absolutely comparable to Silicon Valley—probably among the top five ecosystems in the world. But the Israeli Arab ecosystem is far behind—and that although we have more Technion graduates and more people employed in MNCs than before.

He maintains that the Jordanian ecosystem and the Palestinian ecosystem in the West Bank and Gaza are more developed than the Arab-Palestinian ecosystem in Israel. "The Jordanians have access to lots of resources, government involvement, tax breaks accelerators and so on. It is also much easier than here to register a business." He maintains that the Arab-Palestinian economy in Israel is not an integral part of the Israeli economy, although there are, of course, relations. There is exchange of labor and products. "And that is okay, but still, it is not really a part."

He also points to cultural barriers of the Arab-Palestinian population in Israel:

> We don't encourage failure. We don't encourage trial and error, culturally. An Arab Israeli mother's dream is that her kid is accepted to med school and now recently maybe to intel, maybe get a degree in engineering. But she doesn't think he should be an entrepreneur. Everyone would say he is crazy to leave a good job for starting a business.

Sami Saadi, the CEO of Tsofen, talks about the mission of the NGO: "bringing the Arabs closer to high tech and bringing high-tech to the Arabs." For that he believes, "it is important to expose students to the possibilities of high tech but also their parents, who, in the case of Arab students, have significant influence over the course of studies." He talks about the impact of most Arab-Palestinian students not serving in the army: "They are not exposed to the knowledge development, the experience and the network like their Jewish and Druze counterparts, and since they enroll in university or college immediately after finishing high school, they are much younger." Tsofen promotes the integration of Arab-Palestinian companies in high-tech centers and facilitates employment via placement coordination for engineering graduates. In addition, Sami explains the difficulties of graduates in the high-tech center of Tel Aviv:

> We try to empower those already in the tech industry and try to help those graduates who couldn't find work in high-tech in the center. If they don't find work there, they come back to their hometowns in the periphery to work in another field. That has a negative impact on the Arab-Palestinian society as a whole.

He maintains that if those studying tech-related disciplines don't find work in their field, others will not go to study these disciplines. Hence, Tsofen focuses on creating cases of success that will translate to positive social impact. Saad also explains that the NGO is acting to implement government decisions to establish work spaces for high-tech development connected to internet and electricity infrastructure. One of these work spaces is managed by Azem Fatan, as described before. Saad maintains that the elements that are lacking for a startup culture to grow in the Arab-Palestinian society in

Israel concern lack of awareness of entrepreneurship, lack of an ecosystem and lack of access to funds and networks.

Concluding Thoughts

Globally, minorities are often excluded from successful entrepreneurial and technological ecosystems, and the reasons for this exclusion are many and various and dependent upon the context. Since 2014 the OECD publishes a yearly report called *The Missing Entrepreneurs: Policies for Inclusive Entrepreneurship and Self-Employment* highlighting the exclusion of "others" from entrepreneurial ecosystems in general and technological ecosystems in particular. The OECD is concerned with global developments and postulates that this exclusion does not only harm the excluded but also the excluding. Also in Israel, the government and other stakeholders realized that the economy suffers heavy losses because entire populations are not partaking in the high-tech industry. Therefore, much activity has been initiated to change this reality. However, after many years of planning and realizing large-scale initiatives by the government, the Innovation Authority, NGOs and private companies, the results are not promising. Undeniably, between 2012 and 2020, the share of Arab-Palestinian employees in high-tech employment increased, but it stands now on 2.3% following the Start-Up Nation Central report. In other words, only 2.3% of the high-tech employees in Israel are Arab-Palestinians, and the number of Arab-Palestinian-owned high-tech startups is estimated at 1.3% of Israeli startups, about 100–150.

This chapter identified a number of reasons explaining these numbers at least partly: socioeconomic gaps, level of education, lack of financial resources, weak strategic institutional support, insularity of the high tech, challenges of employers in dealing with diversity, cultural issues and geographic location. These reasons reappear in a variety of combinations in policy papers, agendas of NGOs, government initiatives and academic and nonacademic articles. Most of them also came up in the interviews, in those with the high-tech entrepreneurs themselves and in those with the stakeholders. The analysis of all sources indicates that Arab-Palestinians are positioned in a double periphery—a social periphery as a national minority with cultural particularities and a geographic periphery with poor infrastructure, making it difficult to commute to the center. The main reason for the failure to integrate Arab-Palestinians into the high-tech industry—as employees or entrepreneurs—might be located at the intersection of both peripheries. As a national minority, the Arab-Palestinians in Israel were exposed to structural discrimination over many years. This position is reflected not only in an unequal opportunity structure but also in people's perceptions of opportunities and their estimation of capabilities.

Lately, Innovation, Science and Technology Minister Orit Farkash-Hacohen was quoted in the media (Ben-David, 2022). She said the shortage of Arab-Palestinian employees in high-tech was "a national challenge for the

Israeli economy as a whole." In addition, she maintained that incorporating employees from the Arab community into the tech sector was "a highly important social, financial, and strategic need."

Whether or not these insights will translate into an effective and realistic policy plan to increase the number of Arab-Palestinians in the high-tech industry remains to be seen.

Notes

1. In calling the population Arab-Palestinian, I am following the suggestion of Diamond (2020): "Refers to the Arab-Palestinian minority in Israel. Minority communities in Israel self-define their nationality in different ways according to context as combinations of Arab, Arab-Palestinian, Palestinian, Arab-Israeli or Israeli, amongst others. I use the term Arab-Palestinian throughout the paper in order to encompass as wide a range of populations as possible whilst minimizing the risk of identity erasure (Furani & Rabinowitz, 2011)."
2. It was beyond the scope of this book to relate to the Palestinians of the West Bank, Gaza Strip and East Jerusalem. The economic and social circumstances of these people are substantially different from the Arab-Palestinians discussed in this chapter. In addition, comparative data were not available.
3. Takwin is a Haifa-based VC firm promoting high-tech Arab startups in Israel.
4. Tsofen (2000); Holzmann and Halabi (2017); Schneider and Shoham (2018); Blass (2017, p. 4); Bank of Israel (2021).

References

Abu-Asbah, K. M., & Heilbrunn, S. (2011). Patterns of entrepreneurship of Arab women in Israel. *Journal of Enterprising Communities: People and Places in the Global Economy*. https://doi.org/10.1108/17506201111156661

Abu Nasra, K. M., & Oliver, A. L. (2018). The role of founders' human and social capital in the success of ethnic high-tech start-ups. *Academy of Management Proceedings, 2018*(1), 16041. https://doi.org/10.5465/ambpp.2018.16041abstract

Ahl, H., & Marlow, S. (2012). Exploring the dynamics of gender, feminism and entrepreneurship: Advancing debate to escape a dead end? *Organization, 19*(5), 543–562. https://doi.org/10.1177/1350508412448695

Al-Haj, M. (1995). *Education, empowerment, and control—The case of the Arabs in Israel*. State University of New York Press.

Al-Haj, M. (2002). Multiculturalism in deeply divided societies: The Israeli case. *International Journal of Intercultural Relations, 26*(2), 169–183. https://doi.org/10.1016/s0147-1767(01)00048-7

Amara, M., & Schnell, I. (2004). Identity repertoires among Arabs in Israel. *Journal of Ethnic and Migration Studies, 30*(1), 175–193. https://doi.org/10.1080/1369183032000170222

Bank of Israel. (2021). *Arab society in Israel's high tech sector*. Bank of Israel.

Ben-David, R. (2022, January 27). Israel launches $70m program to promote tech entrepreneurship in Arab community. *Times of Israel*. Retrieved April 6, 2022, from www.timesofisrael.com/israel-launches-70m-program-to-promote-tech-entrepreneurship-in-arab-community/

Blass, N. (2017). *The academic achievements of Arab Israeli pupils*. Taub Center.

Boulus-Rødje, N., & Bjørn, P. (2021). Tech public of erosion: The formation and transformation of the Palestinian tech entrepreneurial public. *Computer Supported Cooperative Work*, 1–41. https://doi.org/10.1007/s10606-021-09419-y

Brück, T., Naudé, W., & Verwimp, P. (2013). Business under fire: Entrepreneurship and violent conflict in developing countries. *Journal of Conflict Resolution*, *57*(1), 3–19. https://doi.org/10.1177/0022002712464846

Diamond, A. H. (2020). Minority youth acculturation in third spaces: An ethnography of Arab-Palestinian high school students visiting the Israeli innovation secto. *Journal of Ethnic and Migration Studies*, 1–21. https://doi.org/10.1080/1369183x.2020.1847055

Furani, K., & Rabinowitz, D. (2011). The ethnographic arriving of Palestine. *Annual Review of Anthropology*, *40*(1), 475–491. https://doi.org/10.1146/annurev-anthro-081309-145910

Ghanem, A. A., & Rouhana, N. N. (2001). Citizenship and the parliamentary politics of minorities in ethnic states: The Palestinian citizens of Israel. *Nationalism and Ethnic Politics*, 7(4), 66–86. https://doi.org/10.1080/13537110108428645

Haj-Yahya, N. H., Khalaily, M., Rudnitzky, A., & Fargeon, B. (2022). *Statistical report on Arab society in Israel: 2021*. Israeli Democracy Institute. Retrieved May 4, 2022, from https://en.idi.org.il/articles/38540

Harel, R., Kaufmann, D., & Schwartz, D. (2021). Integrating low socio-economic minorities in a mixed region into technological entrepreneurship and high-tech activities. *Innovation: The European Journal of Social Science Research*, 1–21. https://doi.org/10.1080/13511610.2021.1995333

Hasoub. (2022, April 6). *Hasoub*. www.hasoub.org/

Heilbrunn, S., & Abu-Asbeh, K. M. (2010). On entrepreneurship among Druze. In L.-P. D. (Ed.), *Entrepreneurship and religion* (pp. 313–325). Edward Elgar Publishing. https://doi.org/10.4337/9781849806329.00025

Heilbrunn, S., & Abu-Asbah, K. M. (2011). Disadvantaged and embedded: Arab women entrepreneurs in Israel. *International Journal of Business and Social Science*, *2*(11).

Heilbrunn, S., Abu-Asbeh, K. M., & Nasra, M. A. (2014). Difficulties facing women entrepreneurs in Israel: A social stratification approach. *International Journal of Gender and Entrepreneurship*, *6*(2), 142–162. https://doi.org/10.1108/ijge-02-2013-0007

Holzmann, V., & Halabi, R. (2017). *High-tech entrepreneurship in the Israeli-Arab community*. Eli Hurvitz Institute for Strategic Management—Tel Aviv University.

Inter-Agency Task Force. (2022, April 9). Tsofen—High technology centers. *Iataskforce*. www.iataskforce.org/entities/view/174

Israel Innovation Authority. (2020). *2020 High-tech human capital report*. Israel Innovation Authority. Retrieved March 24, 2022, from https://startupnationcentral.org/wp-content/uploads/2021/04/2020-Human-Capital-Report-Eng.pdf

Israel Innovation Authority. (2021). *Israel innovation authority's 2021 innovation report*. Israel Innovation Authority.

Khamaisi, R., & Abu-Saad, I. (2015). *Education and territory: Charged issues*. The Open University of Israel.

Mahajne, I., Allassad Alhuzail, N., & Bar-On, A. (2022). Challenges facing social work in the indigenous Arab minority in Israel: Voices from the field. *The British Journal of Social Work*, *52*(2), 816–832. https://doi.org/10.1093/bjsw/bcab069

Nasie, M., Diamond, A. H., & Bar-Tal, D. (2016). Young children in intractable conflicts. *Personality and Social Psychology Review*, *20*(4), 365–392. https://doi.org/10.1177/1088868315607800

Rosenberg, D. (2018). *Israel's technology economy: Origins and impact*. Palgrave Macmillan. https://doi.org/10.1007/978-3-319-76654-6

Schneider, A., & Shoham, L. (2018). *Arab citizens' integration into Israeli high-tech: Achievements and emerging issues*. Inter-Agency Task Force on Israeli Arab Issues.

Schnell, I., Greenberg, Z., Arnon, S., & Shamai, S. (2017). Entrepreneurship in the periphery and local growth: The case of northern Israel. *GeoJournal*, *82*(2), 217–229. https://doi.org/10.1007/s10708-015-9676-9

Schnell, I., & Sofer, M. (2002). Unbalanced embeddedness of ethnic entrepreneurship: The Israeli Arab case. *International Journal of Entrepreneurial Behavior & Research*, *8*(1/2), 54–68. https://doi.org/10.1108/13552550210423714

Schnell, I., & Sofer, M. (2003). Embedding entrepreneurship in social structure: Israeli-Arab entrepreneurship. *International Journal of Urban and Regional Research*, *27*(2), 300–318. https://doi.org/10.1111/1468-2427.00449

Shilon, M., Kaufmann, D., Schwartz, D., & Rosiello, A. (2021). Smart specialization: A spontaneous four-step process in the mixed Arab-Jewish region of Haifa and Nazareth. *Regional Studies*, 1–16. https://doi.org/10.1080/00343404.2021.1948524

Tatar, M. (2006). Diversity and citizenship education in Israel. In J. A. Banks (Ed.), *Diversity and citizenship education: Global perspectives* (pp. 377–405). Jossey-Bass.

Tsofen. (2000). *A long-term policy plan for developing hi-tech in Arab society*. Tsofen—High Technology Centers.

Tsofen. (2022, April 6). *Tsofen*. www.tsofen.org/

Weeks, D. G. (2022, March 29). Takwin announces launch of new fund aimed at elevating and empowering high-potential Arab entrepreneurs in Israel to bolster "startup nation." *Businesswire*. Retrieved April 6, 2022, from www.businesswire.com/news/home/20220329005130/en/Takwin-Announces-Launch-of-New-Fund-Aimed-at-Elevating-and-Empowering-High-Potential-Arab-Entrepreneurs-in-Israel-to-Bolster-%E2%80%9CStartup-Nation%E2%80%9D

12 Comparative Analysis of Groups

Introduction

In line with the theoretical framework presented in Chapter 5 of this book, I will analyze the findings of Chapters 6 to 11, which described and discussed a selection of distinct groups and their involvement in the high-tech industry of Israel.

As has been discussed in Chapter 5 of this book, technological entrepreneurship occurs within a variety of contexts that affect its forms and contents. The distinct groups presented in this book are analyzed considering group level and individual level. Accordingly, in each of the relevant chapters, I presented the positionality (Anthias, 2001) of the groups within Israeli society, the position of the group within the tech industry of Israel in general and gave examples as to tech entrepreneurship and individual entrepreneurs. The individual cases introduced are not representative since I searched for tech entrepreneurs who were already actively involved at different stages of their startup. The entrepreneurs whom I interviewed do not necessarily represent their groups, but all exemplify a variety of aspects characterizing the position of their group within the high-tech industry of Israel.

The underlying assumption of the following analysis is that technological entrepreneurship in particular and the high-tech industry in general are entrenched within persistent social hierarchies in which some have more and easier access to critical capitals than others. Therefore, the positionality of the group one belongs to and the respective resources in terms of human, social and economic capital will pose structural and personal barriers (Dy et al., 2017; Dy & Agwunobi, 2019; Martinez Dy, 2020; Maalaoui et al., 2020). Thus, again, I am challenging the meritocracy myth discussed in former chapters of this book.

In the following, I will proceed with a three-stage process of interpretation and analysis of the data. First, I will elaborate on the position of the group in relation to the Israeli high-tech industry and the closeness or distance of the group to the high-tech field and norm circle. Naturally, I will have to rely on generalizations in order to explain the principal idea. Second, I will use the method of constructing "personas" demonstrating typical

DOI: 10.4324/9781003091042-13

high-tech entrepreneurs. Third, I will integrate the two stages and relate to the group specific similarities and differences important for understanding the representation of the groups in the Israeli high-tech industry.

Group-Level Analysis

As has been discussed in Chapter 5, the Israeli high-tech industry exemplifies Bourdieu's concept of field (Willig, 2013). It is geographically located at the center of the country, it is the driver of Israel's economy and there is an undisputable conviction in the public discourse that it is not only a game worth playing but of existential importance for the future of the country. Available venture capital comprises the resources of the tech entrepreneurs, the investors and the policy makers. Applying Bourdieu's concepts of capital for Israeli technological entrepreneurs, I state that their human capital (technical skills and knowledge) is valuable if combined with material capital (savings and investments) and the capability to sell their vision to customers and investors (cultural capital), which is facilitated by prior entrepreneurial successes or degrees from particular universities and military units (symbolic capital). In the norm circle of the Israeli high-tech ecosystem, practices that promote the high-tech habitus are constantly endorsed and enforced, so the members of the circle know they face a systematic incentive to enact these practices. The fact that the Israeli high-tech industry is extremely homogenous reinforces the mechanisms of the norm circle. As has been shown before, the typical Israeli tech entrepreneur is a white Jewish (mostly Ashkenazi) man, belonging to a family with a well-off socioeconomic background, often graduates of tech disciplines from universities and/or elite military intelligent units that function as and are perceived as a springboard to enter the high-tech scene. The following evidences this statement.

Every year on Israel's Independence Day, CTech publishes Calcalist's list of the 50 most promising Israeli startups (Calcalist, 2022). The list includes basic information on the product, the year the startup was founded, the names of the founders and sometimes also pictures, the amount of funds raised and the names of the investors. Based on the names of the founders and their pictures (where available), I compiled a list of the 50 most promising Israeli startups in Israel in the years 2018, 2019, 2020, 2021. Even when taking into account a small number of misevaluation of the origins of the names of the founders, the emerging picture does definitely not reflect diversity.

In 2018, 44 of the 50 most successful startups in Israel were founded by Jewish men, two were founded by Jewish men with female partners, and three were established by Jewish men together with Jewish immigrant men from the former Soviet Union. One startup was founded by men and women immigrants from the former Soviet Union.

In 2019, 44 of the 50 most successful startups in Israel were established by Jewish men, two were founded by Jewish men and female partners and two were founded by Jewish men together with Jewish immigrant men from the Former Soviet Union. One startup was established by Jewish Israeli and American men and one by ultra-Orthodox men.

In 2020, 40 of the 50 most successful startups in Israel were established by Jewish men, four were founded by Jewish men with female partners and four were founded by Jewish men together with Jewish immigrant men from the Former Soviet Union. One startup was set up by Jewish Israeli men and immigrant women from the Former Soviet Union.

In 2021, 38 of the 50 most successful startups in Israel were founded by Jewish men, two were established by Jewish men with female partners and five were set up by Jewish men together with Jewish immigrant men from the Former Soviet Union. Three startups were founded by Jewish Israeli and American men, and two were set up by Jewish men and immigrant women from the Former Soviet Union.

Undoubtly, the trend over the years shows a growing diversity of the owners of the 50 most successful startups in the Israeli high-tech industry, but the relative homogeneity in terms of gender, nationality and origin remains considerable. I could not find a single Arab-Palestinian man or women in the lists, and only one startup that made the list in 2019 is owned by ultra-Orthodox entrepreneurs. Moreover, there is only one startup owned by immigrants alone, without Israeli-born partnerships. The 2022 Report of the Innovation Authority reflects this trend and states that "high-tech is preserving is standing as an exclusive industry in which growth is primarily that of the (non-Orthodox) Jewish population in central Israel. An examination of the changes in the composition of salaried high-tech employees reveals that only 200 Arabs joined high-tech in 2021 while the number of ultra-Orthodox high-tech employees dropped by 500" (Israel Innovation Authority, 2022, p. 7).

Distance of the Groups from the Center

The data presented previously show that being part of the Israel tech-industry is not only about talent but also about hierarchies, access to resources and structural and cultural barriers. On the macro level, the distance of the group from the center will be estimated based on the data presented in the former chapters. More specifically, for each group, I will estimate its distance from the center using the following dimensions: nationality, social and geographic peripherality, estimated political power, and social and human capital of the group.

In the Israeli context, two rather particular categories are important and relevant for understanding the positionality of the groups under investigation in this chapter. One concerns citizenship and the other nationality. The only category that is common to all groups in this book is their Israeli citizenship.[1] In Israel, the term "nationality" concerns Jewishness versus non-Jewishness. The Jewish majority constitutes the dominant majority in the country. Of the groups discussed in Chapters 6 to 11, all belong to the Jewish dominant majority except for the Arab-Palestinians, discussed in Chapter 11. The chapter on women includes both Jewish and non-Jewish tech entrepreneurs.

Group Analyses

In the framework of this book, I analyzed six distinct groups. For three of the groups, namely the ultra-Orthodox, the Arab-Palestinians and women, data as to their participation in the high-tech industry as employees exist. For women, the Innovation Authority also provides data on the rate of high-tech employees and technological startup founders. There are no respective data for Kibbutz members, Ethiopians or immigrants from the former Soviet Union; therefore, concerning these groups, it is necessary to rely on estimates.

The Ethiopian community is part of the national Jewish majority, constitutes a visible minority in Israel, and is often described as at the margins of society. Processes of marginalization locate them in the social periphery and often in the geographic periphery of cities in which they reside. As a community and due to their relatively small size, they have no political power or influence on the public sphere. Over and again, there are incidences of open discrimination against members of the community. As presented in Chapter 6, the socioeconomic position of the majority of the Ethiopian community is low, with relatively high rates of poverty and unemployment. The educational achievements of Ethiopian high school pupils and students are comparatively low, with few of them qualified to study technological disciplines at institutes of higher education. In addition and as consequence of their low matriculation profiles, generally, the young Ethiopian women and men are not recruited to the technological intelligence units in the military. Therefore, it is safe to state that the majority of members of the Ethiopian community have little or no access to the high-tech industry since they typically lack adequate human and social capital. As Mekonen mentioned rightly in the interview, there are no meeting places, no opportunities to interact, and therefore no awareness of the centers' realities.

Chapter 7 of this book presented the Israeli Kibbutz as a unique form of organization and community. Kibbutzim are typically located in the geographic periphery of Israel. Kibbutzim, once perceived as an elite of the Israeli society, have undergone profound processes of changes during the last decades. In general, the Kibbutz phenomenon is still perceived as an economic and social success (Abramitzky, 2018), and the educational system of the Kibbutz is overall evaluated as excellent (Dror & Prital, 2020). While during the early decades after the state building in 1948, Kibbutzim were closely engaged in national politics and intertwined with and part of the government, today, Kibbutzim and their leadership play only a minor role in the country's political arena (Galanti et al., 2020). Kibbutz members belong to the Jewish majority of the Israeli population and usually serve in the Israeli army, young men and women alike. They often serve in technological elite units and achieve higher education in technological disciplines. In the geographical periphery where most of the Kibbutzim are located, they are often perceived as the privileged (Topel, 2011). Thus, the group characteristics of the Kibbutzim place them at the geographic periphery of Israel but certainly not at the social periphery.

Immigrants from the former Soviet Union are discussed in Chapter 8 of this book. These immigrants arrived in Israel under the Law of Return. Consequently, they are part of the national Jewish majority. Following former research, the overwhelming majority of FSU migrants are secular, and a large number of them are well-educated professionals. Their pattern of integration to Israeli society has been termed "segmented acculturation" (Raijman & Geffen, 2018). They have a rather low sense of belonging to Israeli society. This low sense of belonging has been explained by the challenges to translate their relatively high human capital into assets in the Israeli labor market (Amit, 2010), the existence of the rather exclusive co-ethnic circle and the feelings of superiority over Israeli culture (Remennick, 2003). The rate of students in technological disciplines among this group is high, and many serve in technological intelligence units of the Israeli military. Nonetheless, as a group, they are underrepresented among successful high-tech entrepreneurs as indicated previously. Israelis from the Former Soviet Union are involved in the political arena in Israel and have substantial political power. Avigdor Liberman, a Soviet-born Israeli politician and founder of the political party Yisrael Beiteinu,[2] has been serving as Minister of Finance since 2021. Overall, the group can be located in a self-selected semiperiphery of the Israeli society, with a relatively high degree of visibility in the Israeli high-tech industry in terms of employment, but not in terms of entrepreneurship.

As has been discussed in Chapter 10, the ultra-Orthodox community lives largely separated from the rest of the Israeli society. Even if they reside in cities located in the center area of the country such as Bnei Brak, they are still concentrated in separate neighborhoods often at the geographic margins of the cities. About 60% of all ultra-Orthodox high school pupils do not study core curriculum such as mathematics, sciences and English in school, and the majority of ultra-Orthodox young men and women are not serving in the Israeli army (Rosenberg, 2018). The share of poor households is high and labor market participation significantly lower than the Israeli average (Black et al., 2021). The ultra-Orthodox parties have partaken in almost every government over the years. In sum and based on the information provided in Chapter 10 of this book, the group can be located at the social periphery of the Israeli society, with extremely low participation in the Israeli high-tech industry.

Chapter 11 of the book discussed the Arab-Palestinians of Israel, who amount to about 21% of the population. The socioeconomic status in the majority of the Arab-Palestinian municipalities is extremely low due to the long-lasting unequal division of public resources, inadequate opportunity structure, lack of proper infrastructure and inaccessibility of capital. The poverty rate among the Arab-Palestinians is significantly higher in comparison to the Jewish majority (Haj-Yahya et al., 2022). Their political parties have been part of the Israeli parliament for many years, but it has only been since the 2021 elections that an Arab-Palestinian party has participated in the governing coalition. In sum, Arab-Palestinians are positioned in a double periphery—at an intersection of social and geographical periphery. The national minority status, religion and cultural differences from the Jewish majority reflect the social peripherality (Mahajne et al., 2022). The geographic distance from the center, in combination with poor infrastructure, reflects the geographic peripherality.

Chapter 9 of this book presented the case of women, a different group category from those previously discussed. Women are more than half of the population of all groups presented. In light of ongoing global and local gender inequality, they are discussed separately in academic and public discourses in general and concerning the high-tech industry in particular. Data presented in the Chapter 9 show that about a third of high-tech employees in Israel are women, a high share in comparison to other population groups. Female students and women do not underachieve in school and higher education frameworks, but they are less likely to focus on disciplines enabling participation in the high-tech industry later on. Their pipeline is significantly thicker than that of the ultra-Orthodox and the Arab-Palestinians, and around 9% become technological entrepreneurs. Therefore, in line with former research, for women who did manage to enter the high-tech industry, barriers for becoming a high-tech entrepreneur are most probably located in structural and cultural particularities of the high-tech industry (Brush et al., 2019; McAdam et al., 2019).

Personas

I related to the group characteristics in terms of human and social capital relevant in the context of the high-tech industry and their respective location concerning geographic and social peripherality. In order to exemplify the positionality and the relative distance from the norm circle of the high-tech scene, I will use the methodology of constructing personas. The concept of "persona" relates to purposefully generalizing stereotypical features of a "typical" representative of a group, based on information gathered beforehand (Fergnani, 2019; Schäfer et al., 2014; Nielsen et al., 2015). In the following, I will present "personas" of imaginary tech—entrepreneurs—relying on the group characteristics, the interviews and the desk research presented in the respective chapters. In addition to the personas associated with the chapters, to enable the understanding of distance, I added the typical high-tech entrepreneur persona.

The Ethiopian Persona—Moshe

The Ethiopian tech entrepreneur. His imaginary name is Moshe. Moshe will most certainly be male and come from a rather socioeconomically weak neighborhood in one of the midsize cities of Israel. His parents immigrated from Ethiopia; his mother had a cleaning job, and his father worked in public gardening. Both are retired. Moshe went to a local school and graduated holding a matriculation certificate, which would allow him to enter certain colleges but not the high-quality universities. He served in the military for three years and was then exposed to the high-tech industry when visiting a friend's house. While starting to investigate about the possibility to study electronic engineering, he discovered that his matriculation exams needed substantial improvement. He therefore attended a one-year pre-academic program, focusing on English, mathematics and computer sciences. At the end of this program, Moshe was accepted into a college and enrolled for electrical engineering. His parents and extended family did not support this choice. They had no awareness of the high-tech industry and thought he should aim for a more secure career path, such as bus driver or nurse. During his four-year engineering studies, Moshe worked as a waiter and gave mathematics and physics lessons to Ethiopian high school children in his community. He lived in the dormitories of the college during the week and at his parents at weekends and semester holidays. During the last year of his studies, he tried to get a student job at a high-tech company but did not manage to pass the job interviews. One reason could be the fact that there are very few Ethiopians working in the high-tech industry; thus, there is a liability of "otherness," in his case mainly based on color. In addition, his English proficiency is extremely low, something he did not manage to improve during the pre-academic preparatory program. Eventually, a friend from the college offered him to join a group of engineers, developing a startup idea in the field of cybersecurity. Moshe agreed since he was disappointed that he could not find a job in one of the big high-tech companies. In the process of developing the product and business idea, Moshe was mostly engaged in the technological field since he had no business knowledge and no acquaintance in the investor landscape. The commercialization efforts of the group were not successful, and eventually they joined a technological incubator, where they stayed for two years. The group did not manage to move the product idea into the growth phase, and they separated a couple of months after having to leave the incubator. Moshe moved back in with his parents. He is now married and has two small children and is working at a small manufacturing company as a shift manager in the neighborhood where he was born.

The Kibbutz Persona—Amir

The Kibbutz tech entrepreneur. The typical Kibbutz tech entrepreneur will probably be male and come from a Kibbutz in the northern periphery of

Israel—his imaginary name is Amir. The Kibbutz has a successful manufacturing plant and is operating a hotel and developing innovative agricultural products. His father was born in the Kibbutz and is the general manager of the hotel; his mother is originally from Tel Aviv, studied medicine and works as a medical doctor in the nearby town. Amir has three siblings, two of them living in Tel Aviv. Amir attended the high school operated by a number of Kibbutzim and graduated with an excellent matriculation exam. He served in one of the technological intelligent units in the military for six years. When he was released, he already held a BA in computer sciences. During the service, he met his wife, and today they are a family of five. The family lived for a couple of years in Tel Aviv but decided to relocate to the Kibbutz. Since Amir is Kibbutz-born, he had the legal right and opportunity to apply for membership in the Kibbutz. Nowadays, not all Kibbutzim are ready to accept new members, and for non-Kibbutz born persons, it is extremely difficult and expensive to be accepted as a member into the community. Amir and his wife utilized the possibility since they were looking for a rural and more relaxed lifestyle and a since they believed that the Kibbutz is a better place to raise children than Tel Aviv. Consequently, Amir quit his job at an Israeli high-tech startup and decided to become a tech entrepreneur himself. His wife quit her job at the hospital and was offered a managing position at one of the medical clinic centers in the nearby town. The three children integrated in the school system of the area, two of them in the same high school where Amir studied as a child. Amir's family and his Kibbutz friends were supportive to the relocation decision of the family and offered much physical and emotional help. The children and his wife adjusted quickly and successfully to the new environment. Amir—after a three-month break—started to initiate the development of his startup idea. Although well established in the social network of the military veteran circle, he found commuting to the center extremely challenging. Although, due to Covid-19, many meetings were held via Zoom, Amir evaluates the geographical distance from Tel Aviv—where the tech-industry is located—as a major obstacle. He was used to attending events and meeting his friends weekly, a mission more difficult for him in light of a two-hour drive in each direction. Eventually, after not being able to set up a team to work with him together on his idea, he approached an innovation center located in the northern periphery about 40 kilometer away from the Kibbutz. Amir is optimistic and hopes he will be able to realize his idea and set up his startup eventually in the Kibbutz, but he is worried about the relative distance from the high-tech center and not certain that he will be able to overcome the liability of geographic peripherality. Since his wife has a permanent and well-paid job and the living expenses in the Kibbutz are much lower than in Tel Aviv, he decided to give it a trial and invest two or three years in the startup, even without a salary. He is certain that he will always be able to find a job in a high-tech company in the future.

The Immigrant Persona—Sasha

The Former Soviet Union immigrant tech entrepreneur. The typical Former Soviet Union entrepreneur will probably also be male and come from a city close to Tel Aviv. His imaginary name is Sasha, and he might not become an entrepreneur. Sasha's parents immigrated to Israel form Moscow; when they arrived in Israel, he was 5 years old. His father was a mechanical engineer, and his mother held a lecturer position in mathematics at one of Moscow's universities. They decided to immigrate to Israel in order to provide their two children with better educational opportunities. Sasha's father found employment in a mechanical plant in a town 50 kilometers away from his home. He worked below his initial professional status but received a decent and permanent income. His mother was not accepted to any of the Israeli colleges or universities and worked as a high-school teacher for many years. Today Sasha's parents are retired and live in their own flat. Sasha moved to his own flat a year ago. His sister is married and has one son. She is working as a chemist in a pharma company, and her husband has a job in marketing. Sasha attended the high school in his neighborhood, which was dominated by immigrants from the former Soviet Union. He was selected to join a school program for gifted children, together with many Russian-speaking friends. Together they spend their high school years until matriculation in an environment characterized by the strive for high academic achievements, Russian culture and language and within close family and friend circles of their parents. In the social circle of Sasha and his parents, army recruitment was considered important and meaningful, and the rate of acceptance to prestigious military units was high. Sasha joined the army for a combat unit and served for three years. He then decided to apply for academic studies at Israeli universities in order to study software engineering. Due to his excellent matriculation exams, he was accepted to three universities and chose the one closest to his parents, with whom he was still living when starting his academic studies. Sasha graduated after four years with an engineer diploma and found a job in a multinational company rather easily. There were a couple of other Russian-speaking employees, and therefore, he adjusted rather easily. Sasha was sent to international branches of the company for a couple of times and therefore had the opportunity to improve his English skills and learn about the high-tech culture in other countries. When offered a three-year relocation opportunity, he declined since he wanted to stay close to his family. Over the years of working with the company, Sasha has had a number of ideas for technological innovation in his field of expertise. However, until recently, he has not proceeded with the ideas since he did not know how and with whom. The vast majority of his Russian-speaking friends in the Israeli high-tech industry are employed; in fact, he does not personally know anyone who is a tech entrepreneur. His parents and sister expressed concern with his idea to become a tech entrepreneur; they think he should not take the risk and give up a secure and high-paying job. For now, Sasha has decided to continue at his present job in order to secure ongoing income while, at the same time, promoting his startup idea. He is currently in the process to enter a technological incubator, where he hopes to receive support.

The Ultra-Orthodox Persona—Reuven

The ultra-Orthodox tech entrepreneur would be from Jerusalem, probably also male, and his imaginary name is Reuven. Reuven grew up in an ultra-Orthodox neighborhood in Jerusalem, where he attended the typical religious schools, teaching boys Tora studies from the age of three. Reuven's father was a famous rabbi, and he and his wife had eight children. When Reuven was ten years old, an ultra-Orthodox community in Brooklyn, New York, offered his father to teach Tora studies in a high-profile college for ultra-Orthodox boys. Eventually, the family relocated to the USA for a couple of years. During the family's stay in New York, Reuven learned English and was exposed to core curriculum studies such as mathematics and sciences, subjects not taught in the ultra-Orthodox school system for boys in Israel. Reuven, less interested in religious studies, excelled in mathematics and sciences and managed to convince his parents to allow him to attend a technological college after finishing high school in New York. He received a technician diploma at the end of the two-year study program. Back in Israel, his family understood that Reuven would not proceed with religious studies and was not interested to become a rabbinic scholar, a fact not easily accepted by his parents. However, in the end, they understood that they would not change Reuven's mind but insisted that he get married and maintain an ultra-Orthodox lifestyle. By that time, he was already 23. During the first year after coming back from New York, Reuven attended a number of coding courses proposed by government agencies and NGOs in the neighborhood. He got acquainted with Kamatech, an NGO aimed at integrating ultra-Orthodox men and women into high tech, and started to take part in the events and lectures they proposed in Jerusalem. Although his parents and wife tried to convince him to apply for a decently paid job in a high-tech company not too far away from his home, he was less interested and continued to dream about becoming an entrepreneur himself. By then, Reuven had a solid business idea for a software-related product in the field of digital medicine. He believed that due to cultural particularities and restrictions of the ultra-Orthodox community, the development of digital medicine was extremely important. Kamatech introduced Reuven to potential investors and assisted him in setting up a professional team to promote and develop his idea. The team included ultra-Orthodox as well a non-ultra-Orthodox members but no women. After two rounds of successful investments, Reuven and his partners are now owners of a startup in the field of digital medicine. The company is located in Jerusalem and operates nationally and internationally. Reuven and his partners are considering selling the company in the near future. Reuven and his wife, Zipporah, live with their six children in Jerusalem.

The Arab-Palestinian Persona—Ahmed

The Arab-Palestinian entrepreneur from an Arab city not far away from Tel Aviv will probably also be male, and his imaginary name is Ahmed. Ahmed grew up in a well-established neighborhood of the city. His father owns an accountancy firm, which he inherited from his father, and belongs to a well-known and large family with long-standing roots in the community. His mother studied English and arts at the Hebrew University in Jerusalem and worked as a freelancing language editor. Ahmed has two sisters and one brother. Ahmed attended the local elementary school. He and his siblings did not enroll in the local high school but got their matriculation exams at an international school in Nazareth. Therefore, all of them are practically English speakers. In addition, their parents insisted on private Hebrew lessons over the years at school, well aware that the academic colleges and universities in Israel teach in Hebrew. After finishing high school, Ahmed worked in his father's firm for a year but decided that he was not interested in studying economics and accounting in order to eventually take over his father's firm. He decided to study IT engineering and was accepted at the prestigious Technion University in Haifa. Ahmed received a number of rewards for outstanding academic achievements during his four-year engineering studies. During the week, he lived at the dormitories of the Technion, and over the weekends and for semester breaks, he stayed with his parents. After graduation from the Technion, Ahmed enrolled for an MA degree in business administration at Tel Aviv University. He was 24 years old when he graduated in Tel Aviv. His parents financially provided for him and his brother and sisters during their entire period of academic studies. Ahmed had to deal with the liability of otherness when looking for a job in the high-tech industry. For some job opportunities, he could not apply since he did not meet the personal security standards demanded by the companies. These security standards usually imply army service. As an Arab-Palestinian, he stood no chance in any companies directly or remotely connected with security issues. Ahmed's academic record was outstanding, especially since he had relevant degrees from high-profile universities, and was fluent in English and Hebrew in addition to Arabic. However, he had no professional experience and no social network he could recruit when looking for a job. Eventually, after a couple of months, he received a job at a multinational high-tech company through the recommendation of one of his former professors at the university whom he asked for assistance. Ahmed worked at the company for five years in R & D and finally decided to realize his dream and become a high-tech entrepreneur and establish his own company. Backed up with financial resources from his family and himself, he left his job and set up a team of developers in his hometown.

Utilizing his father's business network, he managed to raise money for the first and second round of development, and today he is the owner of a well-established high-tech company with locations in Haifa and Nazareth industrial parks.

The Woman Persona—Caren

The woman tech entrepreneur lives in Tel Aviv. Her imaginary name is Caren, and she holds a PhD in computer sciences. Caren grew up in Tel Aviv, where she lived with her family in a well-to-do neighborhood close to Tel Aviv University. Her father is a university professor in history, and her mother holds a leading position in the public service department of the city. Caren has one brother and a sister. Caren and her siblings attended elementary and high school in their neighborhood, within a circle of friends whose parents were mostly second- or third-generation Israelis from high socioeconomic backgrounds, employed or self-employed with high salaries. The neighborhood was rather homogenous, reflecting the typical Israeli sociocultural elite. Caren excelled in her academic studies from the beginning of elementary school and attended a number of excellent programs throughout the years. She enrolled in a special course in mathematics during high school and eventually graduated from high school with a certificate indicating that she had attended university courses in mathematics and computers. Probably due to this background, she was accepted to the prestigious 8200 technological security unit, where she remained for the five years of her military service. During the army service, she completed her BA degree in mathematics and computer sciences. Immediately after finishing the military service, Caren enrolled in Tel Aviv University for an MA program in data analysis. She then completed a PhD at Texas University in computer sciences. Caren met her husband at an event of the Jewish and Israeli community. He comes from a rich American Jewish family and was already working for a global high-tech company in a leading financial position. After six years in the USA, Caren convinced her husband to return to Israel, and they found a flat close to her parents in the neighborhood where she grew up. Caren was 38 years old and decided to find a job in the high-tech sector. For five years, she worked in the R & D department of a company, and the couple had two children. Her husband was still working for the same company, traveling a lot, and Caren decided that she wanted to move on. Backed by a solid financial basis, she decided to quit her job and set up her own startup, about which she had thought and developed ideas for the last couple of years. Caren recruited two more software experts for the developing stage of the startup, and she rented office space in one of the prominent high-tech we-works in Tel Aviv. Caren explicitly experienced the liability of being a woman when entering the stage of funding. Although she felt well equipped for presenting her business idea, professionally and personally, for the first time throughout her career, she was confronted with reluctance for being a woman. During one sessions with the investors, the CEO of the VC Company asked her whether she intended to have more children. Eventually, Caren managed to secure funding for her startup via the social network of her husband and his company. She is now the founder, partner and co-CEO of a successful young company in the field of digitalization of higher education, and she and her husband did have a third child.

The High-Tech-Entrepreneur Persona—Shahar

The young high-tech entrepreneur lives in Tel Aviv. His imaginary name is Shahar, and in recent years he graduated in computer science from a top Israeli university. Shahar grew up in Ra'anana, a small city situated a few kilometers north of Tel Aviv. His father is a successful businessperson who, throughout his career, served in a number of senior positions in various big companies. Today he is the CEO and partner of a medium real estate company. Shahar's mother is a psychologist working in her private clinic. Shahar has two brothers, one a lawyer working in a well-established law firm and one traveling around the world after having completed his army service. During his teenage years, Shahar was mostly busy with friends and sports activities. However, toward the high school matriculation exams, he took private classes and graduated with high grades in mathematics, physics and English. Accordingly, he was accepted into a technological intelligence military unit, where many friends from his extended circle were serving. After four years of military service, a friend recruited him to work in a startup tech company. He worked there for two years and meanwhile started a degree in computer science. Through the last two years of his degree, Shahar resigned from his job and started working with three friends on a business idea in the tech-marketing sector. He received full support from his family, and his father got them an office to work from and related them to a few key businesspeople for some advice and further connections. Shahar and his partners managed to raise some seed money and tried to develop their idea, but after two years, they understood it would not work, and they resigned. On the one hand, Shahar was disappointed that his idea failed, but on the other hand, he was enthusiastic about the experience of developing his own business. Moreover, his family supported him financially and emotionally through the process, and his father offered him a job in a managerial position at his real estate company. After a year of part-time work at his father's firm, Shahar resigned again and joined two friends from his military unit to jointly develop a new business idea they came up with in the sector of web development. Today, Shahar is the cofounder and CTO of a growing business that recently started working in the US market.

Intersections of Positionalities and Distance from the Norm Circle

The Israeli high-tech industry is geographically located at the center of the country; it is perceived and perceives itself as the driver of Israel's economy. As has been shown in Chapter 4, there is no lack of financial resources; in addition, human and social resources of the major players are high. Those who are high-tech entrepreneurs and startup owners have successfully combined human, social and economic capital and sold their visions to customers and investors, enacting the high-tech habitus generated via socialization and access to symbolic capital such as particular universities and military units. As the data provided on the successful startups over four years showed, the Israeli high-tech industry is extremely homogenous, and that enforces the mechanisms of the norm circle.

The *Ethiopian* community in Israel is located at the social periphery overlapping with a semiperipheral geographic location. The persona exemplified the structural and cultural barriers members of the Ethiopian community have to overcome. The interviews with Salomon and Mekonen in Chapter 6 revealed the liability of otherness, of being black in a very white environment. Salomon reported that he had no access to relevant resources when attempting to recruit investment, little knowledge of doing business and no adequate social network. His immediate environment—friends and family—supported him reluctantly but would have preferred him to stay in a safe and well-paid job. Mekonen stressed the lack of awareness of the high-tech industry as a relevant career path in the community and stressed the lack of the Israeli school system in providing the Ethiopian children with necessary human capital. One NGO, initiated by the community itself, attempts to provide knowledge and skills enabling Ethiopian youth to partake in the center of the Israeli labor market.

Kibbutzim are located at the geographic periphery of the country but certainly not at the social periphery. The persona exemplified the availability of human and social capital, illustrating the fact that Kibbutz members are part of the Israeli sociocultural center. The interviews with Grossman, Klein and Barkan in Chapter 7 revealed high levels of human capital and overall family and social support, maybe except for Grossman's and Klein's wives, who would prefer their husbands to be employed. Two of the three Kibbutz entrepreneurs lacked an initial knowledge of doing business but managed to bypass this deficiency. Overall, the Kibbutz and its environment provide some stability to the families, and there is awareness as to the importance and impact of the high-tech industry. The main obstacles mentioned by all three entrepreneurs are the lack of professional networks in the periphery and the need to commute to the center. The latter, is increasingly challenging in light of the lack of public transport and the intensifying severe traffic bottlenecks.

Immigrants from the Former Soviet Union are mostly living in the geographic center or semicenter of Israel. One could state that they are in a self-selected social semiperiphery, acknowledging what has been called "segmented acculturation." The interviews and results of the desk research showed the existence of a liability of otherness, mainly based on language and culture of origin. There definitely exists a glass ceiling, "annoying and low," faced by migrants from the Former Soviet Union. The persona exemplified the high level of human capital and the integration of group members into the high-tech industry but mainly as employees. The interviews with Weinberg and Solcin in Chapter 8 exposed the access to high-tech networks as problematic, also because both immigrant entrepreneurs are located in the northern periphery. There is awareness and appreciation for high-tech entrepreneurship in their immediate environment, although Solcin's wife would prefer him to be employed. Both Weinberg and Solcin had little knowledge of doing business at the beginning of their entrepreneurial path but had no problems to attain it.

The *ultra-Orthodox* are located at the social periphery of Israel and, similarly to the Ethiopian community, overlapping with a semiperipheral geographic location in separated neighborhoods of the cities where they reside. The interviews and desk research findings point to a liability of otherness, based on the traditional, religious, very restrictive lifestyle of the ultra-Orthodox community, in reality separating them from other populations. The persona exemplified that it is only under rare circumstances that young ultra-Orthodox will be exposed to high-tech and related spheres; they usually have no adequate human or social capital. Although the government launched a number of programs aimed at increasing involvement, the results remain very meager. There is a lack of social support for ultra-Orthodox women and men who are employed in the non-Orthodox labor market in general and in high tech in particular. This is based on fear that exposure to non-ultra-Orthodox environments will undermine the religious traditional lifestyle. Although there are a number of examples of successful ultra-Orthodox tech entrepreneurs, their overall participation in the high-tech industry is extremely low. Kamatech's CEO maintained that many of those interested to join courses and programs of the NGO are not hard-core ultra-Orthodox, a fact that might indicate a stratification phenomenon inside the community.

Arab-Palestinians are positioned in a double periphery—at an intersection of social and geographical periphery. The national minority status, different religion and culture reflect their social peripherality. The geographic distance from the center, in combination with a poor infrastructure, reflect the geographic peripherality. The persona exemplified that high human, social and economic capital can bypass, to a certain extent, the liability of being a minority. However, that is relevant only for a very small section of the Arab-Palestinian population in Israel. The interviews revealed that high human capital is crucial for entering the high-tech industry and that all had experience as employees. They reported on lack of social capital and the inability to join the circles of investors; however, three of them attempted to bypass the lack of social capital by joining incubators/innovation centers. The social environment is generally not supporting high-tech entrepreneurship since it is perceived as taking high risks.

Israel is a country with low *gender* equality, and that also counts for the high-tech industry. However, the share of women is on the rise, at least in terms of employment. Nevertheless, as the persona exemplified, women who do manage to enter the high-tech industry are usually from strong socioeconomic backgrounds, with relatively high levels of human and social capital. Thus, it is safe to assume that the majority of women entering the industry are from the sociocultural center, with low representations of the groups discussed previously. However, even the women who do manage to enter the circle are faced with structural and cultural gender barriers and there are some indications that women tend to leave the high-tech industry at much higher rates than men.

Concluding Thoughts

In Israel, centralization and peripheralization processes (Kühn, 2015) have led to contextual differences privileging or disadvantaging certain groups. To account for the location of groups in respective social and geographic peripheries is important in order to deconstruct the myth that the advantage or disadvantage and success and failure is mainly due to human or social capital, as the meritocracy myth attempts to convince. Consequently, technological entrepreneurship is often presented as accessible to anyone, anywhere and anytime would she/he just try hard enough. The entrepreneurial heroes at the center are presented as generic superstars, talented, self-taught and self-reliant white men, belonging to the sociocultural elite of society.

However, as everywhere, in Israel, socioeconomic inequalities and social injustice are also present in the entrepreneurial realm, undermining the postulate of equal opportunities (Boulus-Rødje & Bjørn, 2021). The analyses of the groups along the lines of social and geographic peripherality, access to relevant capitals and opportunities to bypass structural and cultural barriers highlight the significantly different conditions that entrepreneurs belonging to a variety of groups have when compared with those at the center. The personas, interviews and desk research data presented previously showed that the entrepreneurs are a reflection of their time, place and positions in the Israeli society, shaping types and levels of challenges and opportunities they encounter. In Israel, too, the typical technological entrepreneur is associated with Jewish white men, and masculinity is associated with science, math and engineering. Hierarchies in the high-tech industry generate this ideal type and often exclude those who are different, those who are dealing with what I called the liability of otherness. Also in the cases presented here, the "others" were confronted with a "chilly climate" of excluding networks and hierarchical structures, although many of them had the necessary academic background, experience and skills.

This book is about the Israeli high-tech industry and its winners and losers. The winners are high-tech CEOs, owners, investors, employees and entrepreneurs, interacting in the center, part of the norm circle perpetuating social hierarchies, as reflected in the data provided at the beginning of this chapter. The losers are those groups whose share of high-tech employees is low or practically nonexistent. Per se of course, not everybody has to be in high tech. But since it is currently mainly in the high-tech sector, where people earn enough in order to make a living, those who cannot join are left out. The following chapter, presenting the voices of experts, will continue to clarify these issues further.

Notes

1. In the framework of this book, I did not discuss non-Israeli citizens and their high-tech entrepreneurial activities. Non-Israeli groups would include the West Bank, the Gaza Strip and East Jerusalem. In addition, there are labor migrants living and working in Israel, many of them illegal.
2. A secularist, nationalist, right-wing political party in Israel. The party's base was originally secular Russian-speaking Israelis.

References

Abramitzky, R. (2018). *The mystery of the Kibbutz*. Princeton University Press. https://doi.org/10.1515/9781400888153

Amit, K. (2010). Determinants of life satisfaction among immigrants from Western countries and from the FSU in Israel. *Social Indicators Research*, *96*(3), 515–534. https://doi.org/10.1007/s11205-009-9490-1

Anthias, F. (2001). The material and the symbolic in theorizing social stratification: Issues of gender, ethnicity and class. *British Journal of Sociology*, *52*(3), 367–390.

Black, S., Fadlon, T., & Elran, M. (2021). *Integrating the ultra-orthodox into the labor market*. The Institute for National Security Studies.

Boulus-Rødje, N., & Bjørn, P. (2021). Tech public of erosion: The formation and transformation of the Palestinian tech entrepreneurial public. *Computer Supported Cooperative Work*, 1–41. https://doi.org/10.1007/s10606-021-09419-y

Brush, C., Edelman, L. F., Manolova, T., & Welter, F. (2019). A gendered look at entrepreneurship ecosystems. *Small Business Economics*, *53*(2), 393–408. https://doi.org/10.1007/s11187-018-9992-9

Calcalist. (2022, April 10). Most promising startups. *CTech*. www.calcalistech.com/ctech/home/0,7340,L-5492-234955,00.html

Dror, Y., & Prital, Y. (2020). Education in the changing Kibbutz. In E. Ben-Raphael & O. Shemer (Eds.), *The Metamorphosis of the Kibbutz* (Vol. 49, pp. 119–130). Brill.

Dy, A. M., & Agwunobi, A. J. (2019). Intersectionality and mixed methods for social context in entrepreneurship. *International Journal of Entrepreneurial Behavior & Research*, *25*(8), 1727–1747. https://doi.org/10.1108/ijebr-12-2017-0498

Dy, A. M., Marlow, S., & Martin, L. (2017). A web of opportunity or the same old story? Women digital entrepreneurs and intersectionality theory. *Human Relations*, *70*(3), 286–311. https://doi.org/10.1177/0018726716650730

Fergnani, A. (2019). The future persona: A futures method to let your scenarios come to life. *Foresight*, *21*(4), 445–466. https://doi.org/10.1108/fs-10-2018-0086

Galanti, S. B., Pauker, A., & Hisherik, M. (2020). The post-crisis Kibbutz and its relations with the political Arena. In E. Ben-Raphael & O. Shemer (Eds.), *The metamorphosis of the Kibbutz* (Vol. 49, pp. 166–177). Brill.

Haj-Yahya, N. H., Khalaily, M., Rudnitzky, A., & Fargeon, B. (2022). *Statistical report on Arab society in Israel: 2021*. Israeli Democracy Institute. Retrieved May 4, 2022, from https://en.idi.org.il/articles/38540

Israel Innovation Authority. (2022). Annual innovation report. *State of high-tech 2022*. https://innovationisrael.org.il/en/report/israel-innovation-authoritys-2022-innovation-report

Kühn, M. (2015). Peripheralization: Theoretical concepts explaining socio-spatial inequalities. *European Planning Studies, 23*(2), 367–378. https://doi.org/10.1080/09654313.2013.862518

Maalaoui, A., Ratten, V., Heilbrunn, S., Brannback, M., & Kraus, S. (2020). Disadvantage entrepreneurship: Decoding a new area of research. *European Management Review, 17*(3), 663–668.

Mahajne, I., Allassad Alhuzail, N., & Bar-On, A. (2022). Challenges facing social work in the indigenous Arab minority in Israel: Voices from the field. *The British Journal of Social Work, 52*(2), 816–832. https://doi.org/10.1093/bjsw/bcab069

Martinez Dy, A. (2020). Not all entrepreneurship is created equal: Theorising entrepreneurial disadvantage through social positionality. *European Management Review, 17*(3), 687–699.

McAdam, M., Harrison, R. T., & Leitch, C. M. (2019). Stories from the field: Women's networking as gender capital in entrepreneurial ecosystems. *Small Business Economics, 53*(2), 459–474.

Nielsen, L., Hansen, K. S., Stage, J., & Billestrup, J. (2015). A template for design personas: Analysis of 47 persona descriptions from danish industries and organizations. *International Journal of Sociotechnology and Knowledge Development*, 7(1), 45–61. https://doi.org/10.4018/ijskd.2015010104

Raijman, R., & Geffen, R. (2018). Sense of belonging and life satisfaction among post-1990 immigrants in Israel. *International Migration, 56*(3), 142–157. https://doi.org/10.1111/imig.12386

Remennick, L. (2003). The 1.5 generation of Russian immigrants in Israel: Between integration and sociocultural retention. *Diaspora: A Journal of Transnational Studies, 12*(1), 39–66. https://doi.org/10.1353/dsp.2011.0043

Rosenberg, D. (2018). *Israel's technology economy: Origins and impact*. Springer. https://doi.org/10.1007/978-3-319-76654-6

Schäfer, C., Zinke, R., Künzer, L., Hofinger, G., & Koch, R. (2014). Applying Persona method for describing users of escape routes. *Transportation Research Procedi, 2*, 636–641. https://doi.org/10.1016/j.trpro.2014.09.106

Topel, M. (2011). The changing composition of Kibbutz elites. In M. Palgi & S. Reinharz (Eds.), *One hundred years of Kibbutz life*. Routledge. https://doi.org/10.4324/9781315125749-5

Willig, I. (2013). Newsroom ethnography in a field perspective. *Journalism, 14*(3), 372–387. https://doi.org/10.1177/1464884912442638

13 What Can We Learn from the Experts?

Introduction

The chapter reflects the insights, opinions and evaluations of people I interviewed over the last 15 months. The conversations focused on many themes concerning the Israeli high-tech industry, the periphery and the interconnections and relations between the high-tech industry and the periphery. Short bios of the interview partners are presented here in alphabetical order of family name.

Aharon Aharon—He was the first CEO of the Israel Innovation Authority (IIA and formerly the Chief Scientist's Office) and was responsible, among other things, for the links between academia and industry for the benefit of the growth of the Israeli economy. Prior to his position at the IIA, he worked in a variety of senior management positions at a number of different companies, the most recent of which was Apple, as the first CEO of Apple Israel and Vice President of Hardware Technologies at Apple Global. Today he is active in a consulting company he founded, C-Perto.

Kheir Abdil Razek—Program Manager at the Israel Innovation Authority. Formerly Deputy CEO at Kav Mashve, an organization for the promotion of employment opportunities for the Arab population.

Hassan Abu Shally—Founder, Board Member and Strategic Advisor at Hasoub, an organization working to promote sustainable economic development within the Arab community as well as a culture of insight and data-driven decision-making. Product Manager at RiseUp. Formerly Product Manager at Microsoft.

Ilan Biran—Chairman of the Board at MELODEA Bio Based Solutions. Formerly Director of Itamar Medical, Former Chairman of the Management Committee at the Kinneret Academic College, Director at Discount Bank, Chairman of the Board at Rafael Advanced Defense Systems, CEO at Bezeq, and Director General at the Israel Ministry of Defense.

DOI: 10.4324/9781003091042-14

Izik Crombie—Senior Researcher at the Haredi Institute for Public Affairs. Board Member at Biz-Labs Technology, a "Scalerator" for advanced stage Haredi founders' startup companies. Formerly Cofounder and Managing Partner at Bnei Braq Technology Incubator.

Yossi Dahan—Law professor and the Head of the Human Rights Division at the College of Law and Business. He is the chairperson and cofounder of Adva Center, is an editor and cofounder of Haokets.org, and teaches philosophy at the Open University.

Maisa El Shaik—Founder and CEO of Lotus, a women's space for training and employment in high tech. Lotus is an NGO that aims to empower first-generation Druze women. The NGO is the first in the Druze community to offer to traditional women the opportunity to break the glass ceiling by integrating into quality employment.

Moshe Friedman—Cofounder of KamaTech, a coalition of 50 large high-tech companies to help the ultra-Orthodox integrate into the high-tech industry. He also set up KamaTech, an accelerator for entrepreneurs from the ultra-Orthodox community in Israel.

Uri Gabai—CEO of Start-Up Nation's Policy Institute (SNPI). Formerly Co–General Manager of Start-Up Nation Central, Chief Strategy Office at the Israel Innovation Authority, and Director of Strategy and Economic Research Unit at the Office of Chief Scientist.

Eugene Kandel—Cochair of Start-Up Nation Central's Economic Research and Policy Institute and Professor Emeritus of economics and finance at the Hebrew University of Jerusalem. Formerly, Kandel served for six years as head of the National Economic Council at the Prime Minister Office, then he was appointed for five years as CEO of Start-Up Nation Central.

Naomi Krieger Carmi—SVP at Social Finance Israel. Formerly VP of Societal Challenges at the Israel Innovation Authority, Founding Director of the UK Israel Tech Hub at the British Embassy Israel. Has received her MPP in Public and Economy Policy from the Harvard Kennedy School.

Takele Mekonen—CEO of Tech Career. Former head of Ethiopian program at Ruppin Academic Center and Fidel. Working at the Ministry of education on integrating Ethiopian youth. Holds a master's degree in diplomacy from Tel Aviv University.

Inbal Orpaz—Codirector at Canarias/Israel Innovation Partnership, Research at INSS Israel, Founder of "Woman InTech" initiative, Journalist, Startup Ecosystem Expert and Business Strategy Consultant.

Sami Peretz—Cofounder of The Marker and former Editor in Chief of *Haaretz* newspaper. Peretz publishes a weekly forum focusing on issues of the labor market, inequality, macroeconomics, the financial system, executive pay, competitiveness and more. He is one of the most important journalists in the Israeli media scene.

Jonathan Potter—Head of the Entrepreneurship Policy and Analysis Unit of the OECD Centre for Entrepreneurship, SMEs, Regions and Cities. He directs OECD work streams, including country reviews of entrepreneurship policy. He has worked at the OECD since 1997 and holds a PhD from the University of Cambridge.

Hanna Rado—Founder and President at Group Nineteen and Negev19, President of Supersonas, an organization promoting the presence of women at decision-making and leadership positions in Israel and worldwide.

Sami Saadi—Cofounder and Joint Manager of Tsofen, a nonprofit organization promoting collaboration among Jewish and Arab professionals in the high-tech sector. Formerly an accountant and founder of the Jewish Arab Tech Village.

Izhar Shai—Parliament Member on behalf of the Blue and White Party, Venture Partner at Disruptive AI VC. Founder at Start-Up Stadium, an online community of Israeli Entrepeneurs, Columnist at *Globes*. Formerly, Shai was also the CEO of Business Layers and VP of the company C-Secure, two companies that he led to exits.

Maty Zwaig—Maty is the founding CEO of Scale-Up Velocity, Start-Up Nation Central's human capital arm that focuses on promoting the Israeli high-tech ecosystem by finding solutions for the country's chronic tech talent shortage.

The previous list represents policy makers, opinion leaders, academics, journalists and CEOs of relevant NGOs, along with women and men and representatives of the groups discussed in this book. These are people who have a deep understanding of the Israeli high tech and Israeli society and gave their consent to share their knowledge and thoughts. Again, I would like to express my gratitude that they took the time and effort to contribute to this book.

Insights from the Interviews

In the following part of this chapter, I will present the insights from the interviews following themes that emerged during the process of writing this book and while conducting the interviews. One major question I presented to all interview partners concerned the fact that the achievements of the high tech in the center of Tel Aviv hardly spill over to the geographic and social periphery. Accordingly, the relevant themes are posed as questions in this chapter.

Is There Something Special About the Israeli High-Tech Industry?

Surely, inequality and center and periphery divides are a global phenomena. Naomi Krieger Carmi upheld that naturally, innovation centers tend to be located in larger central cities, where the encounter between academia, industry, young people and startups happens. "Also, the underrepresentation of women and minorities is a common global phenomenon," she maintains. Likewise, on an international scale, Tel Aviv is a city, a metropole. "So we need to develop more flexible approaches to identify opportunities in all areas of Israel."

As has been discussed in the beginning parts of the book, in international comparison, inequality in Israel is very high. Ilan Biran explains that the returns on capital in Israel have grown more than the returns of labor, meaning that the rich have become richer and the poor have become poorer. He evaluates this trend as a problem for Israeli society. Also, Maty Zwaig points to the high rates of inequality and states that "we have two economies—the high-tech and all the rest, and then the high-tech itself is also divided into technological developers and the others." Jonathan Potter from the OECD puts it differently: "To call it the startup nation, that's disguising. Would you take the startup nation out of Israel, then you would see a relatively weak economy, you know, with some major problems."

Summing up, one would argue that center and periphery divides are a global phenomenon, and globally, the high-tech industry is located in centers. However, Israel has an exceptionally high rate of inequality, leading to a dual economy.

Who Are the High-tech People in Tel Aviv?

I have explained in former chapters of the book that the majority of the 10% high-tech employees of Israel belong to a sociocultural elite, positioned at the top of Israel's socioeconomic hierarchy. These are highly talented people with adequate human and social capital. Uri Gabai calls Tel Aviv a magnet attracting talents, companies and investments but barely exporting anything. In addition, he explains, "A Tel-Aviv startup that suddenly says 'I want to move to Jerusalem,' that's weird. A Jerusalem startup that says, 'Okay, I reached the point where I should move to Tel Aviv. That's the mainstream." Tel Aviv is the hub to be when you want to join the club.

Some interview partners talked about a change in attitude of the present second high-tech generation in comparison to the first high-tech generation. Sami Pertez associates the changing narrative with the rise of individualism and profit orientation away from the ideas of collectivism and welfare orientation. "So once there's this switch to individualism, people look to maximize their opportunities and move towards the more rewarding places." During the last 30 years, he maintains, the returns on talent have grown exponentially, and today, those who go to military combat units have no jobs waiting for them when they leave the military, while those who go to 8200 unit have jobs waiting with a 30,000 NIS salary per month, a year before they finish their service.

"That's the illusion of high tech—being worth 100 times more financially doesn't mean being worth a 100 times more in terms of quality."

Aharon Aharon argues along the same line and maintains that high tech became the status symbol. "That's what one wants to do but only in the center." He also complains that the young high-tech people do not give back to society.

> Many are looking for the "quick wins" instead of long-term goals. That is a new phenomenon and not a good one. It appeared about ten years ago. Probably due to the shortage in engineers, the high-tech engineers are moving between companies every two to three years. It hurts building long-term deep-tech technologies. Therefore, my optimism as to the high-tech future is relatively limited.

Arguing along the same line, Ilan Biran believes that the younger generation's values have changed: "It's about 'me' and not about society. They will leave their job for a slightly higher salary." Hanna Rado expects the high-tech people to take more social responsibility: "Who, if not them, will be concerned with future problems?"

Thus, the second generation of high-tech people are perceived and evaluated as very talented by the experts, but seem to prefer to promote their individual interests.

Why Is the Israeli High-Tech Industry So Exclusive?

The reasons for the exclusiveness of the high-tech industry concern partly overlapping phenomena related to the social and the geographic periphery of Israel. Hence, I organized the answers in two separate but intertwined subsections: (1) explaining the fact that there is little high tech in the geographical periphery and (2) explaining the underrepresentation of the population of the social periphery in the high-tech industry in the center.

Explaining the Fact That There Is Little High-Tech in the Geographical Periphery

Sami Peretz lists the reasons for the fact there is no high tech in the periphery. He maintains that high tech needs an ecosystem—academia, companies and infrastructure. High tech requires strong regional councils for building this infrastructure in local industrial zones. Moreover, high tech requires high levels of human capital. "There are no incentives for companies to move to the periphery because it wouldn't have the human capital to grow."

Shai stresses the importance of infrastructure: The geographical periphery of Israel suffers from a weak transportation infrastructure (public transport and traffic bottlenecks), causing travelling from and to Tel Aviv to be time-consuming, he explains. He laments the inappropriate physical infrastructure—"bad roads, badly adapted public transportation, communications, sometimes even electricity, water and sewage." He maintains that this causes significant gaps in opportunities mainly in Arab villages but also in some Jewish ones. "In the periphery, the poor public transportation infrastructure makes it difficult to get to work, and the poor digital infrastructure makes it difficult to work remotely."

An incubator manager who wanted to remain anonymous explains that a startup that enters an incubator in the periphery receives a financial bonus from the state.

> Three million NIS compared to 2 million NIS in the center. Today we demand of companies in the incubator, to have a strong grounding in the North, but it does not always work. The strong and talented CEOs are in the center. We try to make them come here, employ here, use local subcontractors. However, the CEOs are often from other places. They have to travel for an hour and a half each direction. The CEO of the incubator lives in Herzelyia and comes here at least once a week—every week.

In addition, he explains that there is no ecosystem; it is difficult to organize meetups, events, to bring in material.

"And I have an HR problem. I needed to bring an expert in the field of innovation. In the center, you throw a stone and find an innovation expert." Finally, he says the incubator program is for a limited period—two to three years. Often after that, the companies leave back for the center.

Hanna Rado believes that the weakness of the periphery—in terms of infrastructure and human capital—derives from a lack of leadership.

> Leadership in the periphery is far away and very weak, and they have no idea on how to differentiate between what is important and what is not. Have a look and you will find many traffic roundabouts. They spend money on traffic roundabouts and not on education.

Interestingly, she states that the peripherality of the periphery has nothing to do with Tel Aviv but is rooted in 75 years of weak and weakening leadership.

Explaining the Underrepresentation of the Population of the Social Periphery in the High-Tech Industry in the Center

Izhar Shai explains that the social periphery of Israel suffers from an extremely weak educational infrastructure, denying its population the human capital and the opportunity to partake in the high-tech industry. Sami Peretz states that what he calls "tracking[1]" starts very early, leading to selection processes during high school, which expose socioeconomically stronger populations to technological careers and others not. In addition, private spending on education in Israel is higher than in other OECD countries (OECD, 2022), causing a high correlation between the socioeconomic status of parents and educational achievements of children, leaving the social periphery behind. Lately, private schools, colleges and universities are established throughout the country, further increasing the gap between center and periphery. Ilan Biran points to the fact that entire populations in peripheral towns do not receive adequate core education. "They become unemployable and dependent on welfare. That's the real gap between the top and bottom percentile."

Yossi Dahan points out that the main training organization for high tech is the Israeli military.

> Anecdotal data in newspapers show, that there are few and very particular people who end up in the military tech units. There is no bureaucracy that stands in the way of the strong, educated, privileged socio economic groups in Israel. They are strong, sophisticated, well networked. And the military has become a way to advance oneself and one's career.

He further maintains that those who end up there are mostly from the center, from prestigious high schools. There are no Ethiopians or weak socioeconomic groups from the peripheries and, naturally, neither ultra-Orthodox nor Arab-Palestinians. Inbal Orpaz adds that it is difficult to understand the Israeli high tech without the military. "Even if you are an Arab-Palestinian graduate from the Technion with excellent grades, you won't have access to the same opportunities as the military graduates. People go and work for their former unit members." She continues and tells that when she was working in journalism, she did an article on the 8200 unit and the overrepresentation of strong socioeconomic populations from the center. "The HR officer told me that this unit needs high school graduates who did 15 units of cyber studies and have a good command of English and math." So here is the vicious circle—where are the high schools proposing these opportunities? Sami Peretz reinforces this and explained that he talked to a senior officer in the 8200, who told him, "We do have soldiers from the periphery. I'll send you the data." But he never sent them. These are not intentional but institutional problems, Orpaz maintains. "But no one fights hard enough for the young of disempowered communities." Peretz quoted someone saying that the periphery creates either a very strong drive or the opposite—the feeling of incompetence.

Concisely, we are looking at a vicious circle, maintains Aharon:

> So here, we have a circular problem: if we don't solve the problem of health, employment and education, people will not join the periphery, and on the other side, people don't go to the periphery because of the health, employment and education level.

Summing up, geographically, insufficient transportation infrastructure makes it difficult to commute to and from Tel Aviv on a daily basis. Socially, the educational infrastructure does not provide weaker populations with adequate knowledge and skills, thereby preventing their potential participation in the high-tech industry.

Can the Paradox of Chronic Shortage and Exclusion Be Solved?

The paradox of the chronic shortage of high-tech employees parallel to the closed-door phenomenon has lately been discussed increasingly in the public discourse. This discussion is fueled by trends of Israeli companies to increasingly recruit people from countries like Belarus, India and Ukraine, working partly or fully online.

Eugene Kandel expressed his worries and states,

> Everybody thinks that the tech sector that is developed here and is breaking all records over the last couple of years is going to stay just because it's already here. But there is much stronger competition between governments around the world to attract the companies and the people to their locations.

Therefore, as Naomi Krieger Carmi maintains, it is crucial to solve the paradox—the lack of qualified candidates and closed doors at the same time. "Parallel to the shortage, there is the reality of 'closed doors' leaving tech employees not belonging to the center circle outside."

The problem has two roots: One concerns the relative lower knowledge and skill level of potential high-tech employees from the periphery. The other concerns those that are not opening the doors. Krieger Carmi believes that the closed-door syndrome has its roots in the attitude of the CEOs.

> For many CEOs of high-tech companies, the talk about diversity and impact does not sound authentic. If high-tech seniors accept that this might be a the new Zionism, just like the Zionism of having to integrate new immigrants from Russia because they needed the opportunity, then it will work.

Krieger Carmi thinks that then the companies will take responsibility for the training and adjustment of "others"—actively integrate Arabs, women, Ethiopians and ultra-Orthodox and agree to pay the price for cultural adjustment.

In sum, the paradox of chronic shortage and closed doors constitutes a major problem for the high-tech industry. Solutions to solve the lack of qualified candidates demand substantial changes in the education system especially in the peripheries. The closed-door syndrome needs to be addressed and solved by the high-tech seniors.

Should There Be a High-tech Industry in the Geographic Periphery?

Uri Gabai asked whether it makes sense that a small country as Israel should have more than one innovative ecosystem. "I think the answer is no. The fact that we have one is a miracle." And he continues and talks about the pointlessness of handing out grants for companies to expand to the periphery. He maintains that in practice, it encourages companies to keep their activity in the center and pay an employee to commute in order for the company to achieve the funding.

> You set up a big center in the periphery under the assumption that there are stockpiles of human capital up North or down South and give a "push" to companies to tap into these sources. As far as I know, that didn't really work.

Naomi Krieger Carmi maintained in the same context: "There was an insistence that accelerators will be located in the periphery for ideological purposes, and the result was artificial—people would come from the center every day because they had to." She proposes to connect startups in the periphery to local anchors—a local factory, a hospital—having an authentic justification to develop something there, specifically. "But then, in Israel there aren't really that many authentic anchors."

Yossi Dahan adds, "The government invests in high tech but does not invest in infrastructure in the periphery—especially not in education. So even in high-tech startups located in the periphery, the engineers will be from the center."

In sum, there is no need to initiate more high-tech centers in the periphery.

Should Populations at the Social Periphery Be Pushed Into High-Tech Entrepreneurship?

Importantly, the question explicitly addresses high-tech entrepreneurship and not high-tech employment. There are many programs and courses fostering high-tech entrepreneurship of peripheral populations. Is that the right policy? Uri Gabai claims that minority populations should not be pushed into entrepreneurship since they typically do not have the necessary resources. Arguing along the same line, Eugene Kandel maintains that policies promoting the entrepreneurship of minority and peripheral populations are problematic. He explains,

> Let's say because of the fact that you are in an incubator in the periphery, you receive 85% grant for starting a business. Then you still have to finance 15%. If the 15% is 100,000 NIS and you don't have it, then you have to loan from the bank, your parents, friends, etc. There are good

> chances that your startup will fail, because most startups fail. And then you are left with failure and debt.

He maintains that the same counts for subsidies based on population groups such as women, Arab-Palestinians and ultra-Orthodox. Entrepreneurship in high-tech is a privilege of wealthy populations and that policies trying to push peripheral populations into high tech are misleading.

Voices from the Field

In the following, I present the voices of NGO managers and representatives of the Innovation Authority and Start-Up Nation Central on the underrepresentation of peripheral populations.

Firstly, I asked managers of NGOs targeting the integration of underrepresented groups to name the two main obstacles they have identified after working in the field for some years.

Hasan Abu Shally—representing Arab-Palestinians—named lack of professional networks and expertise beyond technological knowledge and lack of trust. "The encounter with HR managers or investors is difficult—it is not necessarily characterized by racism per se but there is obviously a lack of trust, and it's not always on the surface."

Maisa El Shaik—representing Druze women—believes "there's an awareness hindrance internalized in the community," and that the women need a space where they can hold on to the religious requirements.

Tekela Mekonen—representing the Ethiopian community—cites the the geographic and social segregation and the fact that weak neighborhoods stay isolated: "There are no meeting points between the populations."

Izik Crombie—representing the ultra-Orthodox community—believes that the main hurdle is "the misconception about work and career being in conflict with the ultra-Orthodox lifestyle" and the lack of core curriculum in schools.

Secondly, I talked to representatives of the Innovation Authority and Start-Up Nation Central:

Kheir Abdil Razek from the Israel Innovation Authority talks about the outreaching to mainly women, Arab-Palestinians and ultra-Orthodox all over Israel. She maintains that although the number of students in higher education in technological disciplines definitely went up, the results are still very limited. She talks about the plan of the government to invest heavily in the Arab-Palestinian industry. "It took years to reach the point where Israel is a startup nation. It will take years to see the results of policies to integrate these populations."

Maty Zwaig, in her position at Start-Up Nation Central, investigated the underrepresented populations. She explains that many of the existing projects and programs aiming at integrating Arab-Palestinians and ultra-Orthodox women into the high-tech industry are not very efficient and paradoxically prepare the participants for jobs at the periphery of the high-tech industry. However, the industry needs developers at the very center of the deep technology.

> There at the center, we have to deal with very profound cultural obstacles, also to uproot stereotypes of the HRMs and do work so that these populations get to the center of the high tech. It will not just happen.

She sums up the main obstacles: geographic distance and segregation, lack of infrastructure in the periphery, lack of English proficiency, mutual biases, lifestyle demanding segregation (especially for ultra-Orthodox women), lack of willingness to move (especially for the Arab-Palestinians), lack of self-efficacy in presenting one's skills and competencies and lack of experience. She maintains,

> The roots of the gap are so deep that we need a very meaningful and even disturbing change. Without a concrete plan of how to bring this change about, the chances that these populations will integrate in the high-tech industry are low.

In sum, the voices from the field reveal that some of the obstacles hindering the integration of underrepresented groups into the high-tech industry are group specific, and others are systemic.

Is There a Spillover Effect from the Center to the Periphery?

Aharon Aharon believes that there is a spillover effect. However, the spillover effect does not necessarily benefit the periphery immediately. Uri Gabai says,

> I'll put the term "spillover" aside because it's a lot about interpretation, and mine is a bit different. I'll tell you what I mean. Does the ecosystem of Israeli innovation "spill" from Tel Aviv to other places in Israel? The answer is in a very, very minor way—very, very minor

Potter argues differently:

> True, most of the high tech is in Tel-Aviv, but they pay high income tax and there's corporation tax and there's value added tax, and those taxes are redistributed inside of Israel to enable public expenditure on the periphery, on schools, to pay for the welfare system.

He stresses that the future of Israel depends on the ability of the high-tech cluster to compete on the international markets. He continues and maintains, "There are benefits to Israel from having a thriving high tech even if it seems to be disconnected from the rest of the economy." He also believes that there are limits to the extent to which you can engineer that cluster and finally argues, "I think you need to let the high-tech thrive and prosper, but you also need to develop alternatives."

Inbal Orpaz understands the spillover problem in a somehow different way and maintains,

> I do think without a doubt there is a spillover problem. High tech is an opportunity. I try to think where the springboards are to closing social gaps. High tech is supposedly a meritocracy, but in fact, it is a closed circle, not open to everyone.

She believes that the government and its agents have to understand that if the high tech is the main resource Israel has, "the country's business model, its comparative advantage," then in order to maintain this advantage, "you need to let in more populations." "And this," she continues, "requires long-term planning and thinking outside the box." The grim conclusion is that "since governments change a priori every four years, there is no interest in long-term planning." Eugene Kandel puts the same line of thought a bit differently and cautioned that

> unless the Israeli government matches in terms of thinking strategically and puts a coordinated effort into making sure that we have the leadership in the next ten years, we may wake up in five or six years and not find high tech here at all.

While Israel's high tech is generating income and taxes that are reinvested in the entire society and not only in the high-tech industry, which means per se a spillover. Nonetheless, there is a need to increase the circle of those partaking in the industry and the generated revenues beyond the borders of Tel Aviv.

What Needs to Be Done to Solve the Paradox and Generate Spillover?

Potter states that Israel has to decide whether it is trying to make the high-tech sector more equal or attempts to balance the high-tech sector with the rest of the economy. "If you want to do both, open up access to high-paid high-tech jobs to other parts of the population. Then you have to address education, cultural issues and discrimination."

In contradiction to Kandel, Gabai and others, Potter believes that Israel needs to develop an additional high-tech cluster. He says,

> In pragmatic terms, high-tech clusters benefit the country. They bring inequality with them, and you don't want to "chase them away" but

find ways to render them more equal internally as well as with the rest of society through public spending and investment in education and infrastructure.

Therefore, he recommended to relax planning constrains, invest in infrastructure and transport to allow the cluster to grow, and invest in education and integrate poorer populations. Taxation generated from high-tech "enables to develop places like Eilat and Nazareth, not necessarily for high tech, and to try and integrate more populations into the labor market, to businesses that are not necessarily high-tech."

Inbal Orpaz points to the lack of long-term planning and compares between Singapore—planning 20–30 years ahead—and Israel. "In Israel five years is considered long-term planning, but that does not work for infrastructure and education." Ilan Biran expressed frustration with the bureaucracy and regulations hindering changes in the infrastructure that would render the periphery more attractive. He believes that infrastructure level changes in all domains and persistence over at least one generation are needed in order to improve the situation in Israel.

Yossi Dahan maintains that for a real change to occur, the solutions need to be systemic. The allocation of budgets to the places where it is needed can solve infrastructure problems. He thinks that government policy is very rewarding to high tech and that even the Bank of Israel recommends rechanneling this support toward traditional industries in the periphery to generate growth. "The high tech does not need this growth."

Hanna Rado upheld that one way to deal with the low level of leadership in the periphery would be to raise wages of public service positions in order to make these positions more attractive. "Why not pool many small municipalities to bigger clusters? Then there would be more money for wages." She also believes that it is crucial to rely on people from the periphery when setting up initiatives and not "export people from the center." She maintains that there are no people from the periphery in the decision-making bodies. "That could change in five years. Why not develop a leadership cadre in the periphery?"

Solutions mentioned by the experts include taxation, investment in infrastructures, municipalities and education in the peripheries. This demands long-term planning and rethinking the allocation of budgets. It seems, though, that it is widely known what should be done, but it is also rather clear that it will not be done.

Concluding Thoughts

As has been suggested in the first chapters of this book, the advancement of the high-tech industry in Israel depended on state policies and investments, and some of the interview partners maintained that clearly Israel will depend on them to overcome inequalities and address the challenges of climate and demographic change.

Indeed, Sami Peretz raised the question of whether the state needs to "step in" in order to regulate the increasing gap between the high tech and all the rest. He elaborates, "Once the high tech becomes so much more rewarding than all the other sectors, should it be taken care of?" In particular, when considering the statement of Inbal Orpaz, "being in high tech is almost the only way to survive here, as life is so expensive."

The interviews and other material presented in this book show that the Israeli high-tech industry is not a free market story. Accordingly, Potter maintained, "We can say it's a neoliberal country, but then again it's not, in that the state has got a tremendous role to play, not only in the military. This is what stimulated the high-tech sector."

Regulating the increasing gap between the high tech and all the rest does not necessarily imply that everyone has to work in high tech. Instead, other sectors and industries should be strengthened. As Gabai put it,

> People should not have to work for a low salary. A teacher should not earn 5,000 NIS. People have to work for a fair salary but not necessarily in high tech. Not all fit high tech and high tech does not fit all.

Whether or not there will be a political agenda to regulate increasing inequalities, implement long-term planning to improve the infrastructures and foster diversity in employment and industries remains to be seen. Yossi Dahan put it very pessimistically but with a potential perspective:

> We'll end up a technologically advanced nation of ignorants, a non-democratic nation. people with very narrow horizons, occupied with their own personal financial interests—a pretty horrendous society to be honest, even if exports grow another 200%. In this sense, the high-tech vision doesn't knock me off my feet. But there are possible steps to take.

Note

1. 'Tracking' means directing certain populations towards professional, nonacademic, routes, lowering expectations. This happened for many years in the Israeli school system and some state it is continuing till today. The outcome is that certain environments do not promote technological higher education and others do.

References

OECD. (2022). *Private spending on education (indicator)*. OECDiLibrary. https://doi.org/10.1787/6e70bede-en

14 Conclusion

During the last decades, Israel has undergone processes of transformation from a developmental to a neoliberal model, configurating a specific version of national neoliberalism. A significant step toward this transformation process were innovation policies, intentionally initiated and embedded within national strategy. The aim of this strategy was to increase Israel's competitive advantage in the international arena and create an economic reality that compensates for and counters international pressure in relation to Israel's continued occupation of the Palestinian territories. Over the years, this innovation policy, in combination with additional market-oriented policies initiated by the government, have led to a rather stable and high growth economy. However, the model of economic growth is based almost exclusively on the high-tech industry and has generated increasing economic inequalities. Technological entrepreneurship and innovation are considered engines of national growth and competitiveness, as reflected in a vibrant and successful high-tech scene, accumulating resources and enabling constant growth. At the very center of the Israeli high-tech industry, like everywhere, the entrepreneur is the hero. He—yes, he—is the actor taking risks and making profits. He relates to himself as if "he was a business, actively embracing risks, capably managing difficulties and hide injuries" (Scharff, 2016, p. 108). The typical high-tech entrepreneur is a white Jewish Ashkenazi man embodying success. He is addressed as the cultural hero combining freedom and independence with hard work, accumulating wealth and supposedly creating benefit for the economy and society. The successful high-tech entrepreneur has become Israel's cultural icon, symbolizing its values—at least at the center of the country.

However, as often explained in the academic and public discourse, the achievements and fruits of the high-tech industry in Israel have hardly spilled over to the periphery. Consequently, a dual economy emerged, exemplified extensively throughout the book. The success of the high-tech sector—which consists of only about 10% of all employees, does not benefit the Israeli workforce as a whole. Figure 4.1 in Chapter 4 reveals extraordinarily high wage differences between the high tech and the rest—consistently over the years. The average non-high-tech employee earned only 46% of

DOI: 10.4324/9781003091042-15

the average high-tech employee in 2016; in 2020 it decreased to 40%. The high wages of the high-tech industry benefit a small, overwhelmingly Jewish and highly educated elite, thereby contributing not only to high income inequality but also to a dual economic and divided social structure.

In the past, the Israeli government knew how to balance technological innovation with traditional industries and create a symbiosis between the private and public sectors. As has been shown in Chapter 3 of this book, the state conditioned government subsidies for high-tech companies and required the establishment of factories in the periphery, thus ensuring that the surplus portion of the fruits of the new industry would be translated into job creation. In the 2000s, changes in the law to encourage capital investment removed these restrictions and, in effect, allowed high-tech companies to copy the production process to countries where the cost was lower. In addition, the rise of the venture capital funds has driven high-tech companies to move to a Silicon Valley–like model, a model based on early exits and an emphasis on research and development stages rather than on company establishment and broad-based economic activities. The venture capital industry in Israel has a major impact on the economic disparities. According to Breznitz (2021), "More than 95% of the venture capital industry's investments in Israel are foreign, so when exits occur all that money and profits leave the Israeli economy and return to the foreign bank accounts they came from." Breznitz (2021) calls it two economies sharing one place. He maintains that the fact that Israeli high-tech focuses on financial exits further contributes to the split, since growing companies would also demand non-technological workers. Furthermore, he explains that 95% of the venture capital invested in Israeli companies is foreign; therefore, when a company exits, so does the money. Breznitz (2021) provokingly calls Israel a startup VC nation, with 10% highly skilled and the rest left behind.

This book addressed some of the consequences of this dual economy and tried to argue, why these consequences generate problems that should be addressed? As has been discussed in the introduction of this book, inequality drives economic insecurity and social fragmentation, erodes traditional collective structures and might foster calls for authoritarian leadership. Inequality is intrinsically undesirable. The quote from Piketty's *Capital in the Twenty First Century* catches it in a nutshell: "Every human society must justify its inequalities: unless reasons for them are found, the whole political and social edifice stands in danger of collapse (Piketty, 2014)." Israel has high levels of inequalities. It is also a highly heterogeneous country, with a kaleidoscope of very different population groups. Unsurprisingly, the rates of poverty are high and significantly higher in certain groups than in others. Two of those population groups, with extremely high rates of poverty—the Arab-Palestinians and the ultra-Orthodox, which are so-called minorities and are addressed in this book—consist together about 35% of the population and thus can hardly be referred to as minorities. The share of the

Arab-Palestinian population of Israeli society is predicted to stay at about 20% of the Israeli population. However, the share of the ultra-Orthodox population is predicted to be 1 out of 4 Israelis in 2050, which is less than 30 years from now. Since the ultra-Orthodox population has high rates of poverty, it can be expected that the overall inequality in Israel will rise with the relative increase of this population group. The ultra-Orthodox population's labor market participation is extremely low, their share in the high-tech industry is less than 2 % and they can hardly be expected to provide high-tech employees in the future. Inequality will remain to be a problem for the Israeli economy and society.

In order to continue to grow and drive the economy, the Israeli high tech needs more talents. The chronical shortage of people with adequate knowledge and skill level has been discussed throughout the book. However, the very features of the dual economy may prevent the opportunity to recruit more talented employees from the second economy at the periphery. Following a report published in 2018 by the Taub Center for Social Policy studies in Israel, there is a very limited potential supply in the current labor force. The report shows an exceptionally high disparity of the wage and skill level between high-tech and non-high-tech workers. This disparity is significantly higher than in other countries (Brand, 2018). Furthermore, due to the generally low skill level (including English proficiency), vocational training programs aimed at integrating Arab-Palestinians and ultra-Orthodox into the high-tech industry are not very effective. Following Brand (2018), women—still underrepresented in the high-tech industry—are considered the most plausible untapped pool of potential high-tech employees. But as has been shown in Chapter 9 of this book, in order for women to be willing to enter the high-tech and to stay in the industry, its organizational culture needs to change, allowing for more work-life balance possibilities and adapting a less masculine feature.

In sum, the very existence of the dual economy is not only problematic from a normative perspective but also because of a high level of knowledge and skill disparity, it affects the growth potential of the high-tech industry itself.

Similarly to other countries globally, the dual economy overlaps to a large extent with the center and periphery divide. This divide has been tackled extensively throughout the book; therefore, I will relate to it only briefly here. The main questions arising concerning the periphery-center divide and Israeli high tech are two: should high-tech be exported to the periphery and should people from the periphery be imported to the high-tech center? Chapter 13 discussed these questions in detail, and not all experts are of the same opinion. There is overall consensus that it will be extremely difficult to export high-tech companies to the periphery since the periphery lacks adequate infrastructure and human resources. Furthermore, there are examples for failures of policies aimed at attracting high-tech companies to the periphery: In 2015, the Israeli government launched the 528 plan to subsidize employees' wages by 20% for cyber companies that reside in Be'er Sheva, hoping to attract more companies to the southern city, that in addition to subsidies for new high-wage positions in National Priority Regions, made almost entirely of peripheral municipalities. However, these initiatives failed to initiate a substantial drift of tech companies to the Negev and other peripheral regions. In 2021, the Innovation Authority declared on an additional 25-million-shekel plan to support innovation in Be'er Sheva. Moreover, majority of companies that received the support of a government-franchised cyber-incubator in Be'er Sheva have relocated to the center of Israel after graduating from the incubator. Overall and despite the government's efforts to position Be'er Sheva as an innovation and technology hub and specifically as "the cyber city," many budgets and allocations were left unutilized, and a significant change of balance toward Be'er Sheva did not occur.

Also, other government-led and NGO-led programs aimed at increasing the share of populations from the geographic and social periphery in the high-tech industry did not succeed. In the end, the data confirm that the high-tech industry is still homogenously located mainly at the center—with all the rest lagging behind.

Surprisingly—or maybe not—lately, the government has discussed yet an additional package of benefits targeting the high-tech industry. The package addresses tax benefits and is not likely to tackle the problem of shortage of high-level employees. Maybe also not surprisingly, OECD data show that in 35 OECD countries, there is a strong positive correlation between R & D investment and welfare spending, meaning that as the rate of R & D spending increases, so does the welfare spending. Unfortunately, this is not the case for Israel, although it is one of the countries with the highest R & D spending. Welfare spending, especially long-term investment in the education of poorer population groups, would have the potential to solve part of the knowledge and skill shortage. Thus, in Israel 2022, the government aims at benefiting the strong high-tech industry; what is presented as the sole and highly successful driver of the economy has no agenda to deal with inequality. Targeting welfare spending is a long-term process that demands long-term planning, and it will happen only if the rising inequality will be postulated as a societal problem.

To date, however, inequality in Israel is still high, and the related public discourse is more concerned with saving the high-tech sector than with moral concerns of its consequences.

In Israel, there is an unsurprising absence of public discourse on the intersection of technology and ethics. The public is hardly interested in what of the Israeli high-tech products is sold to who for what purpose. Typically, a public outcry concerning the use of technology occurred only, when the Israeli police was suspected to have used surveillance technologies inside Israel. As long as Israeli cybertechnologies have been sold to other countries, that was of minor concern. However, in February 2022, the *Washington Post* published a report (Washington Post Staff, 2022), stating that

> military-grade spyware licensed by an Israeli firm to governments for tracking terrorists and criminals was used in attempted and successful hacks of 37 smartphones belonging to journalists, human rights activists, business executives and two women close to murdered Saudi journalist Jamal Khashoggi.

The investigation concerned the Israeli firm NSO Group's Pegasus spyware and was conducted by a consortium of 16 media organizations and the *Washington Post*. Since the Pegasus affair was exposed, the Israeli and international media published a series of inspective reports on Israeli cybersecurity and warfare firms, and the common denominator of all cases was not violating law but the lack of ethics and internal moral code. A similar trend to avoid ethical questions is emerging when having a closer look at the gambling industry. It is a significant part of the Israeli high-tech industry, but it is "invisible." The Innovation Authority does not write about it in its reports, and government people do not talk about it at events; nevertheless, many high-tech employees are working in the gambling industry, although they prefer not to tell.

Warfare, cybersecurity and gambling companies are an integral part of the Israeli high-tech industry, as they probably are all over the world. However, it seems only natural to expect an extensive and informed discussion on the intersection of technology and ethics. These issues should not be left to the decision of technological entrepreneurs, developers and CEOs of companies. The necessary public discourse could and should be initiated by the state and its relevant agencies.

Naturally, there is a tendency to nationally celebrate the achievements and the international recognition of the high-tech industry. Nonetheless, it is time that the darker sides are acknowledged and tackled, not by the industry alone but in a public and legal discussion. The darker sides also concern a reality in which entire groups of the population are de facto excluded from participating and sharing the outcomes of the high-tech industry. Whether or not this exclusion is intentional does not change its results.

Future Developments

As I have outlined before in this book, in Israel, it was national strategy that led to technological innovation and the high-tech industry, doubtlessly the major engine of today's Israeli economy. However, there is no national strategy dealing with the rising inequalities and its consequences for the Israeli society. Indeed, the rather small group of high-tech people making up the startup nation has happily adopted the entrepreneurial imperative and the neoliberal rationality. This imperative, accompanied by the meritocracy myth, shifts the responsibility for success and failure to the individual. Emerging inequalities then are no longer anyone's but the individual's responsibility.

I believe that the fact that Tel Aviv is the most expensive city in the world is a problem. I believe that it exemplifies the major challenges Israel will have to deal with in the near future. These challenges are multilayered and concern first and foremost and most importantly the sociocultural and socioeconomic gap between center and periphery.

One important aspect concerns the deficiencies of the infrastructure, which should enable easy commuting between center and periphery, as to be expected in a country as small as Israel. There is a discourse on the lack of public transport, traffic jams and bottlenecks, increasing the amount of cars. Government reports and media caution that people will spend increasingly more time on the road for getting to places. Consulting firms produce scenario planning and focused prognoses about traffic bottlenecks and their impact on time people will spend on the road. The experts and policy makers in Chapter 13 talked about the lack of infrastructure, about the need for connectivity in order to improve mobility between center and periphery. Some believed that more high-tech centers should be set up in the geographic periphery of Israel but lamented that in addition to the lack of human capital, the infrastructure in the periphery is inadequate. Others believe that Israel does not need additional high-tech hubs; they lamented the lack of infrastructure since it prevents potential employees to reach the center on a daily basis. Again, to substantially improve the transportation infrastructure in Israel, long-term planning is needed. Israel is not good at that.

Secondly, and as I have hinted at before, the very existence of Israel's dual economy implies the future challenge for the high-tech industry and for the country. The fact that entire populations do not have and will hardly be able to reach the necessary knowledge and skill level to join the industry is directly related to a lack of adequate policy. The expert interviews in Chapter 13 revealed many well-meant policy initiatives by government agencies, engaged NGOs funded partly by philanthropists and operated by engaged volunteers and employees. But the data show that these initiatives have very little—if at all any—impact. OECD policy papers, Bank of Israel reports, academia and politicians point to solutions, all demanding long-term planning, something Israel is not good at, a shortcoming that might be a major challenge to its future. The solutions to the shortage of talent lies in long-term investment in education, from early childhood education to university. It is not only about producing more engineers, programmers and coders who will bravely transform the ideas of others into algorithms. It is not only about English literacy, mathematics and sciences in matriculation exams. There is a need for a broad humanistic education enabling independent and critical thinking and problem-solving based on a deep understanding of realities, be they in engineering, psychology, medicine or religious studies.

There is nothing new about this statement; we know what skills are needed in the complex realities of contemporary times, yet these skills are provided only to a small portion of the Israeli society. The rest are left behind and will stay behind if nothing is done. Surely, as the interview partners in Chapters 6 to 11 show, there are impressive stories of the success of high-tech entrepreneurs coming from the population groups presented in this book. These are women and men who joined the high-tech industry, overcoming external and internal challenges and barriers. However, at least for Ethiopians, the ultra-Orthodox and Arab-Palestinians, we know that overall their integration into the high-tech industry has failed. The examples presented in the book are the exception, and that has to change. I believe that the different situation for women is due to the fact that most of those who joined the high tech—either as employees, investors or entrepreneurs—already belong to the center; they come from sociocultural and socioeconomic backgrounds providing an education that includes the requirements mentioned previously. Therefore, challenging their talent in the direction of tech disciplines is much less of a problem. Although the increased influx of women to high tech is important for the industry, it does not impact the dual structure of the economy and society. If there will be no profound change in the educational system, the high-tech industry will have to look for external solutions to solve the shortage of talented employees, a step that will increase inequalities.

Finally, I would like to turn to a last point, concerning Israel's need to deal with future geopolitical challenges. Climate change is happening globally, and especially in many areas of the Middle East, desertification is on the rise. The World Bank predicts that the region's capital cities will eventually experience up to four months of burning heat every year. Notwithstanding Israel's advances in climate technology, the state controller warned that decades of governmental neglect have left the country unprepared for the coming climate crisis. In November 2021 at the COP26 conference in Glasgow, Naftali Bennett—then prime minister of Israel—promised net-zero emissions by 2050 and plans for a climate-change working group focusing on water solutions and other regional climate issues. But climate change is only one part of the challenge. For Israel, population growth also concerns a major challenge. Following demographic forecasts, in 2065, there will be up to 20 million people living in the country, more than twice as much as today. This forecast includes the populations living currently within the state of Israel, within the green line, and it also includes the Jewish population of the Westbank. It does not include the Palestinian population of the Westbank and the Gaza Strip. The demographic forecasts, combined with the expected climate change, pose a major challenge and threat for Israel, and there is definitely a need for some bright brains to propose sustainable solutions.

But unfortunately, there is no national strategy aiming at sustainable solutions for rising inequalities and its consequences. Neither is there a national strategy tackling the population growth and dealing with climate change and its consequences. The high-tech industry could become a leading player, a catalyst for moving toward sustainable economic models, as what already happens in some parts of the world. The question is whether Israel will be able and willing to utilize its high-tech industry to propose solutions to these urgent challenges.

Concluding Thoughts

Whether technology in itself and for itself is bad or good is yet an unanswered question. Some state that it is neither neutral nor objective but rather a mirror reflecting societal bias, unfairness and injustice (Birhane, 2022). Others maintain that potentially, technology can make the world a much better place but also a much worse one, depending on economic, social and political contexts and players.

Technological innovation can be a significant power to face the challenges of humanity, as presented in the sustainability goals of the United Nations. Innovative technologies can target energy consumption, save natural resources, produce high-quality jobs, improve public service and improve quality of life for all. But this will only happen if countries, including Israel, are willing to tackle the sole profit purpose of high-tech companies who have no concerns for the implications of their services and products, be they moral, environmental or altogether sustainable.

Mariana Mazzucato, in her book titled *Mission Economy: A Moonshot Guide to Changing Capitalism* (2021), maintains that technological innovations themselves are not the aim of the entrepreneurial state but rather the tool to achieve societal missions. A change of discourse is needed; governments must step in but with a mission directed at the well-being of all.

For Israel, that means to rethink the blind celebration of the high-tech winners and suggest alternatives that might enable dealing with the challenges ahead. As Yossi Dahan put it very pessimistically, but with a potential perspective:

> We'll end up a technologically advanced nation of ignorants. A non-democratic nation. People with very narrow horizons. Occupied with their own personal financial interests. A pretty horrendous society to be honest, even if exports grow another 200%. In this sense, the high-tech vision doesn't knock me off my feet. But there are possible steps to take.

References

Birhane, A. (2022, April 11). *The algorithmic colonization of Africa*. Abeba Bihave. https://abebabirhane.wordpress.com/2019/07/10/the-algorithmic-colonization-of-africa/

Brand, G. (2018). *How much can the Israeli*. The Taub Center.

Breznitz, D. (2021). *Innovation in real places: Strategies for prosperity in an unforgiving world*. Oxford University Press. https://doi.org/10.1093/oso/9780197508114.001.0001

Mazzucato, M. (2021). *Mission economy: A moonshot guide to changing capitalism*. Penguin.

Piketty, T. (2014). *Capital in the 21st century*. The Belknap Press of Harvard University Press.

Scharff, C. (2016). The psychic life of neoliberalism: Mapping the contours of entrepreneurial subjectivity. *Theory, Culture & Society*, *33*(6), 107–122. https://doi.org/10.1177/0263276415590164

Washington Post Staff. (2022). Takeaways from the Pegasus project. *The Washington Post*. Retrieved April 11, 2022, from www.washingtonpost.com/investigations/2021/07/18/takeaways-nso-pegasus-project/

Index

Note: Page numbers in *italics* indicate a figure and page numbers in **bold** indicate a table on the corresponding page.